THE TIMES

GREAT LETTERS

A CENTURY OF
NOTABLE CORRESPONDENCE

EDITED BY
JAMES OWEN

Published by Times Books

An imprint of HarperCollins Publishers
Westerhill Road
Bishopbriggs
Glasgow G64 2QT
www.harpercollins.co.uk
times.books@harpercollins.co.uk

First edition 2017

© This compilation Times Newspapers
Ltd 2017

The Times® is a registered trademark of
Times Newspapers Ltd

The contents of this publication are
believed correct at the time of printing.
Nevertheless the publisher can accept no
responsibility for errors or omissions,
changes in the detail given or for any
expense or loss thereby caused.

A catalogue record for this book is
available from the British Library.

ISBN 978-0-00-824949-6

10 9 8 7 6 5 4 3 2 1

Printed and bound in Great Britain by
CPI Group (UK) Ltd., Croydon, CR0 4YY

My thanks and acknowledgements
go to Lily Cox and Robin Ashton at
News Syndication and, in particular,
at The Times, Ian Brunskill and,
at HarperCollins, Sarah Daniels,
Laura Goldie, Jethro Lennox,
Mimmi Rönning, Ewan Ross and
Sarah Woods. Christopher Riches
and Evelyn Sword.

CONTENTS

INTRODUCTION

Before 1914, there was no Letters Page as such in *The Times*. The newspaper had, since its founding in 1785, published correspondence to it. Yet in the era when its front page was still reserved for items of more importance than mere news — club announcements, death notices and public appointments — letters had to be fitted in as space allowed rather than gathered together: let alone considered an attraction in their own right.

Although the change did not become fixed for some years, the decision to start grouping letters onto a single page when possible began to alter their nature and function. Until well into the previous century, those published had often been immensely lengthy (and now almost incomprehensible) political polemics.

That Victorian taste for abundance had begun to dwindle by the time of the First World War and the advent of the motor car and the telephone had led to predictions of an imminent end to letter-writing. But while the constraints of the new lay-out often did encourage correspondents to be briefer, its introduction turned the page into the noticeboard of the Establishment.

Rapidly, it took on the character for which it has become renowned, as a forum for debate, as a playground for opinion-formers and as a billboard for decision-makers. From the start, however, such weighty content was leavened by humour and quirkiness. Moreover, with readers making a regular appointment with the page, another of its features became more pronounced: rallies of letters, with each mail bringing a fresh serving of wit and erudition.

Indeed, what is most striking about this selection of letters, across the years, is the sense of community between readers that emanates from them. Of course, what that community was has changed markedly over time. For much of the first half of this volume, it was largely that which treated the page as an extension of their gentlemen's club. The tone and content accordingly reflects their self-assurance and their preoccupations — cricket features strongly, as do mentions of Eton; and sometimes both together.

Not until well into the post-war years does the mood become more sombre, pondering (if not resolving) the uncertainties of imperial twilight and economic decline. By then, the readership is notably broader, as changes in education, society and at work bear fruit: in the 1970s, more Labour than Conservative MPs took *The Times*. Nonetheless, it is remarkable how frequently the same topics recur in correspondence across the generations — the failings of the young, what is to be done about schools, how best to make porridge.

For it seems to me that the value of these letters lies not just in the great events which often they record, be it the death of Elvis Presley or the onset of the internet, nor even in the changing attitudes that they mirror, but in the window that they offer on the national character. Unconsciously revelatory they may be, but the fascination of so many of these letters is their insight into what it means at any time to be British. They take the temperature of the body politic, map the A–Z of our way of life.

They are a reminder, too, that the writing of letters (and emails), and not just of books, can be an art form. Here are Margaret Thatcher, Benito Mussolini and Theresa May giving glimpses of what took them to the top. Meanwhile, Spike Milligan, PG Wodehouse and Celia Johnson use comedy to have their say.

There are masters of the craft to be rediscovered here, among them AP Herbert and Peter Fleming. Graham Greene, John Le Carré and Agatha Christie demonstrate why they made their living from their pens, even if a taxi driver puts TS Eliot square about the limits of Bertrand Russell's intellect. And Arthur Koestler makes the case for a tax on pleasure (with married love to be zero-rated).

If a Hungarian-born intellectual can be moved to write amusingly in his sixth or seventh language to a newspaper, it must be doing something right. At its best, that is to draw its readers into a long, ongoing conversation about the direction of the nation, what shape it is in and which qualities it should exude.

What is important is that dialogue is open to anyone who reads the paper, not just those who are influenced by its readers' views, or who seek to influence them. Not everyone understands the rules at once, as the first letter hereafter shows ("How to Have a Letter Published").

But it is hard to think of another group of readers who, wanting to protest a decision by local councillors about an exhibition, would spontaneously adopt the personae of literary characters relevant to their cause ("The Curious Case of Sherlock Holmes", which can be found at the start of the book). That ability to make your point whilst retaining your sense of humour is perhaps uniquely — and the best of — British. If newspapers can have a soul, it can be found here, on the Letters Page.

Where it might be helpful, I have added brief contexts to some of the letters which follow. Similarly, the capacities in which correspondents write and their addresses have also been included as seems necessary. Notwithstanding the passage of time, the style and usage of language in the letters, and the views expressed in them, remain those of the original.

JAMES OWEN

STARTING TIMES

HOW TO HAVE A LETTER PUBLISHED

26 January 1970

SIR, YOU'RE JOKING. You must be. "Who will be writing to *The Times* tonight?" is printed on the face of an envelope containing a letter to me from *The Times*. The letter "assures you that your remarks were read with interest". But not sufficient interest to warrant publication. I wonder why when one considers the amount of drivel that is to be found in the Letters to the Editor.

Three times in my life I have written a letter to the Editor. Three times he has found my letter interesting, but not sufficiently so to warrant publication.

The first was on the subject of east Germany, on which I have had a book published. Probably I was not considered an expert on east Germany.

The second was a protest, and an invitation to others to do so, against the victimization of Lieutenant-Colonel Emil Zátopek, the Czechoslovak Olympic athlete. Presumably I was not considered an expert, although, in Prague itself, at the height of his career and for seven years, I advised Zátopek on his training. And wrote two books on sport in Czechoslovakia under the communists.

The third, recently, was a reply to Sir Peter Mursell, a member of the Royal Commission on Local Government, on the implications of the Maud Report. Again, I assume, I was not regarded as an authority on the subject, although the *Guardian* has given a pen picture of my work against Maud spread over four columns and I have been invited to debate Maud with Lord Redcliffe-Maud at University College, Oxford, of which he is Master.

What does one have to do in order to be recognized by the Editor of *The Times*? Bring about a counter-revolution in communist east Germany? Run faster than Zátopek? Become chairman of a new Royal Commission on Local Government in England?

Yours faithfully,
J. ARMOUR-MILNE

Replied on 28 January 1970

SIR, THE ANSWER TO Mr. J. Armour-Milne's question is simple.

Last year I had two letters published in *The Times* and I've been dining out on them ever since. They involved me in an exchange of letters of ever-increasing lunacy with other correspondents. I can bear witness that the prime qualification you need to get letters published in *The Times* is eccentricity.

Yours faithfully,
SYLVIA MARGOLIS

THE CURIOUS CASE OF
SHERLOCK HOLMES

28 October 1950

SIR, IT IS DOUBTFUL whether Mr. Sherlock Holmes will have seen the paragraph in *The Times* to-day recording the singular decision of the councillors of St. Marylebone to oppose the proposal for an exhibition of material of my old friend and mentor for the benefit of visitors to the Festival of Britain. Engrossed as he is in bee-keeping in Sussex, he is unlikely to rally to his own defence, and you will perhaps allow me, as a humble chronicler of some of his cases and as a former resident in the borough, to express indignation at this decision.

There is much housing in the Metropolis but there is but one Mr. Sherlock Holmes, and I venture to assert that visitors from across the Atlantic (who cannot as yet forgotten my old friend's remarkable work in clearing up the dark mystery of the Valley of Fear and the grotesque affair of the Study in Scarlet) would find such an exhibition of interest. Why the councillors of St. Marylebone, in their anxiety to display their work on the clearing of slums, should deny honour to my old friend I find it hard to understand. Perhaps this is time's revenge for the exposure by Mr. Sherlock Holmes of the evil machinations of the Norwood Builder. Whatever the reason, I trust that second and better thoughts may prevail, and in the meantime subscribe myself,

Your humble but indignant servant,
JOHN H. WATSON, M.D. late of the Indian Army.

2 November 1950

SIR, TO-DAY I VISITED Mr. Sherlock Holmes and conveyed to him the welcome news that St. Marylebone will hold an exhibition in his honour during the Festival of Britain. I could see he was deeply moved by this tribute, as also by the correspondence in which your readers have so warmly supported my plea. Several of those letters raise the subject of commemorative material to be placed on exhibition. Alas, but little remains, for a mysterious and disastrous fire at my old friend's Sussex home some years ago (the details of which are not yet ready to be given to the world) destroyed the greater part of the relics of his cases. St. Marylebone, I fear, will have to manage without his help.

May I trespass a little further on your indulgence to reply to two of your correspondents? Mycroft Holmes is, of course, technically correct in stating I was not in the Indian Army, though I did in fact so describe myself on the battered tin dispatch box which until recently lay in the vaults of Cox's Bank in Pall Mall. But it was the custom in 1878, when I was wounded at Maiwand, for those in whatever regiment in India they served, to describe themselves as "of the Indian Army," a point of which Mycroft in his omniscience will be well aware. As for Mrs. Whitney, I am surprised that, in spite of her close friendship, she is apparently unaware that my dear first wife used "James" as a name for him who remains,

Yours faithfully,
JOHN H. WATSON, M.D.

Replied on 2 November 1950

SIR, LONG YEARS OF retirement have failed to break the professional habit of careful examination of the Personal columns of *The Times* newspaper and a necessarily hastier perusal of its other contents. Thus I have learned with no little surprise of the proposal to stage an exhibition perpetuating the performances of my old acquaintance, Mr. Sherlock Holmes. Surely in this correspondence to-day's letter from Mrs. Hudson, his worthy landlady, places the abilities of Mr. Holmes in their right perspective. A place of amusement, such as Madame Tussaud's, is surely the proper setting for a record of Holmes's amateur achievements. It would be ungenerous of me to deny that on occasion the gifted guesswork of Mr. Holmes has jumped a stage in the final solution of a crime. It may not be inappropriate to remind your readers, however, of the fable of the tortoise and the hare, and the true student of criminology will continue to regard as the only true source the so-called "Black Museum" of that institution on the Victoria Embankment which for so many years I had the honour to serve.

I am, Sir, your obedient servant,
G. LESTRADE, ex-Inspector, Metropolitan Police.

THUNDERING

1914–19

MR. BACKHOUSE'S GIFT TO BODLEIAN

7 January 1914

SIR, I READ WITH interest the illuminating account in your issue of December 2 of the Chinese library presented by me to the Bodleian, and thank the writer for correcting an error into which I had carelessly fallen respecting one of the Sung editions, the "Ku Chin Chi Yao." My reason for assigning some date prior to 1085 was that a character identical with the tabooed personal name of an Emperor who reigned after that year was not written with the customary omission of a stroke as a mark of respect. This rule was rigidly enforced under the Sungs, as in later dynasties, and its contravention can only have been due to carelessness on the part of the printer, as your article shows conclusively that the earlier date which I had assigned cannot be correct. It appears from a catalogue which I have consulted that the "editio princeps" of this work was published in 1260, the first year of the Ching Ting of the Southern Sung dynasty, and also the year of Kublai's accession to the northern throne. My belief is that the copy in the Bodleian is the first edition, so that it should be assigned to the Sung and not to the Yuan. Several reproductions of Sung printing which I have seen show the cramped style of printing which your article rightly mentioned as characteristic also of the Yuan period.

In reference to another Sung print in the collection you allude to the light shade of the paper; I do not think that this is exceptional in books of that date. I have before me a Sung edition of the collection known as "Wen Hsuan" from the library of the eminent Viceroy and collector, Tuan Fang, who was murdered by his troops in Szuch'uan during the revolution. This work is mentioned in his catalogue as indisputably Southern Sung, and in this case also the paper is almost white. I may claim some knowledge of the Sung print, "Works of Tu Fu," now at Cambridge, to which your article also refers, as it was formerly in my collection. Personally I believe it to date from about 1230, but a former Tartar general of Canton, Feng Shan, who was an authority on ancient prints, used to tell me that its date is early Yuan, say about 1290. He denied that the colour of the paper was a conclusive test, especially in view of the skilful "doctoring" of the old Chinese prints.

I am, Sir, &c.,
EDMUND BACKHOUSE

Sir Edmund Backhouse (as he later became) was regarded for much of the 20th century as one of the greatest European scholars of China, where he lived for decades until his death in 1944. His reputation stemmed in part from the inside knowledge of the Imperial court which he supplied to *The Times*'s correspondent in Peking. This letter dates from the period when the newspaper was starting to group all letters to it onto a single page and records Backhouse's donation of eight tons of historic Chinese manuscripts to the Bodleian Library, Oxford. Only in 1973 were the provenance of many of these thrown into doubt when Backhouse's biographer Hugh Trevor-Roper unmasked him as a liar, fraudster and fantasist who had wildly exaggerated his expertise and claims of influence.

THE REDRESS OF CRYING SHAMES

28 February 1914

SIR, I AM MOVED to speak out what I and, I am sure, many others are feeling. We are a so-called civilized country: we have a so-called Christian religion: we profess humanity. We have a Parliament of chosen persons, to each of whom we pay £400 a year, so that we have at last some right to say: "Please do our business, and that quickly." And yet we sit and suffer such barbarities and mean cruelties to go on amongst us as must dry the heart of God. I cite a few only of the abhorrent things done daily, daily left undone; done and left undone, without shadow of doubt, against the conscience and general will of the community:

Sweating of women workers.

Insufficient feeding of children.

Employment of boys on work that to all intents ruins their chances in after-life — as mean a thing as can well be done.

Foul housing of those who have as much right as you and I to the first decencies of life.

Consignment of paupers (that is of those without money or friends) to lunatic asylums on the certificate of one doctor, the certificate of two doctors being essential in the case of a person who has money or friends.

Export of horses worn-out in work for Englishmen — save the mark! Export that for a few pieces of blood-money delivers up old and faithful servants to wretchedness.

Mutilation of horses by docking, so that they suffer, offend the eye, and are defenceless against the attacks of flies that would drive men, so treated, crazy.

Caging of wild things, especially wild song-birds, by those who themselves think liberty the breath of life, the jewel above price.

Slaughter for food of millions of creatures every year by obsolete methods that none but the interested defend.

Importation of the plumes of ruthlessly slain wild birds, mothers with young in the nest, to decorate our gentlewomen.

Such as these — shameful barbarities done to helpless creatures we suffer amongst us year after year. They are admitted to be anathema; in favour of their abolition there would be found at any moment a round majority of unfettered Parliamentary and general opinion. One and all they are removable, and many of them by small expenditure of Parliamentary time, public money, and expert care. Almost any one of them is productive of more suffering to innocent and helpless creatures, human or not, and probably of more secret harm to our spiritual life, more damage to human nature, than for example, the admission or rejection of Tariff Reform, the Disestablishment or preservation of the Welsh Church. I would almost say than the granting or non-granting of Home Rule — questions that sop up *ad infinitum* the energies, the interest, the time of those we elect and pay to manage our business. And I say it is rotten that, for mere want of Parliamentary interest and time, we cannot have manifest and stinking sores such as these treated and banished once for all from the nation's body. I say it is rotten that due time and machinery cannot be found to deal with these and other barbarities to man and beast, concerning which, in the main, no real controversy exists. Rotten that their removal should be left to the mercy of the ballot, to private members' Bills, liable to be obstructed; or to the hampered and inadequate efforts of societies unsupported by legislation.

Rome, I know, is not built in a day. Parliament works hard, it has worked harder during these last years than ever perhaps before — all honour to it for that. It is an august Assembly of which I wish to speak with all respect. But it works without sense of proportion, or sense of humour. Over and over again it turns things already talked into their graves; over and over again listens to the same partisan bickerings, to arguments which everybody knows by heart, to rolling periods which advance nothing but those who utter them. And all the time the fires of live misery that could, most of them, so easily be put out, are raging and the reek thereof is going up.

It is I, of course, who will be mocked at for lack of the senses of proportion and humour in daring to compare the Home Rule Bill with the caging of wild song birds. But if the tale of hours spent on the former *since the last new thing was said on both sides* be set against the tale of hours not yet spent on the latter, the mocker will yet be mocked.

I am not one of those who believe we can do without party, but I do see and I do say that party measures absorb far too much of the time that our common humanity demands for the redress of crying shames. And if, Sir, laymen see this with grief and anger, how much more poignant must be the feeling of members of Parliament themselves, to whom alone remedy has been entrusted!

Yours truly,
JOHN GALSWORTHY

TREATING MARRIED WOMEN FAIRLY

6 April 1914

Sir, I think it may serve a useful purpose to enunciate clearly three inevitable results of compelling professional women to give up their professions on marriage. (1) It prevents admirable women of a certain type of character from marrying at all; (2) it deprives the community of the work and the experience of another type of woman, who does not feel able to sacrifice her private life to her career; (3) it leads other women, of a more perfect balance, who demand the right to be both normal women as well as intelligences, to (a) wilfully and "dishonestly" concealing the fact of their marriage from their employers; or (b) living in union with a man without the legal tie of marriage.

Regarding the last alternative, I may say that it is sure steadily to increase if interference with married women's work is persisted in. My own experience of three years of marriage, in which I have discovered the innumerable coercions, restrictions, legal injustices, and encroachments on her liberty imposed on a married woman by the community or sections of it, has brought me to the point of being ready to condone in any of my educated women friends a life lived (if in serious and binding union) with a man to whom she is not legally married. Three years ago such a course would have filled me with horror.

Only by treating married women properly, *i.e.*, by leaving them the freedom of choice allowed to all other individuals, can innumerable unexpected evils be avoided.

Yours faithfully,
MARIE C. STOPES

Dr Stopes was at the time seeking to have her marriage annulled. *Married Love*, the work which made her name, in part by openly advocating that women practise birth control, was published in 1918.

NOT A MANLY GAME

6 June 1914

SIR, THE SOONER IT IS realized that golf is merely a pleasant recreation and inducement to indolent people to take exercise the better. Golf has none of the essentials of a great game. It destroys rather than builds up character, and tends to selfishness and ill-temper. It calls for none of the essential qualities of a great game, such as pluck, endurance, physical fitness and agility, unselfishness and *esprit de corps*, or quickness of eye and judgment. Games which develop these qualities are of assistance for the more serious pursuits of life.

Golf is of the greatest value to thousands, and brings health and relief from the cares of business to many, but to contend that a game is great which is readily mastered by every youth who goes into a professional's shop as assistant (generally a scratch player within a year!) and by the majority of caddies is childish. No one is more grateful to golf for many a pleasant day's exercise than the writer, or more fully recognizes the difficulties and charm of the game, but there is charm and there are difficulties in (for instance) lawn tennis and croquet. It certainly seems to the writer that no game which does not demand a certain amount of pluck and physical courage from its exponents can be called great, or can be really beneficial to boys or men.

The present tendency is undoubtedly towards the more effeminate and less exacting pastimes, but the day that sees the youth of England given up to lawn tennis and golf in preference to the old manly games (cricket, football, polo, &c.) will be of sad omen for the future of the race.

I am, yours, &c.,
B. J. T. BOSANQUET

Bosanquet was himself a cricketer, for Middlesex and England, and noted as the inventor of the googlie – of which more later (see page 139).

THE GERMAN PEOPLE AND THE WAR

7 August 1914

SIR, MAY I ADD MY testimony to that of Lady Phillips published in your issue of to-day? I started from Germany at 3 o'clock p.m. on Saturday last, with my wife and sister-in-law, and during the whole of our trying and anxious journey we experienced nothing but the utmost kindness and courtesy from both people and officials.

Perhaps I may add one thing more. It is too late to believe in the *bona fides* of the German Government; but in that of the German people I still believe. During my short visit I had conversations with many Germans of various classes. All believed that Russia had provoked the war in order to establish the Slav hegemony over the Germans, and that France was an accomplice in the spirit of *revanche*. All hated the idea of war — the look in their faces haunts me yet — but accepted it with a high courage because they believed it to be necessary for the safety of their country.

The German people, believe me, are better than their Government. We have to fight them, but let us do so in the spirit of gentlemen, giving them full credit for the admirable and amiable qualities to which those who know them best bear loudest witness.

W. ALISON PHILLIPS

Phillips was formerly a foreign correspondent with *The Times*. War between Britain and Germany had been declared three days earlier.

OLD SOLDIER

5 September 1914

SIR, I HAVE, BEFORE the war was declared, offered my services as an old soldier in many regiments and as one who has been in service in South Africa (victory and disaster), to the authorities, but no acknowledgment has ever been received. I have got over 100 men to recruit willingly in Fife.

I have had my three servants refused as "unfit" to-day — one for chest measurement, a well set up young man of 22; another very naturally, for varicose veins; a third because at some time he injured his knee and does not work well. The latter is a chauffeur, and long ago offered his services for transport service, and is a good driver. All these men are under 25 years of age. If the medical authority are not allowed to enlist such men for various services how can they render service to their country?

In my own position I consider it scandalous that I cannot fill a position in a cavalry regiment instead of a boy of 17 who has seen no service.

Yours faithfully,
ROSSLYN
The Earl of Rosslyn

P.S. — Of course I want to go to the front after a week's drill.

Lord Rosslyn, the 5th Earl, was then in his mid-forties.

OLD SOCKS WANTED

12 December 1914

SIR, MITTENS ARE WANTED badly by the troops and they are scarce. A sock only wears out in the foot part, and if this is cut off (thrown away) and a hole made in the other part for the thumb to go through, an excellent mitten can be made without any expense. I am paying unemployed typists to sew them over, but in three months I have exhausted my circle of friends. May I ask your readers to send me all the old (clean) socks they can collect, in order in this way to provide more work and more comforts without cost and without interfering with the living of any other class?

Yours faithfully,
GEORGE PRAGNELL

COLONEL CORNWALLIS-WEST

12 January 1915

SIR, LIEUTENANT-COLONEL George Cornwallis-West, who has been in continuous command since September of one of the battalions of the Royal Naval Division which were present at Antwerp, has been much annoyed and feels justly indignant at persistent rumours which have been going round to the effect that he has been "shot in England as a spy."

Colonel West desires us to say that he is alive and well, and he will be much obliged if you will accord him the favour of publishing this letter.

We write as Colonel West's solicitors. He was with us this morning.

We are, yours faithfully,
ROOPER AND WHATELY
Rooper and Whately, Solicitors

Cornwallis-West was primarily known to readers of *The Times* for his marriages. His first wife was the former Lady Randolph Churchill, thus making him stepfather to Winston Churchill — albeit the two men were the same age. He had recently wed the actress Mrs Patrick Campbell, who first played Eliza Doolittle on stage.

MORE LEECHES NEEDED

28 January 1915

SIR, OUR COUNTRY HAS BEEN for many months suffering from a serious shortage of leeches. As long ago as last November there were only a few dozen left in London, and *they* were second-hand.

Whilst General Joffre, General von Kluck, General von Hindenburg, and the Grand Duke Nicholas persist in fighting over some of the best leech-areas in Europe, possibly unwittingly, this shortage will continue, for even in Wordsworth's time the native supply was diminishing, and since then we have for many years largely depended on importations from France and Central Europe. In November I made some efforts to alleviate the situation by applying to America and Canada, but without success. I then applied to India, and last week, owing to the kindness of Dr. Annandale, Director of the Indian Museum at Calcutta, and to the officers of the P. and O. Company and to Colonel Alcock, M.D., of the London School of Tropical Medicine, I have succeeded in landing a fine consignment of a leech which is used for blood-letting in India. It is true that the leech is not the *Hirudo medicinalis* of our pharmacopœias, but a different genus and species, *Limnatis granulosa*. Judging by its size, always a varying quantity in a leech, we may have to readjust our ideas as to a leech's cubic capacity, yet I believe, from seeing them a day or two ago, they are willing and even anxious to do their duty. They have stood the voyage from Bombay and the changed climatic conditions very satisfactorily, and are in a state of great activity and apparent hunger at 50, Wigmore-street, London, W.

It is true that leeches are not used to anything like the extent they were 80 years ago — Paris alone, about 1830, made use of some 52 millions a year — but still they are used, though in much smaller numbers.

It may be of some consolation to my fellow-countrymen to know that our deficiency in leeches is more than compensated by the appalling shortage of sausage-skins in Middle Europe. With true German thoroughness they are trying to make artificial ones!

I am yours faithfully,
A. E. SHIPLEY

The zoologist and Master of Christ's College, Cambridge, Arthur Shipley, an expert on parasitic worms, was knighted in 1920 for his war work, which included letting the Master's lodgings be used as a convalescent home for the wounded.

INTELLIGENT PASSPORTS

17 *February 1915*

SIR, A LITTLE LIGHT might be shed, with advantage, upon the high-handed methods of the Passports Department at the Foreign Office. On the form provided for the purpose I described my face as "intelligent." Instead of finding this characterization entered, I have received a passport on which some official utterly unknown to me, has taken it upon himself to call my face "oval."

Yours very truly,
BASSETT DIGBY

———◆———

RACING IN WARTIME

5 *March 1915*

SIR, I AM AFRAID I cannot follow your reasoning with regard to Epsom and Ascot as set forth in your brief leading article to-day. I put aside the remarks about the affair of the Epsom Grand Stand, as to which there has been both misstatement and misapprehension, which I should have thought the matter-of-fact statement of the Stewards of the Jockey Club would have finally cleared away.

But that is a side, and I may add a false, issue. You say that our Allies "cannot understand how Englishmen can go to race meetings when their country is engaged in a life and death struggle." With all submission I think our Allies understand us better than this. They know that Englishmen do not think it necessary to put up the shutters whenever they are engaged in war. They know that we are paying two millions a day for this war, and do not think that we shall add the sacrifice of our thoroughbred horses, which are so invaluable for the future of our Army. For, make no mistake, if our races are to cease our thoroughbred horses must disappear. No man can afford to keep bloodstock for the mere pleasure of looking at them in the stable. You hope that there will be no attempt to hold meetings at Epsom, and, "above all," at Ascot this year. Of what nature, may I ask, is the original sin attaching to these meetings? You record races of a very inferior character almost daily in your columns, sometimes in impressive print. Why do you sanction these and select for special reprobation the two noblest exhibitions of the thoroughbred in the world?

But you say our Allies will misunderstand us. There are many, however, of our French allies who will remember that the winner of the Derby was announced in General Orders during the Crimean War.

Why, indeed, should we embark on the unprecedented course which you indicate, and condemn all our historical practice? Once before our country has been "engaged in a life and death struggle," at least as strenuous and desperate as this; I mean that against the French Revolution and Napoleon. All through that score of bloody years the Epsom and Ascot Meetings were regularly held, nor indeed does it seem to have occurred to our forefathers that it was guilty to witness races while we were at war. I remember asking the late Lord Stradbroke which was the most interesting race that he had ever witnessed for the Ascot Cup. He replied (I am almost sure, though it is outside my argument) that for 1815, which was run on June 8, eight days before Quatre Bras, 10 days before Waterloo, when Napoleon and Wellington were confronting each other to contend for the championship of the world.

I am and desire to remain remote from controversy, but am anxious to remind you of our history and tradition with regard to this question, and to ask you to pause before you condemn not merely Epsom and "above all" Ascot, but also the principles and practice of ancestors not less chivalrous and humane than ourselves.

ROSEBERY

The 5th Earl of Rosebery — prime minister from 1894–95 — won several classic races as an owner, including the Derby twice.

NO PROFITS FROM WAR

14 September 1915

SIR, IT IS BECOMING plain to the average observer of events that there is only one thing which can cause us to lose this war, or can force us to conclude an unsatisfactory peace, and that is the suspicion between different classes in the nation. It is not my purpose to discuss the question whether this suspicion is justified; it is enough that it exists, and that is a statement which you, Sir, are under no temptation to deny.

So far as one can see the suspicion rages mainly round two topics, the rise in the price of necessaries and the amount of war profits; but these two are really one, for the rise in prices would lose half its sting, but for the idea that it is caused by the undue profits of middlemen. The real question before the Government is, therefore, that of the abolition of all war profits; till that is done suspicion will inevitably continue.

And what is the obstacle? It is not undue sympathy on the part of the Government with profit-makers; Mr. Lloyd George's speech at Bristol has made that plain. It is not the fear of protests in the Press; you have, if I am not mistaken, repeatedly supported such a measure. It is most assuredly not the fear of public opinion, which would be overwhelmingly on the side of such legislation. The professional classes have borne their own burdens as best they could, but they have no more sympathy than the working classes with the abnormal profits made out of the country's need.

It is time, in fact, to ask the plain question, Who *does* want to make profit out of the crisis? When that question has been answered it will be time for the nation to decide what shall be allowed, but I am much mistaken if the demand will be either loud or clear. When every class has given of its own flesh and blood with such splendid readiness, it is impossible to believe that any will haggle over money. We are told that the Government have already dealt with profits in munition factories, and it is no doubt their intention to deal with other war profits by way of taxation. The purpose of this letter is to implore them to make their actions and their intentions plain beyond the possibility of mistake. Vague assertions do not quiet vague suspicions.

When once a clear principle is laid down, be it abolition or curtailment, the question resolves itself into one of fact, and suspicion will die for lack of food. There can be no objection to the fullest representation of working-class opinion on the committee which is to carry out the principle into action. The present situation of half-hearted promises and forced concessions is both humiliating and demoralizing, and to the average man it seems frankly intolerable that a Government in which we all have good reasons to believe should be unable to give expression to an elementary principle of political morality and should allow us to drift, as we are drifting, into a great and needless danger.

I am, &c.,
C. A. ALINGTON
Headmaster of Shrewsbury School

Cyril Alington subsequently became Head Master of Eton and later Dean of Durham.

———◆———

THE VOICE OF A SCHOOLBOY RALLIES THE RANKS

14 December 1915

Sir, May I say one word in reply to the letter of a "Public School Master," which appears in *The Times* of to-day (11 December). As an old headmaster, I am not likely to underestimate the value of school discipline. But long experience has convinced me that we keep our boys at school too long. And, as to the commissions to boys, Clive sailed to India at the age of 17; Wolfe, "a lanky stripling of 15", carried the colours of the 12th Regiment of Foot; Wellington was ensign in the 73rd Regiment at the age of 17; Colin Campbell gained his commission in the 9th Regiment of Foot at the age of 16. We keep our boys in leading strings too long.

I am, Sir, your obedient servant,
JOSEPH WOOD

The writer had been headmaster of Tonbridge and Harrow schools.

BODY ARMOUR OR SHIELDS

28 July 1916

Sir, IT IS A YEAR NOW since you were good enough to allow me to express some views about body armour in your columns. Since then, so far as I know, nothing has been done, but now we have got so far that the Minister of War admits that something of the kind may some day come along. To me it seems the most important question of any, and I earnestly hope that you will use your influence to keep it before the notice of the authorities.

Upon July 1 several of our divisions were stopped by machine-gun fire. Their losses were exceedingly heavy, but hardly any of them from high explosives. The distance to traverse was only about 250 yards. The problem, therefore, is to render a body of men reasonably immune to bullets fired at that range. The German first-line trenches were thinly held, so that once across the open our infantry would have had no difficulty whatsoever.

Now, Sir, I venture to say that if three intelligent metal-workers were put together in consultation they would in a few days produce a shield which would take the greater part of those men safely across. We have definite facts to go upon. A shield of steel of 7/16 of an inch will stop a point-blank bullet. Far more will it stop one which strikes it obliquely. Suppose such a shield fashioned like that of a Roman soldier, 2ft. broad and 3ft. deep. Admittedly it is heavy—well over 30lb. in weight. What then? The man has not far to go, and he has the whole day before him. A mile in a day is good progress as modern battles go. What does it matter, then, if he carries a heavy shield to cover him?

Suppose that the first line of stormers carried such shields. Their only other armament, besides their helmets, should be a bag of bombs. With these they clear up the machine-guns. The second wave of attack with rifles, and possibly without shields, then comes along, occupies and cleans up the trench, while the heavily armed infantry, after a rest advance upon the next one. Men would, of course, be hit about the legs and arms, and high explosives would claim their victims, but I venture to say that we should not again see British divisions held up by machine-guns and shrapnel. Why can it not be tried at once? Nothing elaborate is needed. Only so many sheets of steel cut to size and furnished with a double thong for arm-grip. Shields are evidently better than body armour, since they can be turned in any direction, or form a screen for a sniper or for a wounded man.

The present private contrivances seem inadequate, and I can well understand that those who could afford to buy them would shrink from using a protection which their comrades did not possess. Yet I have seen letters in which men have declared that they owed their lives to these primitive shields. Let the experiment be made of arming a whole battalion with proper ones—and, above all, let it be done at once. Then at last the attack will be on a level with the defence.

Yours faithfully,
ARTHUR CONAN DOYLE

The first tanks had been demonstrated to the Army command in great secrecy five months earlier and made their first appearance on the battlefield in September 1916.

RUSSELL IN CHAINS

5 September 1916

Sir, Mr. Bertrand Russell's view of pre-war diplomacy is not mine, and it is very far from yours; nevertheless, I hope *The Times* will allow me to protest against the military edict which forbids him to reside in any part of Scotland, in Manchester or Liverpool, or on the greater part of the English coast. Such an edict is obviously aimed at a man who may justly be suspected of communicating with the enemy, or of assisting his cause. Mr. Russell is not only the most distinguished bearer of one of the greatest names in English political history, but he is a man so upright in thought and deed that such action is, in the view of every one who knows him, repugnant to his character. It is a gross libel, and an advertisement to the world that the administration of the Defence of the Realm Regulations is in the hands of men who do not understand their business. Incidentally, their action deprives Mr. Russell, already debarred from entering the United States, of the power of earning his livelihood by arranged lectures on subjects unconnected with the war. *The Times* is the most active supporter of that war; but its support is intelligent, and it speaks as the mouthpiece of the country's intelligence as well as of its force. May I therefore appeal to it to use its great influence to discourage the persecution of an Englishman of whose accomplishments and character the nation may well be proud, even in the hour when his conscientious conclusions are not accepted by it?

Yours, &c.,

H. W. MASSINGHAM

The philosopher, a grandson of the Victorian prime minister Earl Russell, was a pacifist. He had been fined £100 in June 1916 and compelled to resign his Cambridge fellowship because of his anti-war speeches.

POPULAR REPRESENTATION

30 March 1917

SIR, THERE SEEMS TO be a very general failure to grasp the importance of what is called—so unhappily—Proportional Representation in the recommendations of the Speaker's Conference. It is the only rational, honest, and efficient electoral method. It is, however, in danger of being thrust on one side as a mere fad of the intellectuals. It is regarded by many ill-informed people as something difficult, "high-browed," troublesome, and of no practical value, much as science and mathematics were so regarded by the "practical" rule-of-thumb industrialists of the past. There are all too many mean interests in machine politics threatened by this reform, which are eager to seize upon this ignorant mistrust and use to delay or burke[1] the political cleaning-up that Proportional Representation would involve. Will you permit me to state, as compactly and clearly as I can, the real case for this urgently-needed reform—a reform which alone can make Parliamentary government anything better than a caricature of the national thought and a mockery of the national will?

The essential point to grasp is that Proportional Representation is not a novel scheme, but a carefully worked-out remedy for universally recognized ills. An election is not the simple matter it appears to be at the first blush. Methods of voting can be manipulated in various ways, and nearly every method has its own liability to falsification. Take the commonest, simplest case—the case that is the perplexity of every clear-thinking voter under British or American conditions: the case of a constituency in which every elector has one vote, and which returns one representative to Parliament. The naive theory on which we go is that all the possible candidates are put up, that each voter votes for the one he likes best, and that the best man wins. The bitter experience is that hardly ever are there more than two candidates, and still more rarely is either of these the best man possible.

Suppose, for example, the constituency is mainly Conservative. A little group of pot-house politicians, wire-pullers, busy-bodies, local journalists, and small lawyers working for various monetary interests, have "captured" the Conservative organization. For reasons that do not appear they put up an unknown Mr. Goldbug as the official Conservative candidate. He professes generally Conservative view of things, but few people are sure of him and few people trust him. Against him the weaker (and therefore still more venal) Liberal organization puts up a Mr. Kentshire (former Wurstberg) to represent the broader thought and finer generosities of the English mind. A number of Conservative gentlemen, generally too busy about their honest businesses to attend the party "smokers" and the party cave, realize suddenly that they want Goldbug hardly more than they want Wurstberg. They put up their long-admired, trusted, and able friend Mr. Sanity as an Independent Conservative. Every one knows the trouble that follows. Mr. Sanity is "going to split the party vote." The hesitating voter is told, with considerable truth, that a vote given for Mr. Sanity is a vote given for Wurstberg. At any price we do not want Wurstberg. So at the eleventh hour Mr. Sanity is induced to withdraw, and Mr. Goldbug goes into parliament to misrepresent us. That in its simplest form is the dilemma of democracy. The problem that has confronted modern democracy since its beginning has not been the representation of organized minorities, but *the protection of the unorganized masses of busily occupied, fairly intelligent men from the tricks of specialists who work the party machines.* We know Mr. Sanity, we want Mr. Sanity, but we are too busy to watch the incessant intrigues to oust him in favour of the obscurely influential people, politically docile, who are favoured by the organization. We want an organizer-proof method of voting. It is in answer to this demand, as the outcome of a most careful examination of the ways in which voting may be protected from the exploitation of those who *work* elections, that the method of Proportional Representation with a single transferable vote has been evolved. It is organizer-proof. It defies the caucus. If you do not like Mr. Goldbug you can put up and vote for Mr. Sanity, giving Mr. Goldbug your second choice, in the most perfect confidence that in any case your vote cannot help to return Mr. Wurstberg.

There is the cardinal fact in the discussion of this matter. Let the reader grasp that, and he has the key to the significance of this question. With Proportional Representation with a single transferable vote (this specification is necessary because there are also inferior imitations of various election-riggers figuring as proportional representation) it is *impossible to prevent the effective candidature of independent men of repute beside the official candidates.* Without it the next Parliament, the Parliament that will draw the broad lines of the Empire's destinies for many years, will be just the familiar gathering of old Parliamentary hands and commonplace party hacks. It will be a Parliament gravitating fatally from the very first towards the old party dualism, and all the falsity and futility through which we drifted in the years before the war. Proportional Representation is the door for the outside man; the Bill that establishes it will be the charter to enfranchise the non-party Briton. Great masses of people to-day are utterly disgusted with "party" and an anger gathers against the "party politician" as such that he can scarcely suspect. To close that door now that it has been opened ever so slightly, and to attempt the task of

Imperial Reconstruction with a sham representative Parliament on the old lines, with large masses of thwarted energy and much practical ability and critical power locked out, may be a more dangerous and disastrous game than those who are playing it seem to realize at the present time.

I am, &c.,
H. G. WELLS

[1]: meaning "to murder by smothering" and derived from the crimes of the early 19th-century Edinburgh "body-snatchers" Burke and Hare.

VOTES FOR WOMEN

26 May 1917

SIR, MRS. HUMPHRY WARD disputes the authority of the present House of Commons to deal with the question of Women's Suffrage. She seems to have forgotten that at the time of the last General Election the subject was already prominently before the country: the majority of members were more or less definitely pledged to the women of their constituencies to support it; and Mr. Asquith had given a definite assurance that if his party returned to power the matter should be dealt with exactly as it is proposed to deal with it in the present Bill — by a free vote of the House of Commons.

Mrs. Ward prophesies that the age limit of 30 for women voters will not be long maintained. She says nothing of the much more important barrier against complete equality which the Bill proposes to set up; by basing the men's vote on residence, the women's on occupation. The effect of this and the age limit together will be that men voters will be in an overwhelming majority in every constituency in the country. If, therefore, as women hope and believe will be the case, the franchise should be further extended and eventually placed on a basis of complete equality, it can only be because men are willing for it, having become convinced by experience of its actual working that the effect will be beneficial and not harmful.

She says, also, nothing at all of the argument which, perhaps more than any other, has moved many of the most weighty and inveterate opponents of former years to give the Bill their active support. In what sort of position will Parliament be placed, when the time comes at the end of the war to redeem the pledges it has given to trade unionists, if women are still outside the pale of the franchise? Legislation will be necessary, involving probably, as Mr. Asquith has pointed out "large displacements of female labour." Will it be to the credit or dignity of Parliament that it should be open to the charge of bartering away the interests of non-voters in order that it may protect those of its constituents?

The chief argument, however, of Mrs. Ward's letter is that the physical sufferings and sacrifices of women in the present war are not comparable with those of men. This is undeniable. Women have not based their claims to the vote on their sufferings or their services. They have never asked for it as a reward for doing their obvious duty to the country in its time of peril. But the vote, after all, is not a sort of D.S.O. It is merely the symbol of the responsibilities of ordinary citizenship, which requires every one to serve the country according to the measures of his or her opportunity, and to make sacrifices for it, if the call for that comes. Is physical suffering, physical sacrifice, the only kind that counts?

I saw recently a letter from a young wife whose husband had just fallen in the trenches. She wrote — "After all, we have nothing to regret. If it were all to come over again and we knew what would happen, he would go just as cheerily as before, and God knows I would not hold him back."

There spoke the authentic voice of the women of this country, women who have in their blood and their bones the traditions of an Imperial race. In time of peace they may have been bemused by the false doctrine taught by Mrs. Ward and her school, that Imperial and national questions are matters for men, not women. In time of war instinct reasserts itself. They feel as patriots and as citizens, and their citizenship so manifests itself that it compels recognition in the traditional form for which women have asked so long by granting of the Parliamentary vote.

Yours faithfully,
ELEANOR F. RATHBONE

Eleanor Rathbone was a leading campaigner for women's rights and social reform, including the introduction of child benefit. She became an MP in 1929, 11 years after women (at first aged 30 and above) were given the right to vote, and to be elected to Parliament.

AN ACT OF WILFUL DEFIANCE

31 July 1917

I AM MAKING THIS statement as an act of wilful defiance of military authority because I believe that the war is being deliberately prolonged by those who have the power to end it. I am a soldier, convinced that I am acting on behalf of soldiers. I believe that the war upon which I entered as a war of defence and liberation has now become a war of aggression and conquest. I believe that the purposes for which I and my fellow soldiers entered upon this war should have been so clearly stated as to have made it impossible to change them and that had this been done the objects which actuated us would now be attainable by negotiation.

I have seen and endured the sufferings of the troops and I can no longer be a party to prolong these sufferings for ends which I believe to be evil and unjust. I am not protesting against the conduct of the war, but against the political errors and insincerities for which the fighting men are being sacrificed.

On behalf of those who are suffering now, I make this protest against the deception which is being practised upon them; also I believe it may help to destroy the callous complacency with which the majority of those at home regard the continuance of agonies which they do not share and which they have not enough imagination to realise.

LT. SIEGFRIED SASSOON

The poet's celebrated letter of protest was sent originally to the *Bradford Pioneer* newspaper and republished four days later in *The Times*, having been read out in the House of Commons. Sassoon, who had won the Military Cross in France, had been on convalescent leave after being wounded. He wrote the letter after deciding to refuse to return to the trenches. His friend and fellow war poet Robert Graves persuaded the authorities that Sassoon was mentally ill and therefore unfit to be court-martialled. He was treated instead for shell shock at Craiglockhart Hospital, Edinburgh, where he met and encouraged Wilfred Owen in his writing.

POPPIES

17 September 1917

Sir, The subjoined letter has been received by the mother of a young officer in the Household Battalion, and was written from the fighting line in Flanders. It pleasantly varies the story of devastation daily transmitted from the front, and incidentally reveals the sort of young fellow who, in various degrees of rank, is captaining our gallant Armies. This one, impatiently awaiting the birthday that marked the minimum age for military service, went from Eton straight to a training camp, and in due course had his heart's desire by obtaining a commission. He followed close in the footsteps of an elder brother, also an Etonian, killed in his first month's fighting.

"In England there seems to be a general belief that nothing but every imaginable hardship and horror is connected with the letters B.E.F., and, looking at these three letters, people see only bully beef, dug-outs, shell holes, mud, and such like as the eternal routine of life. True enough, these conditions do prevail very often, but in between whiles they are somewhat mitigated by most unexpected 'corners.' The other day we took over from a well-known Scottish regiment, whose reputation for making themselves comfortable was well known throughout the division, and when I went to examine my future abode I found everything up to the standard which I had anticipated. Standing on an oak table in the middle of the dug-out was a shell-case filled with flowers, and these not ordinary blossoms, but Madonna lilies, mignonette, and roses. This vase, if I may so term the receptacle, overshadowed all else and by its presence changed the whole atmosphere, the perfume reminding me of home, and what greater joy or luxury is there for any of us out here than such a memory?

"After having duly appreciated this most unexpected corner I inquired where the flowers had been gathered, and was told they had come from the utterly ruined village of Fampoux close by. At once I set out to explore and verify this information. Sure enough, between piles of bricks, shell holes, dirt, and every sort of *débris*, suddenly a rose in full bloom would smile at me, and a lily would waft its delicious scent and seem to say how it had defied the destroyer and all his frightfulness. In each corner where I saw a blossoming flower or even a ripening fruit, I seemed to realize a scene belonging to this unhappy village in peaceful days. Imagination might well lose her way in the paths of chivalry and romance perhaps quite unknown to the inhabitants of Fampoux. I meandered on through the village until I struck a trench leading up to the front line; this

I followed for a while until quite suddenly I was confronted by a brilliancy which seemed to me one of the most perfect bits of colour I have ever seen. Amongst innumerable shell holes there was a small patch of ground absolutely carpeted with buttercups, over which blazed bright, red poppies intermixed with the bluest of cornflowers. Here was a really glorious corner, and how quickly came memories of home! No one, however hardened by the horrors of war, could pass that spot without a smile or a happy thought. Perhaps it is the contrast of the perfection of these corners with the sordidness of all around that makes them of such inestimable value. Some such corners exist throughout France, even in the front line trenches. It may not be flowers, it may be only the corner of a field or barn; it may be some spoken word or a chance meeting. No matter what it is if it brings back a happy memory or reminds one of home. It is like a jewel in a crown of thorns giving promise of another crown and of days to come wherein, under other circumstances, we may be more worthy of the wearing."

Yours faithfully,
HENRY LUCY

ON THE ETON WORD "ROUGE"

13 October 1917

SIR, I WAS ONCE, about 30 years ago, discussing the Eton word "rouge" and the verb "to rouge" among some English friends at Florence, one of whom was the Hon. Alethea Lawley, sister of Lord Wenlock, of Escrick, in East Yorkshire. (NB — She has been for several years married to a Venetian, Signor Wiel, formerly Librarian of the Biblioteca Marciana.) Miss Lawley exclaimed: "Oh, but 'to rouge' is quite a common word in our part of Yorkshire, meaning 'to push one's way through anything', and I have often, when two people are quarrelling, heard one of them say, 'Now don't ye come a-rouging against me!'" even as at Eton we might have said: "There against was an awful crowd, but I soon rouged my way through it!" Whenever I see a doubtful East Yorkshire word, I always turn to Vigfussen's *Icelandic Dictionary*, wherein I have occasionally found the solution of some difficulties both in Norwegian as well as in East Yorkshire provincialisms. I find in Vigfussen, s.v.: *Rydja* (more anciently *hrjóda*) — *rydja sér til rúms* = "to make oneself room"; again, *rydja sér til rikis* = "to clear the way to a kingdom, *i.e.*, to conquer it"; and III, "to clear one's way, to make great havoc — to throng, to crowd." I never can ignore the possible Scandinavian origin of any word, if it be in use in the east of England.

To give another instance. On one occasion I was reading in Ibsen's *Peer Gynt*, where that rascal is relating a lying tale to his foolish old mother of how he sprang on to the back of a wounded buck and galloped along the Gendin Edge, when suddenly

"paa en raadlös braabraet plet
for ivrejret rype-*steggan*
flaksed, kaglende, forskraemt
fra den knart, hvor han sad gemt
klods for bukkens fod paa eggen."

"*Steggan*" did not appear in any Norwegian dictionary that I possessed at that time, though it is given in Iver Aasen's *Dictionary of Provincial Dialects*, but I bethought me of Vigfussen, and I found "*Steggr* m. *Steggi*, a.m. (properly a mounter); in Yorkshire a *steg* is a gander, from *stiga* (to mount); a he bird, *Andar Steggi* a male duck," &c. Therefore the lines translate:

"(All at once — at a desperate break-neck spot)
Rose a great cock ptarmigan,
Flapping, cackling, terrified,
From the crack where he lay hidden
(at the buck's feet on the Edge)."

Had I not known from Miss Lawley (30 years ago) that the word "rouge" is in common use round Escrick, I might not have thought more about it; but as it is, I cannot agree that it is the same in sound and meaning as "scrooge" (pronounced scroodge) whereas "rouge" is pronounced exactly like the French equivalent of "red".

As it may possibly interest some Old Etonians who know Scandinavia, I venture to send you this for what it may be worth.

I remain yours faithfully,
WILLIAM WARREN VERNON

A letter which gives some indication, perhaps, of the presumed readership of the newspaper and their interests in 1917. A rouge is a scoring play in Eton's Field Game, an ancestor of soccer. Some scholars have seen a link between the attritional nature of it and Eton's other unique sport the Wall Game, the preponderance of Etonian generals in the First World War and the strategy of grim slogging used for much of the conflict.

UNMARRIED MOTHER

25 February 1918

SIR, MR GALSWORTHY, IN his article in to-day's *Times* on "The Nation's Young Lives," strongly advocates the adoption of widows' or mothers' pensions, and the proper protection and care of unmarried girl mothers and their illegitimate children. His words are opportune. No amount of Welfare Centres can do anything radical to help the children of widows or those born out of wedlock, until the State has awakened to its grave responsibility for their welfare.

I have, within the last two days, been present at a meeting of a committee of women Poor Law Guardians in one of our great provincial cities. They were engaged, no doubt unconsciously, in a game which, for want of a better name, I must call girl-baiting. I saw a young expectant mother cruelly handled, and tortured with bitter words and threats; an ordeal which she will have had to endure at the hands of four different sets of officials by the time her baby is three weeks old. These guardians told her, in my presence, that they hoped she would suffer severely for her wrong-doing, that they considered that her own mother, who had treated her kindly, had been too lenient, and that her sin was so great that she ought to be ashamed to be a cost to self-respecting ratepayers.

They added that the man who was responsible for her condition was very good to have acknowledged his paternity, but expressed the belief, nay, rather the hope, that he would take an early opportunity of getting out of his obligation. Meanwhile, a pale, trembling girl, within a month of her confinement, stood, like a hunted animal, in the presence of such judges.

We pray constantly in our churches for "all women labouring of child, sick persons, and young children, the fatherless, the widows, and all that are desolate and oppressed," and yet we continue this oppression of the desolate.

Yours faithfully,
DOROTHEA IRVING

AIR SEWAGE

1 November 1918

SIR, FEW OF US CAN DO more than pass a very short period of the day in the open air. In a country in which a large proportion of the inhabitants spend most of their lives in industrial occupations, it is wiser to teach them the importance of introducing fresh air into their houses than to urge them to the impossible duty of spending much of their time out of doors.

If we devote, on average, eight hours to sleep, then a third at least of our 24-hour day is spent indoors, and each individual who reaches 60 years of life will have passed no less than 20 years of his existence in the one and only room where he is likely to be sole arbiter of the ventilation. Unless there are exceptional conditions, the windows of every sleeping room should be wide open all night and every night. The blinds should be drawn up, otherwise, from their valve-like action, they will only permit intermittent and uncertain ingress of fresh air, while the only egress for devitalized air is by the inadequate route of the chimney. The hours of night should also be employed for regularly and continuously flushing all day-rooms, where sewage air is manufactured in such quantities that it is never adequately scavenged during working hours. I know of crowded offices where the ventilation is imperfect through the day, and where the windows are all religiously closed up every night, so that the next morning the workers start by breathing more or less sewage air. The windows of many workrooms, hotels, schools, banks, churches and clubs are regularly "shut up for the night". It has been shown that the sense of fatigue is more the consequence of breathing devitalized and stagnant air than of any other single factor. There is no harm in a room or railway carriage being warmed, if the air is regularly changed as it is used up. Scavenging our air sewage ensures a supply of fresh air. It is our chief safeguard against the onset or severity of influenza. The possibility of "a draught" — still a bogy to many — is best avoided by remembering that doors should be kept closed and windows kept open.

In 1867 Ruskin wrote: "A wholesome taste for cleanliness and fresh air is one of the final attainments of humanity." Let us hope that this attainment may be advanced by the lessons of science applied in the present epidemic.

ST. CLAIR THOMSON

The letter was written during the 1918 Spanish flu outbreak. An estimated 20 million to 50 million people died worldwide.

DOING YOUR BIT

24 June 1919

Sir, It is now a truism to say that in August 1914, the nation was face to face with the greatest crisis in her history. She was saved by the free will offerings of her people. The best of her men rushed to the colours; the best of her women left their homes to spend and be spent; the best of her older men worked as they had never worked before, to a common end, and with a sense of unity and fellowship as new as it was exhilarating. It may be that in four and half years the ideals of many became dim, but the spiritual impetus of those early days carried the country through to the end.

To-day on the eve of peace, we are faced with another crisis, less obvious but none the less searching. The whole country is exhausted. By natural reaction, not unlike that which led to the excesses of the Restoration after the reign of the Puritans, all classes are in danger of being submerged on a wave of extravagance and materialism. It is so easy to live on borrowed money; so difficult to realise that you are doing so.

It is so easy to play; so hard to learn that you cannot play for long without work. A fool's paradise is only the ante-room to a fool's hell.

How can a nation be made to understand the gravity of the financial situation; that love of country is better than love of money?

This can only be done by example and the wealthy classes have to-day an opportunity of service which can never recur.

They know the danger of the present debt; they know the weight of it in the years to come. They know the practical difficulties of a universal statutory capital levy. Let them impose upon themselves, each as he is able, a voluntary levy. It should be possible to pay to the Exchequer within twelve months such a sum as would save the tax payer 50 millions a year.

I have been considering this matter for nearly two years, but my mind moves slowly; I dislike publicity, and I had hoped that somebody else might lead the way. I have made as accurate an estimate as I am able of the value of my own estate, and have arrived at a total of about £580,000. I have decided to realize 20% of that amount or say £120,000 which will purchase £150,000 of the new War Loan, and present it to the Government for cancellation.

I give this portion of my estate as a thank-offering in the firm conviction that never again shall we have such a chance of giving our country that form of help which is so vital at the present time.

Yours, etc.,

F.S.T.

The writer refers to 'the eve of peace' as the letter was written a few days before the Treaty of Versailles was signed on 28 June 1919.

The initials F.S.T. stood for Financial Secretary to the Treasury — Stanley Baldwin, who would become prime minister for the first time in 1923. His net worth was equivalent to about £50 million now. The scheme he proposed does not appear to have caught on.

HERE'S HOW

15 July 1919

SIR, WILL YOU PERMIT an elderly man, who is not a politician nor a public character, but merely an individual among millions of honest, sober persons whose liberty is attacked by a moral tyranny, to state an opinion with regard to the crusade which is being started against moderate drinkers?

It is not needed even in the cause of morality. That drunkenness has not entirely ceased is obvious, but that it is rapidly declining, from the natural action of civilization, is equally obvious. When I was a child, even in the country village where I was brought up, excess in drinking was patent in every class of society. Now, in my very wide circle of various acquaintances, I do not know of one single man or woman who is ever seen "under the influence of liquor". Why not leave the process of moderation, so marked within 60 years, to pursue its normal course?

It is untrue to say that a limited and reasonable use of alcohol is injurious to mind, or body, or morality. My father, whose life was one of intense intellectual application, and who died, from the result of an accident, in his 79th year, was the most rigidly conscientious evangelical I have ever known.

He would have been astonished to learn that his claret and water at his midday meal, and his glass of Constantia when he want to bed, were either sinful in themselves or provocative to sin in others. There is no blessing upon those who invent offences for pleasure of giving pain and who lay burdens wantonly on the liberty of others. We have seen attempts by the fantastically righteous to condemn those who eat meat, who go to see plays, those who take walks on Sundays. The campaign against the sober use of wine and beer is on a footing with these efforts, and should be treated as they have been. Already tobacco is being forbidden to the clergy!

The fact that Americans are advertised as organizing and leading the campaign should be regarded with alarm. It must, I think, be odious to all right-thinking Americans in America. We do not express an opinion, much less do we organize a propaganda against "dryness" in the United States. The conditions of that country differ extremely from our own. It is not for us to interfere in their domestic business. If Englishmen went round America urging Americans to defy their own laws and revolt against their national customs, we should be very properly indignant. Let crusading Americans be taught the same reticence. It was never more important than it is now for Great Britain and the United States to act in harmony, and to respect each the habits and prejudices of the other.

These considerations may be commonplace; I hope they are. But many people seem afraid of saying in public what they are unanimously saying in private. The propagandist teetotaler is active and unscrupulous. He does not hesitate to bring forward evidence, or to attach moral opprobrium to his opponents. He fights with all weapons, whether they are clean or no. We must openly resist, without fear of consequences, what those of us who share my view judge to be cruel and ignorant fanaticism of these apostles. We should offer no apology for insisting on retaining our liberty.

I am, Sir, your obedient servant,
EDMUND GOSSE

The next year, the sale of alcohol was banned in the United States: Prohibition.

THE FUTURE OF WAR

6 November 1919

SIR, BY LAND AND SEA the approaching prodigious aircraft development knocks out the present Fleet, makes invasion impracticable, cancels our country being an island, and transforms the atmosphere into the battle-ground of the future.

I say to the Prime Minister there is only one thing to do to the ostriches who are spending these vast millions ("which no man can number") on what is as useful for the next war as bows and arrows! — "Sack the lot."

Yours,
FISHER
Admiral of the Fleet Lord Fisher

Postscript.—As the locusts swarmed over Egypt so will the aircraft swarm in the heavens, carrying (some of them) inconceivable cargoes of men and bombs, some fast, some slow. Some will act like battle cruisers, others as destroyers. All cheap and (this is the gist of it) requiring only a few men as the crew.

No one's imagination can as yet depict it all. If I essayed it now I should be called a lunatic. I gently forecast it in January, 1915, and more vividly on July 11, 1918. We have the star guiding us, if only we will follow it.

Time and the Ocean and some fostering star

In high cabal — have made us what we are!

On Friday last the presiding genius at the "Marine Engineers" said, "The day of oil fuel and the oil engine had arrived." In 1885 I was called an "oil maniac." — *Nunc Dimittis*

The former First Sea Lord Jackie Fisher was a prolific and often percipient correspondent to *The Times* on naval matters, and blessed with an inimitable style of writing. He died in 1920, before much of his vision of future warfare was vindicated.

NEW TIMES AND
NEW STANDARDS

1920–29

TO-DAY'S YOUNG MEN

3 August 1921

SIR, MAY I, as a middle-aged spectator, write a few words in your columns to call attention to a curious change in the younger generation of men now, or lately, in residence at the universities, and of ages from 20 to 25?

In many essentials they are the same young men as those of 20 years ago. They are generous and loyal; they are gentle and kind hearted; they are full of spirit and pluck. But there is one great difference. More than ever before in the history of youth do they defy discipline and worship independence. More than ever do they brush aside experience and do exactly as they please.

The writer's observations are based chiefly on recent visits to the universities, on watching cricket matches, and on meeting the younger men in private houses and at tennis and golf.

Many of them, when they are talking to other persons, including people older than themselves, never take their pipes out of their mouths. When asked to luncheon with hostesses in London many of them appear in undergraduate clothes and flannel collars. When they are in London they never dress for dinner except in case of absolute necessity. They often associate with very odd friends, and with the female companions of these odd friends. At the Eton and Harrow match the writer saw in the pavilion a group of young men who were, for any other occasion, rather nicely dressed. They wore blue serge suits, summer shirts and Zingari[1] straw hats. But had they not forgotten that the 1,200 boys who were present were wearing, compulsorily, the kit which for generations had been honoured and welcomed in London as one of the most charming sights of the ceremonial year, and that the great majority of grown-up people who came to the match were showing their respect for the boys by donning the same kind of dress?

The last point I wish to mention is that young men are showing an increasing toleration and fondness for lawn tennis. Breaking away from the general opinion of the masters of our public schools, and from the athletic traditions of many decades of university life, a number of men who might have been fine cricketers devote themselves entirely to "pat-ball," and while Australia triumphs on the cricket field the youth of England wanders from county to county and from tournament to tournament in pursuit of the trophies and tea parties of this effeminate game.

If an older friend ever dares to point out any of these things to them in a friendly and bantering way, the answer is always the same:—"You are the most dreadful snob we ever met. We intend to do exactly as we like."

I leave the issue there. It may be that it is the substance, and not the form, which matters. But for those who value form the question must arise. If this is the form of the beginning of their lives, how will they train their own offspring? How will they save themselves from being judged as

Nos nequiores mox daturos
Progeniem vitiosiorem? [2]

I am, &c.,
OLD ETONIAN

[1] I Zingari ("gypsies" in Italian) is the name of a cricket club that then drew its members from old boys of the leading public schools.

[2] For the benefit of those who did not study Horace at Eton, the Latin tag translates roughly as "We, who are worse than our parents, will soon have children who are even more unbearable."

Replied on 4 August 1921

SIR, MAY I, AS A young man (and, incidentally, an Old Wykehamist), make some reply to the accusations of "Old Etonian"? It would be strange indeed if "a curious change" was not to be observed in the younger generation of to-day. Without making the too common claim that we "won the war," we may at least remind your correspondent that for three or four years we were subject to such a discipline as he and his like have never known, and never will know. We spent a large, an incredibly large, proportion of that time absorbing the notions of "middle aged men" concerning matters of form, matters of dress and "smartness" and sartorial respect. We were told that these things were more than matters of form; they were essential to efficiency. But we saw that many an uncouth miners' battalion was as valiant and efficient in the field as Guards themselves; we saw that those senior officers who were most busy about ritual details of "smartness" were often the most stupid, pig-headed, and inhuman; we saw "experience" fussing about salutes and forgetting about the men's food; and it is not surprising if we have learned to set our own value on matters of form.

Even so, no young man that I have met claims to do "exactly as he pleases" in this respect, though we may have found new standards. It is possible, for example, that the young men in "blue serge suits, &c." regarded their costume as more beautiful and becoming than the funereal top-hattery of the rest of Lord's. But surely, we may be allowed to play what games we like? "Old Etonian" regards lawn tennis as a young woman's game; I regard cricket as an old woman's game. Lethargic, slow, it seems to me to consume a period of time grossly disproportionate to the energy expended by the average individual player; and it seems to me to be a pious myth that cricket is more unselfish than tennis. No doubt there is effeminate lawn tennis, as there is effeminate cricket ("tea parties" and all); but let "Old Etonian" go to Wimbledon, to any tournament, and dare to describe what he sees as "pat-ball."

Nevertheless, I do not object to any man playing cricket, if he can tolerate the game, though I see numbers of men who might have been fine tennis players wandering from county to county and alternately standing about and sitting about in front of ill-mannered and ill-dressed cricket crowds, while America triumphs on the tennis lawn. I only ask for the same liberty for ourselves.

I should not dream of calling your correspondent a "snob." But I would ask him to go a little deeper. If he had pursued his researches at the universities he would have been told by any of the authorities that the average post-war undergraduate displayed an industry or keenness unlike anything that was known before the war. It is conceivable that the young men who go to luncheons in flannel collars do so because they have work to do before and after the meal. If he goes to the stalls on a first night he will see two or three young men in ordinary clothes. They are dramatic critics, and they will be earning their living till 2 o'clock in the morning. Snobbery is not his complaint, but lack of imagination.

As for our offspring, I beg that he will leave them alone. He is right in supposing that they will not be brought up as we were brought up.

I am, Sir, yours, &c.,
A. P. HERBERT

Alan Herbert, the humourist and future MP, had fought at Gallipoli and on the Western Front after leaving Oxford.

Replied on 4 August 1921

SIR, "OLD ETONIAN" DESERVES the thanks of the nation for exposing so lucidly the lack of manners and terrible effeminacy of our young men of to-day. At a reception which I attended recently I was astounded to note that not a single man was wearing knee breeches and ruffles and the ladies had completely discarded the crinoline. Instead of the sweeping bow, the delicate curtsey, and the gentle inquiry as to health, we find a revolting hearty handshake and an indelicate remark about stuffiness of the atmosphere. I was pained to see young men and — *horribile dictu* — young women smoking an abomination called a cigarette, and when I produced my patent folding churchwarden pipe there was a mild sensation.

In my young days we rollicked the summer days away playing croquet and bowls, but now the *jeunesse dorée* indulge in the grossly effeminate pastimes of golf and lawn tennis. It is indeed sad to see that a stalwart soldier like Earl Haig should have deserted the inspiring and breathlessly exciting game of croquet for that of hitting a stupid little ball round the countryside with an iron-headed stick.

"Old Etonian" need have no fear of being dubbed a snob. Far from it. He is of that gallant band who during the war would have insisted, had he been able, upon the tanks being decorated with inscribed standards and being heralded into action by the massed bands of the Brigade of Guards, flanked by the Life Guards in full-dress uniform, or Grand Rounds at dead of night making his inspection of trenches fully cuirassed to a fanfare of trumpets and preceded by a choir of seven lance-corporals chanting "Floreat Etona."

Yours, &c.,
RAYMOND SAVAGE

RATSKIN GLOVES

28 January 1920

Sir, Is it not possible in these times of a world shortage of raw material (especially leather) for such serviceable articles as rat skins to be put to some useful purpose? It will be generally conceded that if a market can be found or created for such skins it will be an incentive for the destruction of these noxious rodents, which is so essential. It is possible there are at present a few buyers, but so far I have been unable to discover them. Any information on this point will be appreciated. For someone with enterprise and imagination rat skins should be a sound commercial proposition — they would make excellent leather purses and gloves.

Yours faithfully,
GEORGE L. MOORE

REPRESSION IN IRELAND

14 September 1920

SIR, ON AUGUST 24 a conference in Dublin of moderate men of all parties demanded, amongst other things, as the preliminary condition of an Irish settlement the abandonment of the policy of repression.

Few Englishmen have any idea of the lengths to which this policy has been carried. Most Englishmen know simply that some 80 members of the Royal Irish Constabulary have been murdered, and they take it for granted that the Government's repressive measures are necessary to put an end to these outrages, and that they are designed for this and no other purpose. Consequently, the actual state of government and justice in Ireland has not been scrutinized carefully, and Englishmen hear little of proceedings that are bringing danger and dishonour upon us. If these proceedings were a kind to put an end to outrages and not to cause further mischief, they would not have called down the condemnation of men like Lord Monteagle, Lord Shaftesbury, Sir Horace Plunkett, and the other leading Irishmen who took part in the conference at Dublin.

The Coercion Act, with the regulations issued for is administration, marks the climax of this policy. Court-martial justice will become the rule. It is provided that men may be kept indefinitely in prison without trial. A Court may sit in secret. If a Court believes that a particular person is able to give evidence, he or she may be arrested. Any person who does an act with a view to promoting or calculated to promote the objects of an lawful association is guilty of an offence against these regulations. As the Gaelic League, which was founded to revive Irish culture, and Dail Eireann[1], which represents two-thirds of the Irish people, are unlawful associations, all but a small minority of Irishmen may be convicted on this charge. This is not a system of justice adapted for the detection and punishment of crime; it is designed for the punishment of a political movement, and it puts every Irishman who holds the opinions held by the great majority of Irishmen at mercy of the military authorities.

These authorities are the officers of an army employed on a task hateful to British soldiers and living in an atmosphere of bitter hostility to the native population. Indignation has been naturally excited in this army by a series of murders which the Government been unable to punish. Discipline has broken down. A sort of military lynch law is in force, applied not to the culprits but to the villages and towns of Ireland. It is not an uncommon experience for whole streets to be burnt, creameries[2] destroyed, and life taken in the indiscriminate reprisals by which soldiers and policemen avenge murder of constables. Not for a century has there been an outbreak of military violence in these islands. The Government have failed to restrain or punish this violence, and they have now taken steps to prevent any civilian Court from calling attention to it. They have issued an order forbidding the holding of coroners' inquests in nine counties. This removes the last vestige of protection from the civilian population. In the "Manual of Military Law" it is laid down that, whereas a man acquitted or convicted by a civil Court may not be retried by military Court, a person subject to military law is not to be exempted from the civil-law by reason of his military status. The Government have now decided that if soldiers or policemen fire a town or shoot civilians they are to be immune from the danger of an inquiry by a Court not under military direction.

In Ireland Englishmen are judged by their actions alone. No assurances of good will have the slightest effect on public opinion there; no English promises make it easier for moderate opinion to get a hearing. Every solution of the Irish question presupposes a friendly feeling between England and Ireland, and we are stimulating hatred.

Thus only by changing our executive policy can we create the atmosphere necessary to the successful working of any solution whatever of the Irish question.

We are, Sir, yours faithfully,
ERNEST BARKER
PHILIP GIBBS
CHARLES GORE
HUBERT GOUGH
J. L. HAMMOND
L. T. HOBHOUSE
DESMOND MACCARTHY
JOHN MASEFIELD
C. E. MONTAGUE
GILBERT MURRAY
C. P. SCOTT
H. G. WELLS
BASIL WILLIAMS

[1] The parliament formed by Irish republicans on declaring independence from Britain in 1919
[2] Butter was an important export and co-operative agricultural ventures, of which dairies were the most numerous, were central to rural Irish life

The Government's measures only fuelled greater violence, which continued to escalate until a truce was signed in 1921. Ireland was partitioned and the next year the Irish Free State came into being.

WIGS AND GOWNS

1 April 1922

Sir, I am glad to say that I do not know the name of any member of the Committee of Judges and Benchers of the Inns of Court whose recommendations concerning the forensic costume of women barristers you publish this morning 31 March. I can therefore criticize their "wishes" without fear or favour.

I have no fault to find with what they recommend about gowns, bands, or dresses. As to wigs, I think they are hopelessly wrong. A wig is, historically and essentially, not a covering, but a substitute for natural hair. I believe the history of the forensic wig to be in substance as follows. About the period of the Restoration, some of the leaders of fashion in France, for reasons of cleanliness and health, took to shaving their heads. They accordingly wore wigs, which soon became very large and elaborate. The fashion found such favour that for something like a century all gentlemen, when fully dressed, wore wigs. During this time they either shaved their heads, or cropped their hair very close, and probably also wore night-caps when in bed.

Then the wig gradually disappeared, and the modern method of cutting the hair short, but just long enough to make an efficient covering for the head, was gradually adopted. Judges and barristers followed this practice like other people, but found that, as long as the hair was short, the wig formed a distinctive, dignified, and convenient headdress for use in court. If women barristers are going to cut their hair short as we cut ours, our wigs will suit them well enough, but I do not believe they will do anything of the kind.

The Committee wish that their wigs "should completely cover and conceal the hair." Why they entertain this wish I cannot imagine. Our wigs by no means completely cover and conceal our hair. Suppose a woman barrister wears her hair "bobbed." Her wig, if it completely conceals her hair, will certainly not be an "ordinary barrister's wig." Suppose she has plenty of hair, and wears it coiled in one of the usual ways. She will then want one pattern of wig when fashion places the coils on top of her head, another when they are resting on the back of her neck, and a third when they approach the situation of the old fashioned chignon, high up on the back of the head. Each of the three will impart to the wearer a hydrocephalous, ungainly, and ludicrous appearance.

It must be apparent to every one, except the Committee, that women barristers ought to wear a distinctive, and probably dark-coloured, headdress, in approximately the form of a biretta, a turban, or a toque. I use each of these terms with very great diffidence.

I am, Sir, your obedient servant,
HERBERT STEPHEN

UNJUST DIVORCE LAWS

11 October 1922

SIR, DURING THE LAST weeks of the Summer Term, at the request of the Lord Chancellor, I undertook the trial of undefended suits for divorce and heard about four hundred cases. They were taken in due order from the list, and included every class, but with a large preponderance of the poor, owing to their numbers, and also to the difficulty of their getting decent homes.

The experience was startling, and explains why it is that practically every Judge on whom a similar duty has devolved has urged an alteration of the law. I believe that the reason why this demand is not universal is that the facts are not known, and false modesty prevents their disclosure. Women's societies pass resolutions declaring that if any change be made, equality must be established between men and women, forgetting, or not knowing, that the present law produces the most insulting inequality, and that it is in the interests of women that reform is sought.

Plain facts need plain speech, and I beg, without apology, to ask attention to the following statement, based on the cases I tried, prefaced only by saying that I scrutinized the evidence with especial care, and that I am satisfied as to the truth of what I state.

A woman marries a man, and is at once infected by him with syphilis. She is an innocent woman, and knows nothing as to what is wrong until the disease has her fast in its grip. The doctor is satisfied that infection occurred immediately on marriage; consequently the law politely bows her out of Court and makes her pay the cost of her struggle for liberty. In the particular case to which I refer, the husband had deserted the woman, and it was possible to prove, though with difficulty, that he had also transferred his "affections" to someone else; but for this his wife was bound for life.

Another woman had been made the victim of the unspeakable savagery of brutal and perverted lust. She also must have remained bound by the bonds of matrimony, enforced by violence, but that her husband went to satisfy his fury elsewhere, and was found out.

A third was deserted, after a week, by a soldier who went to the American continent, where he might have lived unmolested for ever in a life of peaceful adultery, but as he violated two children he also was discovered, and she was able to be free.

I could multiply the recital of individual cases, but lack of space forbids, and the general conditions need attention.

Bigamy was extremely common, but entirely confined to poor persons, for bigamy is not a vice of wealth; the rich can find other less illegal outlets for their emotions. The existing statute, however, provides that bigamy is not sufficient ground for divorce — it must be "bigamy with adultery" — and, though it might be assumed, anywhere outside a law Court, that a man who has risked penal servitude to obtain possession of a woman was not prompted by platonic love, yet the law requires independent proof of the adultery. Further, by a decision now sixty-five years old, this adultery must be with the bigamous wife — adultery with any number of other people is quite inadequate.

On the wisdom and justice of this ancient judgment I will not comment, but it throws great difficulty in the way of a woman who can prove that her husband has been convicted of bigamy, but finds it difficult to trace and obtain evidence of adultery; *quoad hanc*[1], in one case before me, she almost failed.

Among the poorer people desertion was the commonest event: rich folk walk more delicately, and, being in a hurry, obtain a decree for restitution, to be obeyed in a fortnight, instead of waiting two years. It was, of course, only in the rare instances where the deserting husband could be traced and his undoubted adultery legally proved that any relief would be obtained. In one such case the husband, who had first insulted and then deserted his wife, left the country in a ship with the woman with his affection for whom he had often taunted his wife, but, of course, that did not constitute legal proof of adultery, but merely companionship.

In no case that I tried did there appear to me the faintest chance of reconciliation; the marriage tie had been broken beyond repair and its sanctity utterly defiled; nor, again, though I watched with extreme vigilance, was there any single case where collusion could be suggested. With regard to cruelty, there was no case which a competent lawyer, skilled in the knowledge of witnesses, could not have tried.

I was, of course, faced with the question as to what is cruelty, which, we are informed, is so difficult that you want the King's Proctor as an expert in cruelty to keep the law steady. I made my own rules. If a man who was sober kicked his wife in the stomach when she was pregnant, that seemed to me enough; if she were not pregnant, and he was drunk, he might have to do it again or else her complaint might be due to what the most persistent opponent of my Bill called "nervous irritation." So, also, with kicking her downstairs, or making her sleep on the doormat in winter — all of which cases I had to consider. But, however brutal and repeated the cruelty, no divorce must be granted for it, or we shall Americanize our institutions and soil the sanctity of English homes.

I had no case before me involving the question of lunacy or criminality, for these, as the law stands, are irrelevant considerations in connexion with divorce; but the evidence on that is near at hand. Within the last few months two women have been left eternally widowed, with their husbands fast immured in criminal lunatic asylums, and in this unnatural state they will remain while the shadow of the years lengthens and life's day grows dim. Surely the desire to help such people is not, as some appear to think, prompted by a Satan, but is a humble effort to carry out the principle of the supplication which asks that, while our own wants are satisfied, we should not be unmindful of the wants of others.

Parliament will shortly resume its work. Our divorce laws have been condemned by the most competent authority as immoral and unjust. The House of Lords has patiently heard every argument that can be advanced against further change from the lips of the most skilful advocates, and has repeatedly, and by emphatic majorities, demanded reform. Common sense — but for respect to my adversaries I should have added common decency — rejecting the existing law. Is it asking too much to entreat the Government to afford a chance to Parliament to cleanse our laws from this disgrace?

Yours faithfully,
BUCKMASTER

[1] In legal Latin, the sexual impotence of the husband

Viscount Buckmaster had been Lord Chancellor from 1915–16. Men were able to obtain a divorce on proof of a wife's adultery, but women had to prove both a husband's adultery and another reason, such as domestic violence. Despite Buckmaster's efforts, the law was eventually reformed, largely at the instigation of AP Herbert, only in 1937.

THE SPECTACLE OF RESPECTABLE

8 February 1923

SIR, IS IT NOT TIME that the official categories of respectability were revised?

In order to secure the renewal of a passport, it is necessary to obtain a signed declaration of identity and fitness from a mayor, magistrate, justice of the peace, minister of religion, barrister-at-law, physician, surgeon, solicitor, or bank manager, with whom the applicant is personally acquainted; and similar lists are found on many other official forms. On what principle they were compiled I know not, but they cause considerable inconvenience, and defeat their own end.

I never knew a mayor. But I have known many Civil servants of reasonable integrity, and in my neighbourhood are two or three not more unscrupulous than the rest of their profession; I am friendly with two editors; I know a peer; several stockbrokers, baronets, novelists, and Members of Parliament would readily swear that I am a fit and proper person to go to France. But these gentlemen are not worthy, and I am forced to search any casual acquaintance for magistrates and dental surgeons, who, in fact, know nothing about me.

For persons even poorer than myself the difficulty is more serious. As a rule, the only "respectable" people they know are the physician and the clergyman, and why should these alone be bothered with the things? Why not the policeman, the postman, the landlord, the tax collector? Things have come to a pretty pass in this democratic age if the word of an attorney is more than the word of a publisher: and if we cannot trust a policeman, whom can we trust?

The result, in most cases, is that the applicant obtains a solemn declaration from that one of his acquaintance who knows least about him. This is the kind of trivial official rubbish which is allowed to endure forever because no one thinks it worth while to protest. I therefore protest that these antiquated and offensive lists should be revised, as above, or, if that be too daring, abolished altogether. Why not simply "a householder"?

I am, Sir, yours faithfully,
A. P. HERBERT

GATHERING NUTS IN MAY

9 May 1923

SIR, I REMEMBER THAT, when I read the Classics, I had always a liking for the reading of the manuscript and a distaste for emendations. It is probably the same instinct which leads me to think that "nuts in May" are really nuts. (But I remember that, when I joined in the chant some forty years ago, we used to say "nutsimay," and I liked the mysterious sound, and wondered what "nutsimay" was.) If nuts do not grow upon trees in May, I conceive it to be possible that they grow in the ground. Certainly one of my pleasantest memories is that of hunting for nuts in the ground (a long time ago) somewhere about the month of May. They were to be found on a little bank, overshadowed by trees, that overhung a disused quarry. You knew their presence by the tender green shoots which grew from them; and when you saw those shoots, you took your knife, made a small excavation, and had a succulent reward. I have consulted the *New English Dictionary* (my general refuge in all mental perplexities), and I have found there, s.v. groundnut, the admirable entry which awakens a pleased reminiscence and rumination. "*Bunium flexuosum*: Culpepper, *English Physitian*, 64; they are called earth-nuts, earth-chestnuts, groundnuts."

What I cannot really remember is whether we actually gathered *Bunia flexuosa* in May. But while I cannot prove it (except by the obvious device of consulting some scientific work of reference), I flatter myself that it is extremely probable. In any case, there was some real fun in gathering this sort of nut. It was elusive; it was succulent; it was neither so obvious, nor so unsatisfactory, as your hazel nut.

But it pains me to think of these things. They belong to the Arcadia of a vanished youth. *Où sont les neiges d'antan?* Where are the nuts of yester-year?

Yours obediently,
ERNEST BARKER

NESTLETRIPES AND PIGGY-WIDDENS

7 June 1923

Sir, "Tantony" is a new name to me for the small one of a litter of pigs or dogs. Some years ago I made the following collection of names all in use in various parts of the country:

Nisgil (Midlands), Nisledrige and Nestletripe (Devon), Darling, Daniel, Dolly and Harry (Hants), Underling, Rickling, Reckling, Little David (Kent), Dillin, Dilling (Stratford-on-Avon), Cad, Gramper, Nestletribe, Nestledrag, Nestlebird, Dab-Chick, Wastrill, Weed, Dandlin, Anthony, Runt, Parson's Pig (the least valuable to be devoted to tithe purposes), Nest Squab, Putman, Ratling, Dorneedy (Scottish), The Titman (Vermont), Nestledraft, Pigot, Rutland, Luchan, Piggy-Widden.

Yours faithfully,
EDWIN BROUGH

A DIAMOND IN THE ROUGH

28 October 1924

SIR, AS ONE WHO has sampled most British sports, may I say a word upon baseball? It seems to me that in those Press comments which I have been able to see too much stress is laid upon what may appear to us to be a weakness or a comic aspect in the game and not nearly enough upon its real claim on our attention. I fully agree that the continual ragging is from a British view-point a defect, but baseball is a game which is continually in process of development and improvement, as anyone who reads Arthur Mathewson's interesting book on the subject is aware.

The foul tricks which were once common are now hardly known, and what was once applauded, or at any rate tolerated, would now be execrated. Therefore, this rough *badinage* may pass away and it is not an essential of the game. What is essential is that here is a splendid game which calls for a fine eye, activity, bodily fitness, and judgment in the highest degree. This game needs no expensive levelling of a field, its outfit is within the reach of any village club, it takes only two or three hours in the playing, it is independent of wet wickets, and the player is on his toes all the time, and not sitting on a pavilion bench while another man makes his century. If it were taken up by our different Association teams as a summer pastime I believe it would sweep this country as it has done America. At the same time it would no more interfere with cricket than lawn tennis has done. It would find its own place. What we need now is a central association which would advise and help the little clubs in the first year of their existence.

Yours faithfully,
ARTHUR CONAN DOYLE

Conan Doyle was a keen sportsman who had played first-class cricket. He also helped to introduce skiing to Switzerland from Scandinavia, and so popularise the sport in Britain.

LONG LIVES IN THE TIMES

1 January 1925

SIR, ON THE FRONT page of *The Times* last year there were reported the deaths of 402 persons of 90 years of age and over. Of these 123 were men (including 18 clerks in holy orders) and 279 women; of the latter 178 were married. The number of those who reached their century is eight; of these two were men and six women, two of whom were 105 and had been married. Four others (two men, one a clerk) were 99. Besides the above named, 95 attained their 90th year, 28 men (six clerks) and 67 women, of whom 30 were married. The number of nonagenarians who have died in the last ten years is 3,153, a yearly average of 315, ranging from 263 in 1918 to last year's big total of 402. The number of centenarians for the same period is 55, the most in one year being 11 in 1923.

In other parts of *The Times* deaths have been reported of 40 others who had been born before or during 1824. Of these four were 103; six, 104; one, 105; four, 106; and one, 107. Under "News in Brief" on 16 August, John Campbell, of County Antrim, aged 112, is reported dead; and on 18 August, under "Telegrams in Brief," the same is told of Alexa Vivier, of Manitoba, who had reached the, nowadays, patriarchal age of 113.

I am, etc.,
C. B. GABB

Ten years later, Mr Gabb wrote to *The Times* to mark its 150th birthday. He noted that Zaro Agha, a Turk who had recently died, supposedly aged 157, could (and undoubtedly would) have read 46,950 issues of the newspaper — had he not been illiterate.

ALL GREEK TO ME

22 January 1925

Sɪʀ, Rᴇᴀᴅɪɴɢ ᴡɪᴛʜ ɢʀᴇᴀᴛ interest the pleasant controversy between the Headmaster of Christ's Hospital and Mr. Austen Chamberlain, I have noticed that my own beloved and reverend headmaster, Mr. J. S. Phillpotts, is as alert and vigilant as ever.

The issue that has been raised is an old one, and as false as it always has been. Controversialists start on the wrong tack when they assume that learning and teaching grammar must be dull and unstimulating. Nothing is more untrue. There is everything in grammar, the accidence as well as the syntax of language, to make it as stimulating to thought and the imagination and as full of humour as any instrument of education. Witness the inexhaustible romance of the verbs in -μι, the miraculous history of the Greek preposition, or the indefinable wonders of the subjunctive mood!

HUBERT M. OXON:
Hubert Burge, Bishop of Oxford

Replied on 23 January 1925

Sɪʀ, Tʜᴇ Bɪꜱʜᴏᴘ ᴏꜰ Oxꜰᴏʀᴅ's letter gives a delightful picture of cultured boyhood. We see him indulging in a hearty laugh with his headmaster on the vagaries of εἰμί, or walking, a slender stripling, in a summer sunset, tracing with wistful eyes the romance of the subjunctive mood into the glowing West!

I began teaching as an Eton master in 1885, and taught classics there for nearly 20 years, starting with a whole-hearted faith in their merits for educational purposes, and coming gradually and reluctantly to a very different conclusion.

The average boy without literary and linguistic aptitude never seemed to me to get within reach of Latin and Greek as living things at all.

I am, &c.,
A. C. BENSON
Master of Magdalene College, Cambridge

Hubert Burge had been headmaster of Winchester, which no doubt explains his and Benson's differing success rates with their pupils. The latter perhaps exerted more influence over the heirs to Greece and Rome by writing the words to "Land of Hope and Glory".

WITNESSING THE RUSSIAN
REVOLUTION IN 1917

9 March 1925

SIR, SATURDAY WAS the anniversary of the outbreak of the Russian Revolution. No one who was present in Petrograd at the time is likely to forget it. During the morning and early afternoon, sullen crowds thronged all the main streets. Mounted police moved quietly among them. There was no disorder, all seemed to be waiting for something; they might have been workmen outside the gates of a factory before opening time. Nevertheless one felt instinctively that the atmosphere was charged. It reminded one of the strange, gloomy silence that so often comes before a storm.

I boarded a tramway car to visit some people near the Nikolai Station. It was very crowded, but I was able to stand in front near the driver. As we proceeded up the Nevsky Prospect I became aware that a lady I knew was a fellow-traveller. I suggested that she should stay with the friend she was on her way to visit, and not attempt to return, as I felt there was going to be trouble.

I had hardly spoken the words when there rose a dull murmur, and one caught snatches of "Give us bread, we are hungry." The tramway car was not travelling fast owing to the crowds. A university student jumped on to the footboard, said something to the driver, and then turned to the control lever, and the car came to a standstill. This held up all the rest, so my friend and I got off and walked. I took her to her destination, and begged her friends to keep her for the night, and then returned to Nevsky.

There I found everything changed. The placid dullness of these sullen crowds was replaced by alertness and excitement. As I neared the statue of Alexander III, a workman ascended to the plinth, and began to address the people. A policeman approached and remonstrated. The speaker refused either to get down or stop talking, whereupon the policeman drew his revolver, and shot him. It was the match to the fire; the smouldering fuse had reached the powder, and it went off. The Revolution had begun. In 20 minutes there was hardly a vestige of that unfortunate policeman left. Men, women, and even children fell upon him and literally tore him to pieces. One could hardly believe that those sad, silent people of half an hour before could have been suddenly transformed into such savages, lusting for the blood of the wretched man.

After this the crowd moved down Nevsky in one solid mass, were met by police, and were fired on. Every one knows the rest: innocent and guilty alike were shot down until the troops joined the people, and the so-called "bloodless Revolution" began.

I am, etc.,
B. S. LOMBARD

———◆———

A SWINDLE BY TELEPHONE

16 January 1926

SIR, I WISH TO WARN your readers about a swindle, which has trapped even astute men of business. The *modus operandi* is a telephone call from a person claiming to be a friend or to have a business or personal connection with the victim. The gentleman is in distress, having been robbed of his purse.

Would his friend help him with a telegraph remittance in the nearest post office to enable him to return to his home in the counties? This in itself sounds bald and unconvincing, but is elaborated with sufficient circumstantial detail to make the story appear genuine. The device comes from America, where it appears to be very successfully played, and is a very profitable transaction for the swindler, who will continue to make a handsome revenue if the public is not warned.

The most effective answer is to promise the required help and then, immediately, to communicate with the police, who, if the case is genuine, can render the assistance needed, or, if not, can put a stop to these activities. No doubt the trick will appear in varying disguises, so as to keep it fresh, but the net result will be the same.

Yours truly,
VIGILANS

IL DUCE WRITES

26 June 1925

Sir, I am very sensible of the fact that your most important paper attentively follows my political and polemical manifestations. Allow me, however, to rectify some statements contained in your last editorial.

It does not correspond with facts that the last Bills voted by the Italian Chamber are against the most elementary liberties, whereof you will be convinced by carefully considering the article of the aforesaid laws. It is not true that patriots are discontented. On the contrary, the truth is that the opposition is carried on by a small dispossessed group, while the enormous majority of the Italian people works and lives quietly, as foreigners sojourning in my country may daily ascertain. Please note also that Fascism counts 3,000,000 adherents, whereof 2,000,000 are Syndicalist workmen and peasants, these representing the politically organized majority of the nation. Even the Italian Opposition now recognizes the great historical importance of the Fascist experiment, which has to be firmly continued in order not to fail in its task of morally and materially elevating the Italian people, and also in the interest of European civilization. Please accept my thanks and regards.

I am, &c.,
MUSSOLINI

The Times had criticised Il Duce's repression of the press and political opposition. Himself a former journalist, Benito Mussolini was keenly aware of the influence of the media on public opinion, at home and abroad.

MAKING PROPER PORRIDGE

17 August 1925

Sir, The recipe given last Saturday for porridge is not very helpful, nothing being said as to the quantity of water or of oatmeal a person.

The time for preparation given as 1½ hour's boiling, during which stirring is to be frequent and therefore attendance constant, is enough to scare off anyone not cursed with too much leisure from attempting to supply an article of food which has no need to be so costly of one's time and for firing.

It is impossible to make good, appetizing porridge in a double saucepan, the only means of cooking it without stirring at frequent intervals, for the simple reason that it is not possible to bring the contents of the inner pan to the boil, and porridge that has not boiled for some time will not "set" when poured out: and if it will not "set" it is not nearly so palatable as if it does set. Porridge that is set will slide out of your plate a few minutes after being poured into it without leaving a smear behind. It is of a jelly-like consistency, not a viscous half-cooked mess. I repeat that it is impossible to attain this consistency with a double pan, and so far I agree with "E. E. K." I merely mention this to emphasize it. Having, then, a single unjacketed saucepan of a capacity equal to twice the amount of water to be put into it — so as to avoid boiling over, which porridge is very prone to do — put into it, overnight if porridge is wanted in the morning, or, say, for six hours before wanted, for every person or for each small soup-plateful of porridge required, 2oz. of best coarse Scotch oatmeal, and not any of the crushed and mangled or otherwise pre-treated substitutes. Add one pint of water, and leave to soak. About half an hour before it is required bring it to the boil and take care that it does not boil over, stirring nearly all the time. Then keep it gently boiling for 20 minutes, stirring often enough to prevent sticking and burning. Finally boil briskly for five minutes and pour into a tureen or direct into the soup plates from which it is to be eaten. As much salt as will stand on a sixpence may be added per portion when the oatmeal is put into soak, or not, as desired.

To enjoy porridge properly it should be "set," thoroughly swollen, and boiled, which the above treatment ensures, and eaten with plenty, say 1/3 pint per portion, of the best and freshest milk. There may be added salt, or sugar, or cream, or all three; or it may be eaten with treacle. Half an hour is ample for boiling, and I have cooked it satisfactorily in 20 minutes frequently. But it must boil, and not merely stew. Scattering the meal into the water is done to prevent it binding into lumps. It rarely does this if put into cold water for six hours before boiling begins, but it is just as well to see that there are no lumps before leaving to soak. I know of no reason why soaking beforehand should be objected to, and it saves firing and the cook's time and trouble.

W. B. HOPKINS

Porridge, like trains, schools and the younger generation, appears to be a subject guaranteed to raise strong passions in the breast of every generation of *Times* readers.

———◆———

COLD SNAKES

13 April 1926

Sir, The truth of the statement in the last sentence of your note on Puff Adders and Pythons (*The Times*, February 13), about a cold snake being nearly always a relatively safe snake, is well borne out by an experience of my own.

While shooting in the Bindraban nala, in Pangi, in 1913, I was after a red bear one cold, drizzly, wet day. The bear was on a high, grass-topped ridge while I was on a lower one running parallel.

I had looked about for a good place from which to take a lying down shot, and, having found a flat rock with a nice slope, lay down. My knees — bare, as I was in "shorts" — were on the ground at the edge of the stone.

Having wriggled about until I was in a comfortable position, and after having sighted the bear, I concluded it was not good enough to risk a shot at that long range, so sat back on my "hunkers".

To my very great surprise and fear, there was a snake coiled, sitting up and watching me from the very place in which my left knee had been pressing into the ground, and still well within striking distance of my knee! It made no effort either to strike or get away while I remained still, but when I sprawled backwards it made off.

When I had killed it with a stone, I found that it was a very good 26in. specimen of the Himalayan pit viper (*Ancistrodon Himalayanus*). The height up would be somewhere between 10,000 ft. and 11,000 ft., and it was, as I have already said, a cold day, with a thin rain falling every now and again; but as my left knee must have been actually pressing upon the snake, it was fortunate that it was a "cold" snake with which I had had to deal.

I am,
T. H. SCOTT
United Service Club, Simla.

MR MACDONALD'S HONORARY DEGREE

8 June 1926

SIR, SINCE THE RECENT unfortunate occurrence may easily be misinterpreted outside, or even inside, this University, may I express what I know to be the feeling of others also, from the point of view of one who has twice voted for Mr MacDonald's party at General Elections, but who would probably have abstained from voting either way on the question of his degree?

A memorial has been circulated in Cambridge deploring that this incident will embarrass, or even destroy, the convention of offering honorary degrees to politicians as such, apart from any direct services which they may have rendered to learning, letters, or art. Some of us, on the other hand, while deeply regretting this incident on other grounds, would welcome that result, and rejoice that some good, at least, had emerged from the present evil. Many, even among Mr MacDonald's political opponents, have the greatest admiration for what he did, as Foreign Minister, in the cause of this country and of world-peace. They heartily regret that, practice in these matters having been what it has been, the first break in that practice during the last few years should seem to imply personal discourtesy to Mr MacDonald. But they cannot agree with the memorialists in branding the small group of determined opponents as persons whose political intolerance humiliates this University; they feel that this would come perilously near to denying the right of conscientious objection to all persons whose objections we ourselves do not happen to share.

Is there any real way out of this difficulty, so long as universities are in the habit of offering Doctorates in Law to politicians or soldiers *as such*? It is argued that the honour is here offered not to the politician but to the distinguished servant of the Crown, *ex officio*. If that were clearly understood on all sides; if it were generally known that the Prime Minister is thus to be honoured automatically, while others must take their chance of an adverse vote, this would certainly remove the misgivings felt by many at the present moment. Although an honour is certainly somewhat lessened by being automatic, yet such a clear understanding would relieve us from our present attempt to fly in the face of nature, and to combine the advantages of free will with those of absolute obedience to rule. We should be a very dead University if there were not strong differences of political opinion, accentuated by the present crisis.

Is it not a contradiction in terms to say that we offer degrees to politicians *qua* politicians, yet without reference to their politics? At least, this is contrary both to reason and to practice in normal cases, where the scholar, the *littérateur*, and the artist are chosen with the directest and most explicit reference to the value of their performances in scholarship, literature, or art. There are men here who joined in a similar public protest against Lord Randolph Churchill's degree; this did not prevent Lord Randolph from receiving his degree on a majority vote. It is as certain as anything can be that Mr MacDonald would have had a sweeping majority; to doubt this would be to suggest, by that very doubt, the strongest possible justification for the opposers' action. In the absence of absolutely clear understandings and precedents, this matter could not possibly have been emptied of all political significance. Some people (as things are at this moment) would have found political significance in the unopposed grant of a degree; even more will find political significance in the fact that it was opposed. Therefore (to repeat my earliest question in a different form), must not a politician be always ready to face a politician's chances?

If universities deliberately intend that a certain studied gesture, when made to a politician, should mean something essentially different from that identical gesture towards a scientist, then ought it not to be understood beforehand, beyond any possibility of misconception, that this offer of a degree is simply an automatic sequel to the King's offer of the Premiership?

Yours, &c.,
G. G. COULTON

Cambridge University had been debating whether to award the customary honorary degree to Ramsay MacDonald, the Labour leader, after he became Prime Minister. Some dons took issue with his opposition to the First World War and his recent encouraging of the General Strike. MacDonald eventually let it be known he did not want the honour. Nearly 60 years later, Oxford would find itself in the same position – see page 360

THE YALE'S HORNS

15 June 1926

SIR, A FEW YEARS AGO, when the King's Beasts were placed on the bridge over the moat leading to the gateway at Hampton Court Palace, I was distressed beyond measure at the effigy of the Yale[1]. Both its horns were directed backwards! I drew the attention of the late Lord Harcourt to this on more than one occasion, and he was genuinely vexed and said that something must be done. But judging by a picture postcard I have recently received, nothing has been done.

My distress and grief have been increased by the action of those who are responsible for restoring the King's Beasts on the outside of the Royal Chapel at Windsor, for here again the Yale has both horns pointing backwards. The Dean of Windsor kindly lent me for a day or two a little book which clearly shows this appalling lack of appreciation of what a Yale really is. For it is in the very essence of a Yale to have one horn pointing forward over the nose and the other horn pointing backwards. I have traced the history of the Yale back to the fourth or fifth Egyptian dynasty, back to the old kingdom, nearly 3,000 years BC. One finds them repeatedly throughout Egyptian art. Herodotus describes them as ὀπισθονόμοι, because their horns curve forward in front of their heads so that it is not possible for them when grazing to move forward, as in that case their horns would become fixed in the ground. Aristotle gives a similar account. Pliny describes their horns as mobile, so that should the front horn be injured in a contest the horns are swivelled round and the hinder horn now comes into action. But in spite of Pliny's uncritical mind and unbridled fancy, he could hardly have invented the Yale. At the present time certain of the domesticated cattle in the great territory of the Bahr-el-Ghazal, to the south of the White Nile, have their horns trained by the natives, one to project forward and one to project backwards.

One of the Canons of Windsor states that the new King's Beast on the outside of the Royal Chapel was copied from one in the interior of the chapel. Should this be the case, those who have been or are responsible for the King's Beasts at Windsor are doubly guilty, for they are misleading the public not only without but within the walls of the sacred edifice. It is impossible to test the accuracy of this statement owing to the present reparations to the building. A distinguished archaeologist in the neighbourhood of Windsor who has been kind enough to inspect for me the false Yales on the outside of the chapel, writes that "we can do little but mourn." But surely that is a counsel of despair. At Hampton Court Palace, and still more on or in the Royal Chapel at Windsor, under the very shadow of Royalty, we might at least expect a certain degree of historical and heraldic accuracy in such matters as the King's Beasts, and the horns of the Yales should be set right.

I am, Sir, yours faithfully,
A. E. SHIPLEY

[1] A mythical beast akin to an ibex used in heraldry and associated with the arms of the Royal Family since Tudor times. It also figures in those of Christ's College, Cambridge, of which Shipley was Master.

———◆———

TIMED OUT

5 July 1926

SIR, THE ETON AND Harrow match is again at hand. May an imponderable quantity, who with countless other such, has suffered from four consecutive draws, venture a suggestion?

Whatever the rule, could it not be the practice in this match for the ingoing batsman always to leave the pavilion gate for the wicket as the outgoing batsman reaches the pavilion gate? Considering that there are 30 to 40 intervals on the fall of wickets, during each of which at least a minute (on the average) is lost, more than half an hour would be saved. Last year's match would have been finished and not impossibly that of the year before. In fact, one has seen several draws in this match which another half-hour would have converted into a win.

This definite practice would have one other advantage: it would automatically save whichever side was tempted in that direction from lingering to the legal limit between wickets to avert defeat. Good sportsmanship, as a rule, takes care of that, but one remembers hearing shouts of "Hurry up!" The reasons against this saving of time no doubt will now be given to him, for they are with difficulty imagined by

Your faithful servant,
JOHN GALSWORTHY

The Nobel Prize-winning novelist had been captain of football at Harrow. His suggestion did not bear fruit until 1980, since when incoming batsmen can be given out unless they get to the wicket within a short time, now 3 minutes.

The annual cricket match against Eton was a highlight of the summer Season.

SILLY POINT

11 August 1926

SIR, DOWN 'ERE WE be 'mazed along o' they writer chaps an' the goin's on o' they Testës. Laws be laws, an' rools be rools, an' they as makes 'em should keep 'em. Paarson — they sez as 'ow the rev'rend gentleman played fer the Blues afore 'e was so 'igh — tell'd us: "Once they arm-chair crickets gets yer into the papers, yer 'ave to be'ave yerself 'cardin'lye. That be the crucks of the matter." I never learned French lingo, but we agrees along of 'im. So do Joe Rummery, as 'as umpir'd fer us nigh fitty yers.

Laast Saturday we at Firlin' played a side from Lunnon — furriners, they be — an' we 'ad two goes apiece, though I knaws we only played from foor till eight, cuz Farmer Beckley said Eb an' me must finish that ten-acre field first. I was out twice leg-afore, an' it bain't no use sayin' "wot fer," cuz Joe wunt be druv. "If it 'its yer leg, yer goes out, sartin sure," sez Joe, who knaws the rools. Joe 'as the same coppers to count over-balls as when he started, with picturs o' the Good Queen on 'em.

We thinks as 'ow they chaps at Lunnon be narvous, else 'ow should they be allus callin' fer tay as soon as they be done dinner? An' these paper chaps makes 'em wuss, a-tellin' us wot it be about, pilin' up pettigues (Paarson sez "worries"), till they batters wunt knaw whether they should be ther at all, or som'eres else.

Firlin's played 'ere 'unnerds o' yers, long afore that ther Mary Bone lady started 'er pitch at Lards in Lunnon, though we likes 'er, an' 'opes she'll keep purty blithesome an' not fergit that we be cricketers too. We ain't wantin' foor stumps, as we finds three a plenty, an' we ain't thinkin' that they pros an' such like 'ave read the rools. If they did as Paarson sez his Irish friend did — when yer sees a 'ead, 'it it— ther wouldn't be no cause fer this gurt talk o' foor days.

I am, &c.,
F. CARTWRIGHT

It was felt in cricketing circles that, because of advances in preparing pitches, modern batsmen were scoring too freely off bowlers. Reforms to what was then regarded as the national game were mooted by correspondents to *The Times*. The options generally favoured were widening the wicket with an extra stump or extending the duration of first-class matches from three to four days in the hopes of enabling fewer to be drawn. In the event, no changes were made, prompting England some years later to target Australian batsmen rather than their wickets: see Bodyline p. 116.

BRITISH FILMS

18 March 1927

Sir, I hope that Mr. Percival's excellent letter in *The Times* last Wednesday will persuade those who still have minds to make up of the folly of the Government's muddle-headed proposals for meeting mediocrity more than halfway. Professed patriots are at times very hard to understand. They prefer the word "British" to cover a multitude of sins rather than wishing it, as the more arrogant and less noisy of us do, to stand as a symbol of merit. Why a sandbag rather than a lantern?

On another page of your paper I read that a number of eminent authors and actors have placed their services at the disposal of a new enterprise called "British Incorporated Pictures." This is, I think, the only country in the world that has not yet realized that films must be conceived and interpreted as films. None of the really great pictures have been adapted from books and few of the great performances, with the exception, of course, of Miss Pauline Frederick's, have come from stage actors. Until literature and the theatre realize that the cinema is not a subsidiary concern to be despised intellectually and exploited financially we shall never get down to the real problem of producing good British films. After all, painters do not tell us that they are taking up the violin in order to help music!

Yours faithfully,
ELIZABETH BIBESCO

Elizabeth Bibesco was an author and the daughter of Herbert Asquith, the former Prime Minister, and his second wife Margot Tennant.

HATS OFF

22 April 1927

SIR, A DUTY ON HATS would be no new thing. A century ago no self-respecting gentleman could visit France without bringing back a Paris bonnet as a present for a lady friend. But the gift was of no value unless it was smuggled. At the landing port a number of bareheaded women used to board the packet-boat on arrival. For a consideration, one would don a bonnet and go on shore with it thus making it free of duty. As soon as it was safely on land it was returned to its rightful owner. When I was a boy my father used to tell me stories of the filthy heads on which the Paris creations were brought on to British soil.

There is a legend that one of the Imperial crowns of Delhi, in the possession of an English officer after the Mutiny, was similarly brought to England, but on the head of the owner's baby. That baby it is said, later became a distinguished General.

I am, &c.
GEORGE A. GRIERSON

"SARAH WAS RIGHT"

2 September 1927

SIR, OUR WEATHER prophets are sadly incapable of interpreting the future. I was confronted this morning with the problem of a hay crop that might have been carried but would be far better for a few hours' sunshine. Daventry told me last night that I might expect two or three fine days. So did this morning's paper. And the 10.30 broadcast gave a special message to farmers to the same effect. So I decided to wait a day.

But my cowman said: "Sir, you're wrong; Sarah says it's going to rain." Now Sarah is a rheumaticky cow that has previously shown great talent in meteorological prediction, and she was very lame this morning. But I trusted the human experts.

Sarah was right.

I wonder if the Meteorological Office would buy her. Her lameness affects her milk yield, and her milk record this year is deplorably low.

I am, Sir, &c.
H. C. HONY

GONE TO THE DOGS

23 December 1927

MAY I BE PERMITTED to express, on behalf of the executive committee of the Girls' Life Brigade, strong disapproval of greyhound racing and its appalling effect upon the girlhood of our nation? It has come to our knowledge that girls of tender years are to be found at the racecourses betting on the various races. If such things are allowed to continue, what can be the outlook for the future of womanhood in our land? We are firmly of opinion that immediate and strong action should be taken to protect the youth of our country from these new and growing menaces, and we should like to take this opportunity of associating ourselves with every effort made to resist the opening of courses at the Crystal Palace (where so many young people assemble) and throughout our land.

Miss DORIS M. ROSE
Headquarters Secretary, The Girls' Life Brigade

ELOCUTION LESSONS

6 June 1928

Sir, The subject of elocution in the theatre being closely akin to speaking in our churches, may I suggest some few useful rules?

(1)   Read or speak so that a person sitting at two-thirds of the total distance of the space to be reached may hear.

(2)   Stop at the mental pictures the words are to convey – the punctuation marks are mainly the concern of the grammarian and the printer, e.g., "There was a man of the Pharisees (slight pause) named Nicodemus."

(3)   The speaker should acquaint himself with the acoustic properties and peculiarities of the building.

(4)   If we are young or not too old to learn, a visit to the Law Courts, there to hear our leading barristers, or to the theatre to hear Sir Johnston Forbes-Robertson, who tells us, I believe, that "our syllables should be like pistol shots," would be helpful.

(5)   Our pauses must be at the right pace, lest we say, for instance, "a man going to see (sea) his wife, desires the prayers of the congregation."

I am, &c.,
REV. W. WILLIAMSON

SLEEPING OUT OF DOORS

21 July 1928

SIR, I WAS MUCH interested in your article "Sleeping Out of Doors." As I have myself slept out of doors every summer since 1912, perhaps some personal experience may be of use to others. My house is just ten miles from London Bridge, and, fortunately, my garden is not much overlooked, although I live in the centre of Bromley, in the High-street.

I first tried sleeping in a hammock, but found it draughty and difficult to turn over, so I soon took to sleeping on a canvas Army bed, which is easy to pack up if required. If the weather is fine, I always sleep under the stars, with no covering on my head, in a sleeping bag, with an extra rug if necessary. If the weather is cool or likely to rain, I sleep in a wooden shelter I had made facing south-east, just large enough to take the bed. I begin sleeping out when the night thermometer is about 47deg. to 50deg., that is, as a rule, early in May. This year I started on 20 April. Having once started, I go on through the summer till October, and have even slept out in my shelter on into November, when the temperature has fallen as low as 25deg. during the night. If it should be a wet night I stay indoors, but then usually feel the bedroom stuffy, although the windows are wide open, and not refreshed as I do outside. If it rains when I am in my bag, I do not mind, and have often slept out in a thunderstorm. This last week I slept six hours without waking and got up feeling fresh and keen like a schoolboy, though I am well past 60.

Friends say, what about midges and insects? Well, all I can say is that in 16 years I have only been bitten once by a mosquito. As to midges, they are very busy up till 10, but evidently go to bed before I do. As to other animals and insects, they have never worried me, and the secret, I believe, is that my bed stands 1ft. from the ground. I hate the cold weather, and look forward to the spring that I may sleep out; and to hear the "birds' chorus" in the early morning in May is worth waking up for; it only lasts about 20 minutes, but must be heard to be appreciated. In June it dies down, and few birds sing after Midsummer Day.

When sleeping outdoors I never get a cold. I do not require so much time in bed, and wake refreshed in a way I never do indoors, with such an appetite for breakfast as no tonic can give. I enjoy the best of health, and wonder more people do not try it. During this summer weather I have never had any difficulty in keeping my rooms cool. My study has never been higher than 70deg., while outside in the shade my thermometer is 84deg. and 88deg., simply because I shut my windows at 9 a.m. and pull down the blinds, and open them at 8 p.m.

and leave them open all night. I bottle up the cool night air and shut out the air which is baked by the hot road and pavement. My study faces due west and has the sun streaming down nearly all day. Bedrooms may be kept cool in the same way.

Yours faithfully,
H. WYNNE THOMAS

The writer was a former president of the British Homeopathic Society.

VERY LITTLE BRAIN

23 August 1928

SIR, I MUST MAKE my contribution to cricket history; the only one I am likely to make. In 1899 I was playing for Westminster v. Charterhouse, the match of the year. Somehow or other the batsman at the other end managed to get out before I did, and the next man came in, all a-tremble with nervousness. He hit his first ball straight up in the air, and called wildly for a run. We all ran — he, I, and the bowler. My partner got underneath the ball first, and in a spasm of excitement jumped up and hit it again as hard as he could. There was no appeal. He burst into tears, so to speak, and hurried back to the pavilion. Whether he would have run away to sea the next day, or gone to Africa and shot big game, we shall never know, for luckily he restored his self-respect a few hours later by bowling Charterhouse out and winning the match for us. But here, for your Cricket Correspondent, is a genuine case of "Out, obstructing the field."

Yours, &c.,
A. A. MILNE

MORAL OF THE STORY

19 October 1928

SIR, IT IS A CURIOUS thing that when they speak of "immorality" in literature our moral reformers seem to have in mind only one department of misbehaviour. They complain that they see nothing but "sex" in the modern novel: and serious writers are entitled to complain there is too much "sex" in many of their sermons. For the majority of the population are not reading books about successful sexual aberration: they are reading books, and seeing plays, about successful murders, robberies, and embezzlements, about charming crooks and attractive burglars. And if there is any substance in the view that the literature of wrongdoing has a demoralizing effect upon popular conduct, we should be suffering now from an unprecedented wave of crime (which is not the case), and Mr. Edgar Wallace should be locked up (which would be a pity). Does the Home Secretary think that so many murders are good for "the little ones"? For my part, I would rather give my children a book which dealt with the difficulties of married life than a book which illustrated the simplicity of homicide. But I do not give them either. And I wish to assure the Home Secretary that my wife and I are capable of watching over our family's reading without any Jixotic[1] assistance from him. But I fear that it is no use talking; and very soon, I suppose, we shall see him tilting fearlessly at John Stuart Mill.*

I am, Sir, your obedient servant,
A. P. HERBERT

* "We can never be sure that the opinion we are endeavouring to stifle is a false opinion; and even if we were sure, stifling it would be an evil still."
J. S. MILL

[1] The decidedly authoritarian Home Secretary, William Joynson-Hicks, was known as "Jix".

IN PRAISE OF BREAD

10 December 1928

SIR, AMONG THE VARIOUS ways in which agriculture is encouraged by the present Government of Italy is the institution of a yearly festival for the glorification of bread, with a hymn in its praise, to which Signor Mussolini has appended his name. The festival is held on April 13 and 14, and the "hymn" is one which surely no one but a countryman of St. Francis could have conceived. It is printed on cards which may be seen on many cottage walls in all parts of Italy. Below is a translation.

I am, Sir, yours very truly,
G.H. HALLAM
S. Antonio, Tivoli (Roma)

IN PRAISE OF BREAD
Italians!
Love Bread.
Heart of the home,
Perfume of the table,
Joy of the hearth.

Respect Bread,
Sweat of the brow,
Pride of labour,
Poem of sacrifice.

Honour Bread,
Glory of the fields,
Fragrance of the land,
Festival of life.

Do not waste Bread.
Wealth of your country,
The sweetest gift of God,
The most blessed reward of Human toil.

MUSSOLINI

"CADDIE!"

6 February 1929

SIR, THIS WILL never do! For five days in the week we avail ourselves of *The Times* as it so competently deals with the less important affairs of life: politics, domestic or foreign; the imminence, hopes, fears of a General Election; the arrivals or departures of great people; the steady depreciation of our scanty investments; another century or two by Hobbs; or a stupendous break by Smith. But on the sixth day *The Times* is exalted in our eyes; for then your "Golf Correspondent," in a column of wisdom, humour, and unmatched literary charm, deals with the one real thing in life.

This week for the first time he has deeply shocked and disappointed us all. I am but a "rabbit." I confess to a handicap of 24 (at times) and a compassionate heart (always). I cannot bear to see a fellow creature suffer, and it is for this reason among others that I rarely find myself able to inflict upon an opponent the anguish of defeat. To-day I suffer for a whole world of caddies, wounded in the house of their friend. They learn in a message almost sounding a note of disdain that the verb which signifies their full activity is "to carry."

By what restriction of mind can anyone suppose that this is adequate? Does not a caddy in truth take charge of our lives and control all our thoughts and actions while we are in his august company? He it is who comforts us in our time of sorrow, encourages us in moments of doubt, inspires us to that little added effort which, when crowned with rare success, brings a joy that nothing else can offer. It is he who with majestic gravity and indisputable authority hands to us the club that he thinks most fitted to our meagre power, as though it were not a rude mattock but indeed a royal sceptre. It is he who counsels us in time of crisis, urging that we should "run her up" or "loft her," or "take a line a wee bit to the left, with a shade of slice." Does he not enjoin us with magisterial right not to raise our head? Are we not most properly rebuked when our left knee sags, or our right elbow soars; or our body is too rigid while our eye goes roaming? Does he not count our strokes with remorseless and unpardonable accuracy, keeping all the while a watchful eye upon our opponent's score? Does he not speak of "our" honour, and is not his exhortation that "we" must win this hole? Does he not make us feel that some share of happiness, or of misery, will be his in our moment of victory or defeat? Does he not with most subtle but delicious flattery coax us to a belief that if only we had time to play a "bit oftener" we should reach the dignity of a single-figure handicap? Does he not hold aloft the flag as though it were indeed our standard, inspiring a reluctant ball at last to gain the hole? Does such a man do nothing but "carry" for us? Of course, he does infinitely more. He "caddies" for us, bless him.

Yours,
BERKELEY MOYNIHAN

THE TELEPHONE KIOSK

22 May 1929

SIR, IF THIS LETTER should meet the eye of the Postmaster-General, perhaps he will explain why he has christened the telephone box near the Royal Academy a telephone kiosk! It would not be easy to find a more ridiculous word.

Yours, etc.,
ALGERNON LAW

Replied on 23 May 1929

SIR, TO SIR ALGERNON LAW's question anent the name "kiosk," as applied to the street telephone box, the Postmaster-General could reply with official hauteur, as did Humpty Dumpty to Alice, "When *I* use a word it means just what I choose it to mean, neither more nor less." Actually the word has travelled from Persia via France, gathering *en route* a veneer of Western civilization plus Post Office vermilion and shedding some of its Eastern trimmings, such as its veranda and balustrade. When the out-of-door telephone call station (open to the public day and night, Sundays and early-closing days) had to be given a name, "box" was already assigned to the first-born, the indoor public telephone. The resemblance to the Paris "kiosk" paper stall naturally suggested kiosk as the appropriate name.

Yours, etc.,
H. S. POWELL-JONES
Secretary, Telephone Development Association

SIR, MR POWELL-JONES seeks to defend the Postmaster-General for the adoption of this ridiculously inappropriate name for an out-of-door telephone station by the irrelevant argument that it is applied by Parisians to a newspaper-stall and that the word "box" had already been applied to the indoor public telephone. But "box" is not the only word in the English language. For instance, "stall" or "booth" or, better still, "hut." We shall next have the General Post Office called the Yildiz Kiosk and the P.M.G.[1] the Padishah.

Yours, etc.,
ALGERNON LAW

[1] The Postmaster-General

Replied on 25 May 1929

SIR, IN VOICING A horror of foreign word immigrants that one would scarcely expect from his distinguished career at the Foreign Office, Sir Algernon Law is hardly consistent. In his short letter he uses at least 13 words of foreign derivation which at some time must have been as alien as "kiosk" is to-day. He does not even boggle at "telephone," though one might well fancy that with its Hellenic ancestry it would feel itself more at home in an Oriental kiosk than in a Nordic hut, booth, stall or byre. After all, does it matter greatly what we name their local habitation so long as we are provided with public call facilities on a more adequate scale?

Yours, etc.,
H. S. POWELL-JONES
Secretary, Telephone Development Association

WHEN LONDON WAS NOISY

23 September 1929

SIR, WHAT IS ALL this noise about noise? Only a few genuine antiques like myself remember what London was like when there were no quiet motor cars running on wood or asphalt pavements, and when all the traffic was drawn with iron tires running on either stone setts or macadam. If you want to know what the noise was like in those days you have to go to the docks or to one of those stone paved streets in a factory town and hear the horse-drawn lorries.

In spite of the motor-omnibuses which make most of the noise, you can talk going along Piccadilly. When I was a boy you could not, because the crashing of the hooves and the rattling of the iron tires made hearing impossible. And in those times on a wet day the windows of the shops in Bond Street were splashed waist-high with mud squirted out of the puddles by the air compressed by the hollow hooves of the horses. People have forgotten all those unpleasantnesses.

And the congestion in the streets was just about as bad. A hansom for two took up more room on the road than the biggest Rolls-Royce. And a pair-horse carriage cumbered the earth more than does a motor-omnibus. The old horse-omnibuses took up nearly as much room as a motor-lorry and trailer. The shouting of drivers and cracking of whips and whistling for cabs made far more noise than does the mild tooting of motor horns to-day. Let us thank Heaven that we are quit of those bad old times.

Yours faithfully,
C. G. GREY

NEWSPAPER OF RECORD

1930–39

THE CONSTANT READER

12 January 1935

SIR, A LETTER IN *The Times* of 4 January signed "A Forty Years' Reader" tempts me to tell you what has led to my having read *The Times* for over 74 years. In October 1857, at Florence, my father called me into his study and said: "My boy, circumstances beyond my control oblige us to remain in Italy for some years. I want you to be an English boy and to grow into an Englishman. What will do that more than anything else and teach you all about England will be reading *The Times*. Every morning after breakfast you shall read me one or two paragraphs." I was filled with pride, and the one or two soon became a goodly number.

In 1862, when my father died, I had no *Times*; but I managed to obtain a copy when a week old and to keep it for one day. It made a heavy inroad on my slender pocket money. Pride gave way to interest, and I read *The Times* from cover to cover till I started for England in 1868.

In London I at once tried, and succeeded, in obtaining *The Times*, and interest gave way to habit. In 1870 I became a successful "competition wallah," and since then I have bought or subscribed for *The Times*. I never missed one in Egypt nor in South Africa during the Boer War, nor during my time in India. In 1873 Delane showed me over *The Times* office. I was ill in the spring of last year. *The Times* was carefully kept, and I have devoted the last Christmas Day and the Bank Holiday to reading 13 back numbers. I was happy, for habit had given way to obsession.

Your obedient servant,
GUY FLEETWOOD WILSON

STALIN'S POLICY IN RUSSIA

5 February 1930

SIR, APART FROM ALL questions of diplomatic relations, may I call attention to the critical importance of the present moment for the fate of the Russian peasantry! Stalin, on his 50th birthday in December, wrote that 1930 is to be the year of the great change and of that there is no doubt, whichever way the change may go. On the anniversary of Lenin's death, he denounced Lenin's last political act, the so-called New Economic Policy. We are already well on in an entirely new period.

The change, for all careful students of Russia, is fully explained by the evolution of the preceding period. From the Communist point of view the New Economic Policy, except in one very important respect, failed. It was being eviscerated by the trend of life in the country. The whole period was full of glaring ironies. A mathematical demonstration was given to the population that in practice Communism—that is, the elimination of personal initiative—meant decay; that economic recovery was proportionate to the abandonment of Communism. Every instinct suppressed by the Communists, the religious, the academic, the economic, received a new vitality from the repression. There was only one big success, a negative one it is true—namely, that a number of hard young hooligans have been brought up in blinkers and in complete ignorance of the outside world and its laws.

All this has been very intelligible for many years past. It has been emphasized with monotony in all serious evidence; but at last its effect became manifest within the Communist Party itself, and, though this small party has a complete monopoly of power and of the Press, the cracks appeared only too visibly on the surface, and the party has been torn by all sorts of dissensions. In the main the trend of policy has for long been an alternation between big drifts to the right and vehement tugs to the left, and it is the latest of these that we are now witnessing.

Stalin, whose violence was always feared by Lenin, has now expelled or subdued all his colleagues, and is determined by violence to force through at all costs the whole programme of militant Communism. It was the peasants who defeated Lenin, as Lenin himself admitted. He recognized, as all of us do who have spent long periods among them, that the peasants were the worst material for Communism, that they were essentially small-property men. This essential character is what Stalin is out to alter by force. As is known, the Bolshevists hoped to win in an industrial country, and had no real agricultural policy till they found themselves the rulers of Russia. A more or less mechanical attempt to apply Communism off-hand to the Russian peasantry broke down in 1921—because the peasant, when told that, except for the allowance assigned to him for his own needs, he was to grow grain, not for the market, but for the State, stopped growing what he was not allowed to keep, and the result was a colossal famine which is still a nightmare to those who survived it. Stalin is now going through at all costs. He will mechanize agriculture; and he hopes that the difference in output created by State-owned tractors on military farms will cancel the inevitable loss caused by the simultaneous elimination of thrift. At the best he seems in for another great famine, and as likely as not for assassination.

That is the position; and, as one who has lived long among the Russian peasantry, I want to call attention to their plight under this grisly experiment; for the peasants are the mass of the Russian people, the raw material of the Army and the main producers of the country. The bulk of their long and dreary history was the story of serfdom, abolished in 1861, and it is really serfdom that Stalin is trying to restore. Then, as now, it was instituted for State purposes—recruitment and taxation; and the Russian gentry were not squires in our sense but local officials; the peasants, not without reason, looked at them as intruders, and took comfort in the fact that at least the land remained with them. After Napoleon's Moscow campaign, when promises of emancipation had been issued, there was instead of this an actual militarization of agriculture in many districts, which produced peasant risings, and has always been regarded as one of the worst blots on the rule of the Tsars. Now we are back at that again.

In the name of a ridiculous and fantastic theory, which has already gone bankrupt once under the Bolshevists, the peasant is to be deprived of all interest in the produce of his toil, and that by a Government which has the effrontery to style itself the "Government of the Workers and Peasants," but is, of course, in spite of its complicated system of castrated elections, nothing else but the present master of the inner ring of the Communist Party. The peasants are naturally divided into those who are laborious and produce and those who do not; but the label of "kulak," earlier applied to the three or four hard-fisted and avaricious peasants in a village, has now been made to cover all the former section; so Rykov himself was saying a few months ago. Of course the peasants will resist, for even the poorer peasant generally owed his means of living to his more prosperous neighbour. But all the machinery of the State has been turned against them, and executions and wholesale confiscations are going on every day.

What will be the issue? Who can say, except that in any case it will be terrible?

There are still arm-chair theorists who regard it all as an interesting experiment, perhaps worth the sacrifice of a generation of peasants, and there are capitalists who, if payment is secured, will be glad to supply the tractors. But, though its name has been eliminated from the State title, there is still Russia, a country with only 3,000,000 industrial workers and close on 120,000,000 peasants, and there is still enough of the love of liberty in this country for voices to be raised against this new slavery.

Yours faithfully,
BERNARD PARES

Sir Bernard Pares was one of the first British scholars to study contemporary Russia and, at a time when many Western intellectuals still believed that the Soviet government was essentially benign, among the earliest to reveal the excesses of Stalinism.

THE PERFECT WAITER

5 April 1930

SIR, THAT THE TRUE waiter should receive his accolade, if not a step in the peerage, has long been my conviction. Consequently, although I have not the honour to be a waiter myself, I read your appreciation in *The Times* this morning with profound satisfaction, even while deprecating somewhat a touch here and there of the frivolous in treating a subject so inherently serious. Permit me, Sir, to assert, and I do so without hesitation, that the true waiter, in order to live up to the high standard of his calling, must be possessed of a greater variety of gifts and acquirements than the representative of any other profession. There are unquestionably to-day more good lawyers in Great Britain than there are good waiters — due to no other cause than the less exacting requirements of the Bar.

The waiter, as he should be and as he is expected to be, must have outward details such as the setting of the table or the pouring of the wine — matters of form as distinct from those of content — so completely mastered that at no time can there appear any flaw in his technique. He should have such knowledge of the viands and wines he has to offer as will command the respect of the most fastidious gourmet. He should be able to command at least two languages besides his own. He should be able so to control his temper as to receive even insults in accordance with the high and honourable traditions of his class rather than to attempt to compete with the lower standards of other classes.

But there are qualities, less self-evident, which he is expected to display. He must have infinite tact, so as to enable him to handle appropriately any human situation or disposition, a knowledge of character such as to give him to read promptly that of the guest of the moment and shape his course accordingly, as well as a sixth sense, which I shall call "anticipatory," informing him what the guest wants before the guest knows himself, that he may supply it unobtrusively. He should have true, not assumed, kindliness and sympathy, but with an insight that will enable him to display it in the manner most acceptable to the case in hand. In fine he should have the will, education, and natural gifts to produce in each patron, however trying and diverse the circumstances, a pleasant feeling of well-being, which alone can give food the final touch of the delectable that makes a perfect meal.

These qualities are rare. The combination of them is so unheard of that it is expected from no other calling. We do expect it from a waiter, thus rendering him an unconscious tribute.

I am, &c.,
WILLIAM MUMFORD

A FLORAL CONFESSION

7 June 1930

Sir, Your leading article to-day on the indiscriminate picking of flowers prompts me to tell you of an incident in my own experience.

In the early spring my eye was suddenly gladdened by the sight of a bunch of pussy-willows in the arms of a dingy gentleman in the drab streets near Victoria. "How much are they?" I asked. "One shilling, lidy," he said, holding out about three twigs. I said that was a great deal, to which he replied that he had to pay 9d. for them off the cart of a man in Covent Garden. When I said 9d. was a great deal for the man to charge him he answered with much feeling, "But, lidy, 'e 'as to steal them. 'E can't get them, only by breaking them off the trees on some gentleman's property. Look at the risk 'e runs—it's worf 9d., that is."

This logical reasoning convinced me immediately. Such courage on the part of one purveyor, such candour from the other could not go unrewarded. I paid the shilling and, though conscious that the transaction reflected discredit on all parties, rejoiced for many succeeding weeks in the breath of spring brought by the pussy-willows into my drawing-room.

Yours faithfully,
ELSA RICHMOND

THE AGE OF OAK TREES

4 July 1930

SIR, AS SOME OF THE letters which you have recently published on the subject of the age of oaks seem to be based on misconceptions, it may be useful to those who are interested in the question to know where such evidence may be found, and the value which may be attached to it.

Doomsday Book may be ruled out. It does not cite those boundary surveys of lands in which mentions of individual trees are frequent, partly, in all probability, because those boundaries were already centuries old at the time when Doomsday was compiled, and were therefore well known, partly because the citation of the bounds of all the lands included in the work would have entailed the compilation of a record of gigantic size, the cost of which could hardly have been faced by a Government of that age. Furthermore, the object of the survey was to record the rights of the Crown, rather than to protect the rights of the tillers of the soil to the lands they tilled.

I have not made use of the whole of the Doomsday record; but I have had to examine a large part of it, and I do not remember any instance of the mention of an individual tree. Woodland is frequently mentioned in reference especially to rights of swine pasturing, the felling of timber and the supply of firewood. The rights cited are those which the village communities had held before the Conquest; and though a rough estimate of the area of the woodland is usually given, there is nothing of the nature of a detailed account of its bounds.

The pre-Conquest charters of the Saxon age, on the other hand, cite some thousands of individual trees as boundary marks. It is noticeable that the trees usually chosen are those which are most durable, the oak, the ash and the thorn, though in wet lands the willow is often taken as a boundary mark. It is also the case that even at the present day a tree of the species cited in the old survey may be found on the spot indicated. But it cannot be assumed that that tree is the actual tree mentioned in the Charter, because the land-holders were naturally careful to replace trees which formed boundary marks when they decayed or were destroyed.

Lord Leigh, in his letter of this morning, mentions a Gospel Oak at Stoneleigh. The term is not uncommon in mediaeval land surveys. But it had nothing to do with the "preaching" of the Gospel. As many will know, it was customary throughout mediaeval England to make perambulations of parish boundaries, usually on Rogation Days, which for this reason were properly termed Gang Days. In the course of the perambulation the Epistle and the

Gospel were read at certain customary points in the boundary, usually, as it would appear, at an oak tree. The name "Gospel Oak" has survived in numerous instances on the present map. A few examples of "Epistle Oak" survive in Saxon and later documents; but they are far more rare.

G. B. GRUNDY

———◆———

A NOT SO GOLDEN PAST

3 November 1930

SIR, IS IT NOT TIME that certain of the Victorians stood aside for a little while and stopped finding fault with the present generation? We can hardly pick up a paper nowadays without reading the lamentation of pessimists over England's wretched state. A few days ago, someone writing to *The Times* quoted "a middle-aged masseur" who considered there was no one left in the country to be trusted. Now another has been bewailing our vanished dignity and the golden days that will never return. Well, were they so very golden? For the comfortable classes in their great houses, yes; but what of the Crimean heroes who walked the streets and lanes destitute and hopeless, and the great gulf fixed between rich and poor; derelicts for whom there was nothing save haphazard charity between starvation and the workhouse; and the jerry-built homes that directly caused the slum problems of to-day?

It is true that the young are not easily discouraged. But it is scarcely helpful to be constantly reminding them that the country is completely decayed, and that they can never hope to do as well as those who have gone before them. When a great life is closed the usual wail is raised about "the last of his kind" and "a torch gone out in the dark," and so forth. It is not true. Let our pessimists stop their croaking and watch the glorious achievements of this generation; things unheard of, undreamt of, in their day.

Yours obediently,
SYBIL CUST

KEEP OFF THE GRASS

13 August 1930

Sir, The delightful leading article on "Keep off the Grass" in *The Times* of August 1 has reached me down here. It points out how difficult it is for those in authority to enforce discipline, and it expresses the disquieting truth that forbidden fruit is often more coveted than other kinds, although less alluring and less sweet, so that prohibition unhappily becomes sanction. But why is this?

Psychologists say it is all due to counter-suggestion, for every suggestion carries with it a counter-suggestion. If I suggest a straight line it implies it is not curved. If I say a statement is not true I imply it is false. If I am miserable it implies I am not happy. Suggestion—which transforms ideas into acts—plays a much more important role in human affairs than is usually believed and accepted: and, as we know, suggestion is either direct—"Keep off the grass," don't pick the flowers, ten-mile limit, wipe your feet, no smoking, and many others—or it is indirect, less conscious, yet much more powerful and of much greater importance than direct. Indirect suggestion is the basis of education. It forms the background or the mental basis of the trend along which all actions in later life are likely to develop. It is the work of the moral teacher to supply and to transform direct into indirect suggestion, so that good suggestions may automatically create a desire for fight conduct.

Unfortunately, however, some, especially the ill-balanced children, often act upon counter-suggestion. Ask a child to shake hands and it immediately puts its hands behind its back. In certain forms of mental illness persons are described as "negative," for they do the very opposite of what is suggested. Indeed, in a voluntary effort we are simultaneously conscious of a resistance and we suffer from two or more conflicting promptings or ideas and may arrive at the opposite result to the one originally desired, because the opposed stimuli have upset the balance of the total relevant stimuli and counter-suggestion has won. My sleepless friend who repeated "I am sleeping" twenty times and then failed is the victim of counter-suggestion—the "law of reverse effort" has prevailed, as explained by the late M. Coué. This is why we do not all "keep off the grass," a failing shared by all the "cussed" fellows we all know so well, who are also victims of counter-suggestion, who defy custom and ceremony and reason and who constitute the cranks, oddities, singularities and eccentrics, yet are nevertheless interesting because they afford such excellent examples of abnormal psychology.

I am, Sir, your obedient servant,
ROBERT ARMSTRONG JONES, M.D

The writer, a psychiatrist, was the grandfather of the 1st Earl of Snowdon, the photographer and husband of Princess Margaret.

SILENT, UPON SOME TEAK
IN FARNHAM

21 January 1930

SURELY THERE IS one most important time of the day which has not been suggested for silence—namely, that essentially British institution breakfast. Breakfast is a meal that should be eaten in complete silence. It is bad for a Briton to be asked to talk at this time of day. He is probably liverish and certainly disgruntled at having been routed out of bed at what always seems an unreasonably early hour. If unnecessary conversation at breakfast were punished by the lessening of the bacon and egg supply, tongues would cease to wag, and the results of General Elections would be different.

MR. CHRISTOPHER BARLOW

ITALIAN ARTISTS

13 February 1930

Sir, While public attention is being riveted on Italian art in all its glory, it may be of interest to direct attention to the use of woad as one of the sources of blue pigments used by Italian painters during the 13th, 14th and 15th centuries.

Our chief authorities for the presence of woad on the artist's palette are two MSS, one at Bologna, the other at Venice.

The pigments derived from woad were mainly shades of blue which went by the name of "indum" (or indigo) and "azure."

These pigments were usually manufactured from the scum or "flower of woad," which floats on the surface of the woad vat during the process of dyeing textiles. At times woad paint was used alone, at other times it was mixed with exotic indigo, according as a sober or more brilliant hue was desired.

The superb blue used for the adornment of saints, and especially for the mantle of the Virgin, was probably obtained from ultramarine or from indigo. The darker shades of blue, however, were in many cases painted with woad dye, which was not only more durable, but much less expensive than indigo, and therefore better suited to the purses of poor artists.

The interesting question arises: why was woad eventually abandoned in favour of exotic indigo? The reply is that the discovery of the route to India via the Cape in 1560 and the development of America as a dye exporting country led to an immense reduction in the price of indigo which hitherto reached Europe by the long overland journey through Persia and Baghdad, and consequently was sold as at exorbitant price.

The cheaper and more brilliant foreign dye gradually superseded the indigenous woad.

Yours faithfully,
J. B. HURRY

ONE AMUSEMENT AFTER ANOTHER

22 September 1930

SIR, NOW THAT OUR boys and girls are on the eve of going back to school, may we parents not seek through your columns to ascertain one another's views on these long holidays, now just over? Am I alone in thinking that those dear boys and girls of ours have got into a most alarming habit of requiring one amusement after another? They seem quite incapable of putting in two quiet days running. Either it must be money for a round of golf, or money to hire a hard court for lawn tennis, or money to take them to the cinema, which is probably pronounced scornfully to be "rotten" on return home. They cannot bid a friend to tea unless some definite scheme is first prepared, perhaps to convey them off to the river where a boat must be hired.

This is very bad, especially when parents have such a terrific struggle to pay these enormous public school fees. How can we stop it? The charming children seem to wilt and be puzzled if they are denied, and everybody else invites them to such entertainments, so they feel they must do likewise. Above all, they won't go walking or for a picnic stroll or woodland expedition.

Yours truly,
ALARMED

SOCIALISM

3 October 1930

SIR, THERE IS ONE sentence in the letter of my friend, Sir Martin Conway, in your issue of to-day, against which, as a Tory, I am moved to an emphatic protest. "If the country wants Socialism," he writes, "let it get it from an openly Socialistic Government."

It is a familiar plea, and not a very cogent one. The assumption seems to be that Socialism is a definitely malign thing wholly inconsistent with Conservative principles. But surely it is the primary business of a Government or a party to look at facts and to select the method of dealing with them. In certain circumstances the solution may lie in individual effort, in others in the use of the corporate powers of the State. It is a question of fact in each case. To Socialism as rigid and universal creed the Tory is as much opposed as he used to be to the atomic individualism of the Whigs, for he disbelieves utterly in abstract dogmas. But, as I read the history of our party, we have never shown any narrow jealousy of State action when such action was warranted by the facts. Why should we be asked to resign an important weapon in our armoury merely because some people want to make an extravagant use of it? No dry-fly purist will prevent me fishing my fly wet if it is the best way to catch trout.

I am, &c,
JOHN BUCHAN

The author of *The Thirty-Nine Steps* and *The Blanket of The Dark* was at the time also an MP representing the Combined Scottish Universities.

DIVIDED BY A COMMON LANGUAGE

2 May 1931

SIR, I HAVE BEEN READING a publication which purports to deal with American life—and death—in Chicago. Not being much of a hand at foreign languages, may I enlist your assistance or that of your readers in getting a translation of the words and expressions which I have extracted and grouped roughly under initial letter below?

Some of course, one knows the meaning of: "tuxedo," for instance, is meant for dinner jacket. I believe: "hot squat" is the electric chair used (or not used) for capital punishment—and so on: but I have made the list comprehensive. Certain other words are apparently English but are intended, I think, to have a meaning other than the normal.

It is interesting to note that though there are plenty of words beginning with "H" there are under "A" one: "E" nil; "I" two; "O" one; and "U" one. Can it be introducing the aspirate before a vowel? I cannot say that I have noticed this failing when listening to American conversation; but then, of course, it is difficult to notice anything when listening to American conversation.

LIST FOR TRANSLATION

Alky-cooking

Ballyhooer, Bailiwick, Boloney, Belly-gun, Bunkie, Broad, Back-drop, Break, Bouncer, Barter-house, Bourbon, Bum, Bulging-hip, Blind-pig, Big-shot, Bootlegger, Brass-knuckle, Boss-killer, Black-jack, Beer-baron, Black-hander, Black-and-tan.

Cinch, Capper, Craps, City-sealer, Class-proms, Candy-kid, Carbarn, Cased, (go) Cuckoo.

Dingbat, Drummer, Dough, Dumb-bell, Dive, Dickering, Dime.

Flop, Fine-pointer, Flaming-vest, Fugle-men, Floater, Fedora hat, Front man, Frame, Flatfoot, Frisking, Fin.

Glad-handing assassin, Gabbing, Gat, G. man, Grand, Gimp, Grape, Go in a hole, Gloze, (to have the) Goods on.

Hook-up, Hijacker, Hard egg, Hot squat, Hoodlum, Horn in, Hokum, Hang out, Hop-toad, Hot-dog, Hustling, Hombre, Hood, H'ist, Heater.

Iron, Indigo-stippled.

Jack, Jake, Jack-roller, Jitney, Jig-time verdict.

Keeled over, Kayo, Katy.

Labour-slugger, Lone-wolf-gambler.

Murder-rap, Mushroom back, Merry-andrew, Muscling, Moonshine.
Nose, Newsie, Needled.
Okey.
Panhandler, Punk, Pure quill, Pineapple, Pipe-line story, Put the fix in, Pander,
   Pistol-toter, Paper-hustling, Pull a boner, Put on the spot.
Ribbing, Rake-off, Roustabout, Rap, Ritzy, Right guy, Redlight enterprise,
   Realty, Rod, Racketeer.
Sob-sister, Stoop, Stall, Squawk, Soda-jerker, Stash, Sucker, Sedan, Snooper,
   Sap, Speakeasy, Spring, Snit, Schooner, Swell dump, Shine, Swell broad,
   Sawbruck, Slugging, Standee, Slug-fest, Snoot, Stir-daffy, Slat, Skullduggery,
   Sorority.
Talk turkey, Typewriter, Tag (in-the) Take, Trimmer, Tailed, Thru, Tote,
   Throw-in-the-can, Tuxedo, Torpedo, Tough baby, Thug.
Ukelele.
Wise crack, Ward-heeler, White-wing, Wild-cat brewery, Whoopee, Wop.
Year-man, (turn) Yellow, Yen.

   Yours faithfully,
   ABNUS

Replied on 6 May 1931

Sir, The letter signed "Abnus" in your columns to-day calls forth the following
glossary. It will be observed that some words have been omitted, either because I
am quite ignorant of their meanings, or because they cannot be accurately defined
apart from their contexts. American slang is used very loosely, and among those
people whose vocabulary is severely limited a word or a phrase is often employed
with wide variations. More often than not a word conveys an emotional attitude
toward the immediate circumstances rather than an idea:-

Alky-cooking — the manufacture of alcohol for beverage purposes.
Bailiwick — usually a district controlled by either a gunman or by a politician.
Ballyhooer — one who persistently and noisily advertises himself or some
   enterprise in which he is interested.
Boloney — a derogatory term used in reply to a misstatement.
Bunkie — a man who shares rooms with another man.
Broad — a prostitute; often, any young woman.

Back-drop — usually the cyclorama of a stage setting.

Break—a term to indicate that circumstances are favourable (or unfavourable) to a desired result; it approximates the word "luck."

Bouncer—one whose duty it is to keep the peace by force if necessary in a dive (*q.v.*).

Bourbon — an excellent native American whisky, now extinct.

Bum—a tramp; any ne'er-do-well.

Bulging-hip — this term refers to those American hip-pockets which bulge either because of a flask or a gun.

Blind-pig — an illegal saloon; speakeasy (*q.v.*)

Big-shot — a prominent and dominating racketeer or gunman.

Bootlegger — one who sells or smuggles alcoholic beverages.

Brass-knuckle — artificial knuckles of great use in fist fights.

Boss-killer — one who is an accomplished murderer; one who controls lesser murderers.

Black-jack — (*a*) a card game; (*b*) a piece of lead pipe or any similar weapon used for the purpose of knocking unconscious the unsuspecting victim.

Beer-baron — one who, as a manufacturer and/or distributor of illegal beer, deserves the feudal distinction implied by the title "baron."

Black-hander — blackmailer; one of a group of Sicilians who carried on extensive blackmail, signing their threats with the picture of a black hand.

Cinch — easy; *e.g.* "It's a cinch"; "It's easy (to do)."

Craps — a popular dice game.

Class-proms — annual dances given by the classes at various American universities.

Candy-kid — a dandy.

Carbarn — a garage for trams.

(go) Cuckoo — to go insane; used very loosely indeed.

Drummer — a travelling salesman.

Dough — money.

Dumb-bell — any extremely stupid person.

Dive — a rough restaurant or speakeasy.

Dickering — careful and exhaustive negotiations.

Dime — ten cents.

Flop — a bed

Fedora — a felt hat.

Frame — to arrange a plot, often by simulating friendship, for the purpose of destroying an enemy.

Flatfoot — a policeman.

Frisking — running the hands over the clothes of a suspected person for concealed weapons.

Fin — a hand.

Glad-handing assassin — one who greets with a cordial handshake and murders with a pistol in the other hand.

Gabbing — being too talkative, dangerously so.

Gat — a pistol.

Grand — one thousand dollars.

Go in a hole — perhaps either "go in the hole," which means to go in debt, or "get in a hole," which means to get into serious trouble.

(to have the) goods on — to know more about the private affairs of a person than that person cares to have known.

Hook-up — an alliance.

Hijacker — one who steals (in transit) liquor smuggled by another.

Hard-egg — anyone who is brutally insensitive.

Hot squat — electric chair.

Hoodlum — one who participates in a disturbance (e.g. a street fight) for no other purposes than to be troublesome.

Horn in — to enter without leave, usually into some enterprise.

Hokum — exaggerated misinformation.

Hang-out — a home; any place which a given individual makes his headquarters.

Hop-toad — A drug addict

Hot-dog — (*a*) an exclamation of pleasurable surprise; (*b*) a peculiar sausage sandwich.

Hustling — to hurry an individual beyond his control.

Hombre — a man.

Heater — a gun.

Iron — a gun.

Jack — money.

Jake — O.K.; all right.

Jitney — five cents.

Jig-time verdict — a verdict quickly returned by the jury.

Keeled over — fell over.

Kayo — a knock-out.

Lone-wolf-gambler — one who gambles without association with any particular group of gamblers.

Muscling — to enter either by guile or force where one is not wanted.

Moonshine — (a) grain alcohol; (b) any spirituous beverage.

Newsie — one who sells newspapers on the streets.

Needled — any fortified alcoholic beverage; usually applied to beer fortified with ether.

Okey — otherwise O.K.; all right.

Panhandler — a swindler.

Punk — (adj) poor; unsatisfactory.

Pineapple — a bomb.

Pistol-toter — one who carries a pistol.

Pull a boner — to make a mistake.

Put on the spot — to plot a person's murder by arranging that he be at a given place at a given time.

Rake-off — a share in the proceeds of an enterprise.

Ritzy — pretentiously elegant.

Right guy — one who may be trusted.

Realty — real estate.

Rod — a pistol.

Racketeer — one who makes a living by indulging in illegal enterprises and protects his position by force if necessary.

Sob-sister — a sentimental woman; usually applied to sentimental women journalists.

Squawk — to turn State's evidence.

Soda-jerker — one who mixes ice-cream sodas and other innocuous beverages in the American drug-store.

Sucker — one who is gullible.

Snooper — a Paul Pry.

Sap — a stupid person.

Speakeasy — any place where alcoholic beverages are illegally retailed.

Schooner — a measure of beer.

Swell dump — any satisfying place, whether a flat or a city; the phrase implies pretentiousness.

Swell broad — an attractive girl.

Sawbruck — ten dollars.

Slugging — hard hitting.

Standee — one who cannot find a place to sit.

Slug-fest — any event during which there is much hard hitting. This may apply to a baseball game or to a riot.

Skullduggery — dishonest dealings.

Sorority — a girls' society (cf. fraternity)

Talk turkey — to talk openly and to the point; to give important information.

Typewriter — machine-gun.

Tailed — followed, usually by detectives.

Thru — through (?).

Tote — to carry.

Throw in the can — to put in gaol.

Tuxedo — dinner jacket.

Tough baby — a hard egg (*q.v.*)

Thug — a tough baby

Ukelele — a stringed instrument reputed to be musical.

Wise-crack — a joke; a repartee.

White-wing —a street sweeper.

Wild-cat brewery — an illegal brewery, usually one which is found to be independent of the great beer organizations.

Whoopee — a word to describe what usually happens at a gay, noisy, and alcoholic party.

Wop — an Italian.

(turn) Yellow — to turn from courageous to cowardly behaviour.

Yen — a desire.

HAMILTON EAMES

SHOP SHY

19 May 1932

SIR, I WONDER IF ANY of your male readers suffer as I do from what I can only describe as "Shop-shyness"? When I go into a shop I never seem to be able to get what I want, and I certainly never want what I eventually get. Take hats. When I want a grey soft hat which I have seen in the window priced at 17s. 6d. I come out with a *brown* hat (which doesn't suit me) costing 35s. All because I have not the pluck to insist upon having what I want. I have got into the habit of saying weakly, "Yes, I'll have that one," just because the shop assistant assures me that it suits me, fits me, and is a far, far better article than the one I originally asked for.

It is the same with shoes. In a shoe shop I am like clay in the hands of a potter. "I want a pair of black shoes," I say, "about twenty-five shillings — like those in the window." The man kneels down, measures my foot, produces a cardboard box, shoves on a shoe, and assures me it is "a nice fit." I get up and walk about. "How much are these?" I ask. "These are fifty-two and six, Sir," he says, "a very superior shoe, Sir." After that I simply *dare* not ask to see the inferior shoes at 25s., which is all I had meant to pay. "Very well," I say in my weak way, "I'll take these." And I do. I also take a bottle of cream polish, a pair of "gent's half-hose," and some aluminium shoe-trees which the fellow persuades me to let him pack up with the shoes. I have made a mess of my shopping as usual.

Is there any cure for "shop-shyness"? Is there any "Course of Shopping Lessons" during which I could as it were "Buy while I Learned"? If so I should like to hear of it. For I have just received a price list of "Very Attractive Gent's Spring Suitings," and I am afraid — yes I am afraid ...!

I am, Sir, your obedient servant,
W. HODGSON BURNET

THE MANLY CHEST

28 July 1932

SIR, SOMEONE IN authority—and what authority could be better than you?—should give the nation a definite ruling on the troublesome question of masculine swimming-wear. At some of our seaside resorts the borough council have boldly announced that it is sufficient for a swimming or sun-bathing male to wear a "slip": others, not only is the "University" costume insisted upon, but beach inspectors and policemen use stern language to the bather if a single shoulder be exposed to the sun, and he is warned "proper" costumes must be worn at these "respectable" places.

The plain meaning of this is that in the opinion of certain borough councillors to expose the male chest and back to the sun and air is an indecent act. It is not clear that a borough council is the proper authority to decide what is decent; but let that pass for the moment. Local councils are, in fact, extending their jurisdiction over more and more of the citizen's life and, it appears, cannot be resisted. But some uniformity in their commands may be reasonably expected; what is decent at Bumbleton-on-Sea cannot be indecent at Bumbleton-super-Mare. But it is.

Is the male chest decent or not? It might be described as indecent—that is, unsuitable—in a church or court of law. But it is not considered indecent in the boxing-ring where delicately nurtured ladies gaze upon it, without surprise, shock, or, so far as we know, moral injury. It is not considered indecent to go on the stage (in ballet) or at the Royal Academy (in sculpture). No sculptor or painter, I believe, has ever thought it necessary to hang one of those careless blue scarves across the manly torso. And it is difficult to see why it should be considered indecent on the beach or in the bath. But (by certain authorities) it is. Why?

This is not a case where the modern is demanding more freedom than the "Victorian" enjoyed. My father was a Victorian (and a Civil Servant); he never wore anything on the beach but what is now called a "slip" (in his wild days it was known as "bathing drawers"), he had never heard of a "University costume," and if you had told him that his manly chest was indecent he would have been both surprised and indignant.

But suddenly (I forget the date) the upper part of the male became indecent; and the reason, I believe, was this. Some clever tailor, hosier, or haberdasher realized that he could charge more money for a long bathing-dress than he could for a short one, and he invented the "University costume." The name attracted the snobs. The rich wore the new garment because it was more expensive; the less rich began to wear it (when they did) because it was more distinguished; nobody, in those days, wore it because it was "proper" or "decent." But it became first fashionable and then a habit; and our aunts and town councillors have converted what was a habit into a rule.

I submit, Sir, briefly, that the rule is nonsense. It may be a small thing, but it is one of the many small things which make our country ridiculous, incomprehensible, and undesirable to the foreigner. There may be many of us whose chests (like our legs and faces) are offensive to the average inhabitant of beach or bath; but these (in these democratic days) will quickly hear of it from those about them: and to deal with real indecency we employ the police. To public opinion and the police we may safely leave the question of what we should wear: borough councillors, most of them elderly and dignified, but not accustomed to bathing, whether in sea or sun, are not always accurate interpreters of public opinion in such matters.

I hope, Sir, that you will give a ruling: and I am,
Sir, your obedient servant,
A. P. HERBERT

THE ORIGINS OF AUSTRALIAN WINE

24 August 1932

SIR, IN THE ARTICLE on Australian wine which you published in your issue of August 18 some doubt is expressed as to the number of varieties of vines that were sent to Australia by my grandfather, James Busby, in 1832. I have before me a copy of the journal which he kept of his tour through France and Spain.

My grandfather had always been interested in wine and had been been greatly struck with the potentialities of the Australian soil and climate in this respect. Before 1831 he had distributed upwards of 20,000 vine cuttings among some 50 individuals, and on visiting England in 1831 he brought with him 10 gallons of a burgundy-type wine of the 1829–30 vintage made by Mr. Sadleir at the Orphan School, Sydney. This was distributed among persons interested in the Colony of New South Wales and was well thought of. James Busby was particularly interested in raisins and determined to visit Malaga and obtain cuttings of the raisin-grape. His tour lasted from September 6 and to the end of December, 1831 and took him through Xeres, Malaga, Catalonia, Perpignan, Rousillon, Rivesaltes, Montpelier, Tarascon, Marseilles, Hermitage, Beaune, Dijon and the Côte d'Or, and Rheims. He collected from the Royal Botanic Gardens at Montpelier and the Royal nursery of the Luxembourg 547 varieties of vines cultivated in France and some other parts of Europe. Of these, with two or three exceptions, he obtained two cuttings. Independently of these he secured "a competent quantity of all the most valuable varieties which I found cultivated in the best wine districts of France and Spain both for wines and raisins." These numbered some 500–600 cuttings of 100 varieties.

The cuttings were packed in sand and earth in cases lined with double-oiled paper, a suggestion of M. Urban Andibert, of Tarascon. With the consent and cooperation of Lord Goderich, his Majesty's Principal Secretary of State for the Colonies, they were sent out in a convict ship, and, arriving at Sydney in excellent condition, were planted and nurtured by Mr. McLean, of the Botanic Garden. Some of the cuttings from the South of Spain which did not arrive till later, were planted in open boxes by Mr. Richard Cunningham, of Kew, afterwards the Colonial Botanist of New South Wales. These were sent to Sydney in the convict ship *Camden*, and not 10 out of the 500–600 cuttings failed. James Busby remarks with some pride that he had

the satisfaction of having transferred to the Colony, without any expense to the public, and almost in a complete state, a national collection of vines which it was for three-quarters of a century the favourite project of writers on agriculture and agricultural societies in France to collect, and which was at length accomplished at a very considerable expense to the country by the Count de Chaptal, when Minister of the Interior under Buonaparte.

There is little doubt that these vines are the stock from which the present Australian vines have sprung. James Busby was afterwards appointed the first British resident in New Zealand, and, with my paternal grandfather, Archdeacon Henry Williams, was mainly instrumental in getting the Treaty of Waitangi signed by the Maori chiefs. It will be remembered that James Busby's residence, Waitangi, in the Bay of Islands, where the treaty was signed, was recently purchased by the Governor-General, Lord Bledisloe, and presented to the New Zealand people as a national park.

Your faithfully,
HAL WILLIAMS

BODYLINE

27 January 1933

SIR, MAY I TRESPASS on your valuable space to discuss the article which appeared in your pages on 19 January with regard to the protest recently received by the M.C.C. from the Australian Board of Control against the employment of a "leg-theory" in cricket?

In the first place, though McDonald and Gregory did undoubtedly send down an occasional ball at the batsman's body, they cannot be said, anyway while playing for Australia, to have employed a "leg-theory," in that such balls were exceptional and were bowled to a field with only two men on the leg-side. It is surely unfair to compare these tactics with the policy of delivering six such balls per over to a field so set as to penalize a batsman who is defending not his wicket, but his head.

Your correspondent further suggests that "so long as a 'shock' bowler is not deliberately bumping down short-pitched balls or purposely aiming at the batsman, his bowling is perfectly fair." Granted; but when six such balls are bowled in each over, either the action is a deliberate one, or else, if the bowler is continuously doing it accidentally, he is a rank bad bowler. You cannot have it both ways. The last thing I wish to do is to bring a charge of malice-aforethought towards the batsman against either our captain or the bowlers he employs. But that our "shock" bowlers bowl deliberately at the batsman's body cannot honestly be denied.

The real objection of the Australians, your correspondent alleges, is to the "array of leg-fielders." I submit that it is to this, in conjunction with body-line bowling, that the Australians, very rightly, in my view, take exception. As long as these tactics are allowed, the batsman will be frightened into giving up his wicket, and if Bradman cannot survive them, I am satisfied that not one of the great players of the past could have fared any better.

It would obviously be impossible for even so august a body as the M.C.C. to dictate to a captain as to how he should place his field. But a short-pitched ball is a bad ball, and one which, without the remotest chance of striking the wicket, stands a considerable chance of doing the batsman bodily harm. And it seems to me that the very least that can be done in the best interests of the game is to empower the umpire to "no-ball" a bowler for pitching his deliveries short. But to my mind the whole question demands consideration from an entirely different angle. Your correspondent urges the point that "Cricket is not played with a soft ball, and that a fast ball which hits a batsman on the body is bound to hurt." Rugby football is also considered by some a fair training ground for manly and courageous virtues. And yet in the event of a player wilfully hacking, tripping, or striking another player, instead of going for the ball, the referee is required by the Laws of Rugby Football to order the offender off the field on the second offence. It seems to me that the analogy between this and the policy of deliberately bowling at a portion of the batsman's body which is not obscuring the wicket is a fairly close one; and the penalty is as well deserved in the one case as the other. In either game enough knocks are given and received in the ordinary course of events to satisfy the most bloodthirsty fire-eater among the spectators. But I would like to see some of the most eloquent supporters of the "leg-theory" step into the arena against a bowler of Larwood's pace and face it for themselves.

Yours, &c.,
LEONARD CRAWLEY

The writer was an outstanding games player who at cricket had represented the MCC. During its tour of Australia in 1932–33, the England team employed intimidatory bowling tactics, dubbed "leg-theory" and "Bodyline". These were intended primarily to counter the skill of the leading Australian batsman Don Bradman, who was thought vulnerable to pace and hostility. The degree of ill-will on and off the pitch rose to such a peak that the issue became a diplomatic incident between Australia and its "mother country". England won the Ashes series 4–1 but the laws of cricket were afterwards changed to prevent any repetition of the controversy.

GEORGE III'S BATHING MACHINE

29 June 1933

SIR, IN REGARD TO your recent article, entitled "Sea Bathing," it may be worth while to put on record that the bathing machine reputed to have been used by King George III at Weymouth was in regular use down to the summer of 1914, when I saw it in its accustomed place of honour on the extreme right of the line of bathing machines.

It differed from the others in its octagonal shape, which gave it of necessity a pyramidal roof surmounted by a small staff, whereas the other machines were oblong in plan with gabled roofs. Further, above the door the Royal Arms, similar in design to those now on your front page, were placed in summer on a strut and removed in winter when the machines were drawn to Lodmoor, where the royal machine retained its pride of place. The last time I saw it was some 10 years ago, when, owing to the popular disfavour which had fallen upon bathing machines, it had been removed from its wheels, and, along with its fellows, had been degraded to some mean use, apparently a tool shed, which I was sorry to see, for I thought Weymouth would have had more regard for this relic of its royal patron.

Your obedient servant,
L. G. WICKHAM LEGG

HIGH TEA

30 June 1933

SIR, WITH MANY OTHERS I have been much intrigued by the third leading article in *The Times* of June 23. Since the War there has been so great a revolution in the habits and customs of the English people in all other respects, it is indeed surprising that our meals have been so immune from the innovators. The late Victorians, as I can testify, conformed with a rigid orthodoxy to both the time and the nature of their meals prescribed for them by tradition. For instance, I was brought up to believe that tea could not be served at any other hour but 5 o'clock, and that its somewhat unsufficing and unattractive fare was as immutable as the laws of the Medes and Persians. I remember that, at a certain house in the highlands of Scotland, where I used to visit, weary sportsmen who returned home at 5 o'clock were allowed tea, but if they came in at a later hour they found the table as bare as the cupboard of the nursery rhyme. I should have thought that the later they came home the more they would have needed and the more they would have deserved refreshment, but my hostess could not bring herself to break with the Victorian tradition. Sherry, cocktails, chipolata, or tea at 6 o'clock would have been right outside her philosophy.

So far as meals are concerned I am a Bolshevist of the deepest dye. Nothing is more palatable to me than the right thing at the wrong meal. Although the sausage, according to all Victorian rules, belongs to the morning, I protest that it tastes far more delicious at any other time of day. The many evening expeditions I am called upon to make to my constituency necessitate for myself an anomalous meal too late for tea and too early for supper, but it is none the less agreeable in that it breaks away from tradition.

Why is it that the right thing tastes so much better at the wrong meal? It may be that the palate undergoes a physical or even a psychological change in the course of the day's work, but I am disposed to believe that the fact that you are doing something which is prohibited by all nice people adds a special flavour which no well-advertised sauce could produce.

For all I care then, let the new generation of epicures rise up and call our meals anachronistic and unsuitable to modern ways and means. Let them exercise to the full their ingenuity to devise meals which in time, place, and substance are at once more convenient and more suitable to our changed and changing needs.

Yours faithfully,
EDWARD CADOGAN

The writer, a son of the 5th Earl Cadogan, was MP for Reading. His dislike of "rigid orthodoxy" extended to painting his head with boot polish when he began to go bald.

GAZING AT "THE GAYS"

19 July 1933

SIR, IN YOUR ISSUE of to-day a correspondent has a Suffolk observation about the "Gays," and you base an article thereon. The landlady bought the illustrated newspaper because her young people liked to look at the "gays." You and your correspondent are, I think, wrong in supposing that the "gays" are "bright creatures of the picture page." The "gays" are the pictures, not the subjects pictured.

I have known Suffolk for 69 years. I remember that the word "gays" meant pictures in illustrated papers, magazines and picture books. That was in the late 1860"s. I have heard an elderly man of those days say: "I'm a child for the gays," expressing his love of picture books. Webster's Dictionary gives one meaning of the noun "gay" (English dialect) as a "picture in a book."

When I was young the plural of mouse in Suffolk was meezen: the plural of nest neezen—spelt phonetically. Those good old Anglo-Saxon plurals have, I fear, disappeared. The old order changeth: but don't let the noun "gay" go to death in dishonour, misunderstood.

I am, Sir, your obedient servant,
ALLENBY, F. M.
Field Marshal Viscount Allenby

ENGLISH HATS IN NAZI GERMANY

1 January 1934

SIR, I WONDER IF you know and feel certain that the vast majority of your readers do not know that *The Times* is to-day used by some foreign visitors to Germany to declare their foreign identity, in order that they may not be subject to the assault and battery which might otherwise be their lot.

I have just heard from a business man of obvious Jewish appearance who has done a great deal of travelling in Germany for some years past that he attributes his escape from molestation to two things only: — (a) The wearing of so English a hat that it seems a little incongruous in a German street; and (b) the fact that he carries at all times of the day in a very conspicuous way a copy of the latest available issue of *The Times*.

Yours faithfully,
F. S. JOELSON

Replied on 9 January 1934

Sir, What constitutes an English hat? This question occurs to me after reading Mr. Joelson's letter, published in your columns, in which he explains that a friend of his was able to escape molestation in Nazi Germany by wearing an English hat and carrying a copy of *The Times* "at all times of the day in a very conspicuous way."

I grant Mr. Joelson that a copy of *The Times* is indubitably English — no one could possibly mistake it for the *Petit Parisien* or *Der Angriff* — but what sort of hat did Mr. Joelson's friend wear which immediately made belligerent Storm Troopers exclaim, "That is an English hat"?

It could not have been a bowler, for that particularly uncomfortable form of headgear is international. Panamas and straw boaters are the hall-mark of the American. Homburgs are much favoured by Germans and Austrians. Soft felt hats known as "Trilby" hats vary very little from one country to another. It seems, therefore, that it could not have been any of these.

Could it have been a cricket cap? Worn with an ordinary lounge suit it might easily have seemed "a little incongruous in a German street." Was it a London policeman's helmet? Was it an English postman's hat? None of these offer an adequate solution to the problem. From my own knowledge of foreign forms of headgear I can only suggest that a truly British hat would be a deerstalker cap, as worn by the immortal Sherlock Holmes. For centuries foreign cartoonists have depicted John Bull wearing a cap of this sort.

During my stay in Germany a few weeks ago it never occurred to me to dress in an obviously English manner to avoid persecution. I admit that I frequently carried *The Times*, but this was merely done with the object of eventually reading it. Although my appearance is not, like that of Mr. Joelson's friend, obviously Jewish, I fully offset it by my journalistic inquisitiveness, which must have been a source of annoyance to the authorities. Despite that, I do not remember one single unpleasant incident either with Government officials or with Storm Troopers. I frequently gave the Nazi salute as a matter of elementary courtesy, just as I would expect a German to take his "German" hat off to the Union Jack. No pressure was brought to bear on me in that respect.

It is unfortunate that all the readers of *The Times* are unable to go to Germany and see conditions for themselves. Apart from furthering international cordiality it would, if they all adopted Mr. Joelson's suggestions, considerably stimulate the "English" hat trade.

I am, Sir, yours faithfully,
MICHAEL FRY

Michael Fry was the author of the soon to be published, and now scarce, volume *Hitler's Wonderland*.

B.B.C. ENGLISH

2 January 1934

SIR, AS CHAIRMAN OF the committee which in the discharge of its frightful responsibility for advising the B.B.C. on the subject of spoken English has incurred your censure as it has incurred everyone else's, may I mention a few circumstances which will help towards the formation of a reasonable judgment of our proceedings?

1. All the members of the committee speak presentably: that is, they are all eligible, as far as their speech is concerned, for the judicial bench, the cathedral pulpit, or the throne.

2. No two of them pronounce the same word in the English language alike.

3. They are quite frequently obliged to decide unanimously in favour of a pronunciation which they would rather die than use themselves in their private lives.

4. As they work with all the leading dictionaries before them they are free from the illusion that these works are either unanimous or up-to-date in a world of rapidly changing usage.

5. They are sufficiently familiar with the works of Chaucer to feel sincerely sorry that the lovely quadrisyllable Christemasse, the trisyllable neighebore, and the disyllable freendes should have decayed into krussmus, naybr, and frens. We should like to vary the hackneyed set of rhymes to forever by the Shakespearian persever; and we would all, if we dared, slay any actress who, as Cleopatra, would dare degrade a noble line by calling her country's high pyramides pirramids. But if we recommended these pronunciations to the announcers they would, in the unusual event of their paying attention to our notions, gravely mislead the millions of listeners who take them as models of current speech usage.

6. We are not a cockney committee. We are quite aware that Conduit Street is known in the West End as Cundit Street. Elsewhere such a pronunciation is as unintelligible as it is incorrect. We have to dictate a pronunciation that cannot be mistaken, and abide the resultant cockney raillery as best we can.

7. Wireless and the telephone have created a necessity for a fully and clearly articulated spoken English quite different from the lazy vernacular that is called modd'ninglish. We have to get rid not only of imperfect pronunciations but of ambiguous ones. Ambiguity is largely caused by our English habit of attacking the first syllable and sacrificing the second, with the result that many words beginning with prefixes such as ex or dis sound too much alike.

This usage claims to be correct; but common sense and euphony are often against it; and it is questionable whether in such cases it is general enough to be accepted as authentic usage. Superior persons stress the first syllable in dissputable, labratory, ecksmplary, desspicable, &c.; and we, being superior persons, talk like that; but as many ordinary and quite respectable people say disputable, laborratory, exemmplary, and despickable, we are by no means bound to come down on the side of the pretentious pronunciation if the popular alternative is less likely to be confused with other words by the new human species called listeners-in.

We have to consider sonority also. The short i is much less effective than the long one; and the disturbance I created in the United States last April by broadcasting privvacy instead of pryvacy was justified. Issolate is a highly superior pronunciation; and wind (rhyming to tinned) is considered more elegant in some quarters than wynd; so that we get the common blunders of trist (rhyming to fist) for tryśt and Rozzalind for Rosalynde; but we recommend the long i to the announcers for the sake of sonority.

Some common pronunciations have to be rejected as unbearably ugly. An announcer who pronounced decadent and sonorous as dekkadent and sonnerus would provoke Providence to strike him dumb.

The worst obstacle to our popularity as a committe is the general English conviction that to correct a man's pronunciation is to imply that he is no gentleman. Let me explain therefore that we do not correct anyone's pronunciation unless it is positively criminal. When we recommend an announcer to pronounce disputable with the stress on the second syllable we are neither inciting him to an ungentlemanly action nor insinuating that those who put the stress on the first ought to be ashamed of themselves. We are simply expressing our decision that for the purpose and under the circumstances of the new art of broadcasting the second syllable stress is the more effective.

Yours truly,
G. BERNARD SHAW

THE PORK SAUSAGE

17 January 1934

SIR, AS ONE OF A family of pork sausage manufacturers, established for nearly 60 years, I claim to be able to answer the questions put by the puzzled "Grass Widower." If one may use the term, a "thoroughbred" pork sausage should contain only the best pork and good seasoning, while a "half-bred" sausage contains a large percentage of bread or biscuit powder. The colour is accounted for in the making. If a pork sausage appears deadly pale, it contains too much fat meat; and that with a pinky tint contains too much lean meat. There is no such thing as a freckled sausage skin, and the "Plymouth Rock" appearance of a sausage is due to the herbs used for flavouring showing through its filmy jacket.

In cooking a sausage needs patient coercion, not fierce cremation, and there would be no shrinking or bursting if it were cooked by the old-fashioned Dutch oven; it would then arrive at table brown-jacketed and retaining its rotund dignity. Sausages should never be cooked in fat. A good pork sausage makes its own bed of fat in which to lie, as it is slowly cooked. Never behave harshly to a sausage by pricking it with a fork, for it is found to retaliate by spitting fat at you and bursting before your eyes. As to the opinion of the legal profession, I once knew a circuit judge who gave pork sausages a splendid character, and taking into consideration the millions of sausages consumed — all different in make and flavour — it is remarkable how the palate of the public is so easily satisfied.

Yours truly,
GEORGE WOOD

NO TO POCKET MONEY

22 April 1935

Sir, The points about children's pocket money raised in the interesting letter by Mr St John Ervine have many bearings of a profoundly fundamental nature, the most vital being character building. The prevalence of regular pocket money is, in my opinion, one of the keys to that lack of adult responsibility about money which is widely deplored. Few parents, however, realize it and think they are being kind to their children when they give them a little money to spend as regular pocket money. They are not being kind; they are wasting one of the most valuable assets they could enlist on the side of independence of character.

I have never given, and never will give, pocket money in my nursery. My son, who is just 11, has earned everything he has spent, with the exception of a few money gifts on recognized occasions, such as birthdays. At the age of four, interested in the household wages book, he asked for a wages book of his own and began to earn money, entering it up in the wages book and signing for it.

Looking back in that little record one finds items such as this: to cleaning white paint in drawing-room, 2d; to laying turf straight in garden, 4d; to chopping wood, 2d; to felling a tree, 6d; etc.

An intelligent and thoughtful parent can find innumerable jobs, especially in the country, where a child can give honest work for pence sufficient to supply him with enough or more pocket money than his less fortunate comrades have given to them. That free gift of money bred in their bones the false idea that money is obtainable without work and that they are entitled to a share of the family income without contributing anything in exchange. Were a wages book established in every home, the national character would undoubtedly gain by it and children have a much greater and more real interest in their occupations.

Yours faithfully,
MARIE C. STOPES

CELEBRATIONS IN VICTORIAN TIMES

3 June 1935

Sir, As I am just completing my eighty-eighth year, more than the first half of which was lived in London, a few incidents in public rejoicings which have occurred in my experience may interest your readers.

Let me say at once that I have heard very many cheering crowds, but never before have I heard anything like the stentorian roar of welcome that I listened to on the wireless on Jubilee Monday[1]. My father sufficiently often referred to the following reminiscence to make it seem to be my own.

On the occasion of Queen Victoria's first visit to the theatre (Drury Lane) in state after her marriage my father, after strenuously struggling in a crowd for two hours, succeeded in getting into the vestibule in front of the pit doors and was congratulating himself on the prospect of getting in when they put up a notice "Pit full."

My own experience begins with the Duke of Wellington. We used to watch my father put on his Wellington boots on Sunday morning, but on one occasion he returned from the office to put them on, and we were told it was to go to the funeral of the Duke of Wellington, which we thought quite appropriate! When a little more than seven years old I was taken by my grandmother to see a display of fireworks which formed an item in the peace rejoicing after the Crimean War. Some years later I walked across London to Ludgate Hill and stood there from 10 a.m. to 3 p.m. to see the Princess Alexandra come into London; but just as she passed a great burly fellow who stood beside me put his hand on my shoulder in order to lever himself up, and all I saw was the tops of the whips! Some months afterwards my brother and I walked from London to Windsor to view St. George's Chapel, where the marriage took place, and there took part in a mild kind of scrimmage in order to kneel down before the altar in the same place that the Princess had knelt.

Among the various public illuminations which took place during the next period, when I was living in Fleet Street, the following stands out prominently. From late afternoon till 1 o'clock in the morning a constant stream of people occupying the whole of the roadway was passing from east to west to see the illuminations. It was like a flowing river, and the noise was not the tramp of soldiers but a more diffused roar. To go from west to east was only possible on the pavements.

Now for Thanksgiving Day, 1872, I was in the crowd at the east of Temple Bar accompanied by a lady when the tragedy occurred, but fortunately we were close to a big man with a broad back, so by placing my hands on his back and pushing with all my might I was able to relieve the pressure a little from my companion. The trouble was caused by every one as they came through the bottle-neck of Temple Bar trying to follow the Royal example and knock at the door. As soon as they had passed the Bar they came against the stream of people coming from Chancery Lane. Three incidents are worth mentioning in connexion with this public rejoicing: — (1) One of the victims of the tragedy was an old lady over 70 who had, unknown to her people, come up to London from Lincolnshire by herself to see the illuminations; (2) one of the casualties treated at Charing Cross Hospital was a dislocated jaw caused by intense yawning while waiting in the crowd; (3) a good many people, our own friends among them, chartered a conveyance to take them along the principal route of illumination, but on attempting to enter from a side street they were stopped, and as they were unable to turn the vehicle round were compelled to sit there for several hours seeing nothing.

Yours faithfully,
G. WILSON BURN

[1] King George V's Silver Jubilee had recently been celebrated.

In February 1872, Queen Victoria marked the recovery of the Prince of Wales, who had been close to death from typhoid, with a service of Thanksgiving at St Paul's Cathedral. (The future Edward VII had marked his recovery by calling for a Bass ale.) Vast crowds thronged the route, especially at Temple Bar on Fleet Street, where in the crush several people were trampled, with fatal consequences.

STUMPED

4 September 1935

SIR, MOST SUGGESTED reforms in the rules of cricket break down because they are not equally applicable to all types of matches. A new l.b.w. rule, for example, may be desirable for the first-class cricket, but unsuited to the village green. But one reform would escape this criticism. Let us get rid, once and for all, of the fetish that the wicket must consist of three stumps, irrespective of the conditions and of the class of cricket. Instead, let the rules permit of two, three, four, or five stumps.

The object to be aimed at is to secure the best chance of a good game and of a finish within the time available. All Test Matches could properly be limited to three days, if played with five stumps at the most or four at the least. First-class county cricket would always be played with three or four stumps; a small sub-committee of the M.C.C. after consideration of the weather forecast, might decide. We should soon learn to listen every Tuesday and Friday for the B.B.C. announcement, "All first-class matches starting to-morrow will be played with four stumps." At the other end of the scale many of the half-day matches on bad wickets would be played with two stumps – encouraging to many of those enthusiasts who play often, but whose scores are usually small.

It is, however, in club cricket, I believe that the benefits of this change would be the greatest. If four stumps were allowed we should hear little, even in a dry summer, of those one-day club matches in which the less expert members of the side are bracketed week after week under the heading "did not bat"; and in two-day club matches, in which the batting is almost invariably stronger than the bowling, decisions would be possible without the rather artificial declarations made to give the other side "a sporting chance" (to which, incidentally, their out-cricket has probably not entitled them). An increased interest, too, would be given to a match such as that between Eton and Harrow when it was realized that the choice of four stumps would make a decision within two days a probability rather than a remote possibility.

The plan which I suggest is less revolutionary than it sounds, and it has the merit of simplicity. It creates no new problems for umpires; it changes none of the principles of the game. But it does allow the rules to be adapted according to the varying conditions under which the game is played.

I am, Sir, your obedient servant,
J. C. MASTERMAN

The historian John Masterman played tennis and hockey for England and, at 46, toured Canada with the MCC. During the Second World War, he chaired the XX or Double-Cross Committee which famously turned Germany's network of spies in Britain back on itself, feeding the agents' spymasters with misinformation and deceiving them about the Allies' plans for D-Day.

NEWS FROM TARTARY

23 November 1935

SIR, MR. T. B. MONEY-COUTTS's suggestion that *The Times* should present me with a .256 Mannlicher is an admirable one. The rest of his letter is nonsense.

He charges me, in the first place, with inefficiency because I attempted a journey through Central Asia armed only with a rook-rifle and a useless .44 Winchester. The answer to this charge, and to the implication that I do this sort of thing as a stunt, is that these two weapons were the best I could get. Sporting rifles and ammunition are practically unprocurable in China. My own preparations were made in Peking in the brief intervals between journeys to Shanghai, Tokyo, and Inner Mongolia; time was short, and much of it was devoted to obtaining passports, getting inoculated against typhus, writing articles for *The Times*, and other sordid activities. In the end, having ransacked Peking without success, I wired to a resourceful friend in Shanghai, who got the rook-rifle from a lighthouse-keeper: even so, the train bringing it up to Peking was wrecked and it only arrived at the last moment.

The .44 was kindly but rashly lent to me by Sir Eric Teichman and now awaits the imminent arrival of its owner in Kashgar. I took it with me largely for reasons of "face"; anything with a magazine commands great respect among people who are mostly matchlock owners. From his reference to Allan Quatermain, your correspondent seems to imagine that a .44 Winchester is an elephant gun, or something very like it. He should brush up his ballistics, my .44 weighed about 5lb.

Mr. Money-Coutts writes from Berkhamsted and can perhaps be forgiven for his ignorance of the armaments market in North China. But when he complains that in Central Asia, as in Brazil, only a rook-rifle "stood between Mr. Fleming and an untimely death," he is being less venially fatuous. Mr. Money-Coutts evidently belongs to the "keep a bullet for the woman" school, and has no doubt shot his way out of many a tight corner among the savage nomads of Hertfordshire. Further afield, however, such heroics are suicidal; the last foreigners to enter the Tsaidam—two Frenchmen—did not survive to earn Mr. Money-Coutts's approval of their adherence to the traditions of melodrama.

As for the question: "Does Mr. Fleming never learn from experience?" the answer is: "In this instance, yes." It was precisely my experience in Brazil that convinced me of the value of a rook-rifle in country where the game has little reason to dread the rare human beings that it sees, and is more puzzled than alarmed by the discreet report of a .22. The first shot from a big rifle or a shotgun is liable both to clear the ground of fauna for some distance and to attract the unwelcome curiosity of the local inhabitants; and shotgun ammunition is, of course, extremely heavy.

But, after all, the proof of the pudding is in the eating, and I should like to know how Drake, after circumnavigating the globe, would have answered those critics who felt "slightly annoyed" at his inefficiency in not providing himself with a larger and more commodious vessel than the *Golden Hind.*

It may reassure Mr. Money-Coutts to learn that Mlle. Maillart started on the journey in possession of a large automatic pistol. This weapon was left behind in Lanchow: whether in a fit of intrepidity or of amnesia, I see no reason to disclose.

I beg to call your attention to the first sentence of this letter, and remain. dear Sir,
Yours expectantly,
PETER FLEMING

P.S.—To forestall further accusations of inefficiency in not bringing a battery of rifles out from England, I should perhaps add that before starting on the Central Asian journey I had been travelling continuously for six months through the Caucasus, the Soviet Republics of Central Asia, the Maritime Province, Manchuria, and Mongolia. If I had set out from England with a rifle I should indeed have escaped the wrath of Mr. Money-Coutts: for I should still be filling up forms somewhere between Samarkand and Sinkiang.

Peter Fleming made his name as a writer long before his younger brother, Ian. As well as being a roving correspondent for *The Times*, he published a scintillating parody of the stiff upper-lip school of travel writing, *Brazilian Adventure*, and in the mid-1930s crossed Central Asia in the company of the Swiss writer Kini Maillart. He was also a magisterial letter-writer.

HANDEL OR BARK?

16 January 1936

SIR, THAT DOGS OF ALL breeds and sizes are musical is generally known and agreed; but the reason they are unable to carry their talents further has been overlooked by your correspondents.

Dogs lack rhythm: What, after all, is the difference between a howl and a note but the question of knowing when to stop? Dogs, in common with Italian prima donnas, are inclined to hang on to a good thing. It is not that they cannot hit the note, but that they do not know when to come off it. They have not, like Mussolini, learned the value of the "indispensable pause." They have tone, they have colour; they understand the glissando and the tremolo; some have fine lungs and a good ear (I once knew a bitch with absolute pitch); but, Sir, they cannot master the 3:4 nor the 6:8.

Now the horse can waltz. The snake, though science assures us it is deaf, will move its hips at the lure of the flageolet. The sea lion, as visitors to Olympia will observe, has "rhythm in a great big way" and can syncopate and shimmy with the best hula from Havana. But the dog, the friend of man — alas, it is a sobering thought — cannot, after years of broadcast jazz, master the blues.

No doubt your columns could be filled for weeks with diverse instances of the canine love of the vocal line; but will anyone come forward and claim they have a dog with rhythm? Should the phenomenon exists, vistas of possibilities blossom. Such a creature, under expert tutelage might acquire taps, routines, and breaks that, having four legs and a tail to accomplish them with, might astonish the world.

Darwin played the trumpet to a row of runner beans to see if music would affect their growth. He was unable to detect any reaction; but who knows? Such things, in this age of surprising discoveries, should be investigated. Will no one give a poodle to Fred Astaire?

Yours faithfully,
CECIL LEWIS

Cecil Lewis had a remarkable early career: First World War air ace as a teenager; with John Reith, one of the five founders of the BBC; and, in 1938, co-winner with George Bernard Shaw of an Oscar for the script of *Pygmalion*. "You should live gloriously, generously, dangerously," he wrote in his memoir; he himself lived to almost 100.

QUEEN VICTORIA'S FUNERAL

28 January 1936

SIR, IN YOUR ISSUE of January 25 you refer to the historic gun-carriage to be used [at George V's funeral]:

"At Queen Victoria's funeral there was an unfortunate contretemps in connexion with the horses which were to have been used to draw the coffin up the hill at Windsor, and the bluejackets manned the drag ropes in the emergency."

It would, perhaps, be more accurate to say that the *contretemps* was in connexion with the so termed gun-carriage than "with the horses" or their handling by the Royal Horse Artillery. February 2, 1901, was a bitterly cold day with some snow, and the gun-carriage, under the charge of S Battery, R.H.A., and under the independent command of Lieutenant M. L. Goldie, had been kept waiting at Windsor Station for a considerable period. When the Royal coffin, weighing about 9cwt., had been placed on the carriage, drums began muffled rolls, which reverberated under the station roof, and the *cortège* started. Actually when the horses took the weight the eyelot hole on the splinter bar, to which the off-wheel trace was hooked, broke. The point of the trace struck the wheeler with some violence inside the hock, and naturally, the horse plunged. A very short time would have been required to improvise an attachment to the gun-carriage. However, when the wheelers were unhooked the naval detachment promptly and gallantly seized drag ropes and started off with the load. The "gun-carriage" had been specially provided from Woolwich and was fitted with rubber tyres and other gadgets. This was due to Queen Victoria's instructions, as also was the prohibition of the use of black horses. On February 4, I conveyed the Royal coffin on another carriage, from Windsor to the Royal Mausoleum at Frogmore by means of the same detachment.

I have the honour to be, Sir,
Your obedient servant,
CECIL B. LEVITA

KING GEORGE'S FUNERAL

8 February 1936

SIR, IT IS A COMMONPLACE to observe that the radio is a modern miracle, but this morning, the 28th of January, in Florida, I have had an unusual demonstration of the manner in which wireless transmission has annihilated distance.

At half-past 8 I rose with the glorious sunny morning around me. Out of my window I looked upon the green plumes of royal palms, on the tall feathery coconut trees, with their encased fruit hanging like footballs on the silvery leaves of the eucalyptus, and the spreading foliage of the many-rooted banyan tree. Below me shone an emerald swimming pool, set in a frame of green turf. Thus early, gorgeous butterflies are flitting from flower to flower, visiting the blue bells of the thurnbergia and the flame-like blossom of the *Bignonia venusta* that falls like a sheet of fire over the pergola. The morning is noisy with birdsong. Loudest, for the moment, is the call of the scarlet-winged Cardinal bird, whose wings flash for a moment as he dips to the rockery cascade and disturbs the self-important fantail doves strutting, snow-white, against a screen of scarlet azaleas. Across the lawn, in the aviary, the cries of the java sparrows, the parrot, and the masked lovebird, with ringed eyes and iridescent plumage, a comedian among the budgerigars, compete with the shrill singing in the patio of the canaries. But over all the sound of this birdsong there comes the sudden deafening, palpitating drone of another bird, an immense steel bird of flight that has arisen with its 40 passengers from the great Pan-American aerodrome on the blue Bay of Biscayne, a mile distant, and which is now winging its way south to Brazil.

Having dressed myself in midsummer fashion, for it is already 75deg. Fahr., though the day will get no hotter with the beneficent south-east wind that keeps this coast temperate while sub-tropical, I descend to the patio, the customary adjunct of these Florida houses modelled on the styles of Spain and Italy, its roof shadowed with palm leaves, and through the arches, supported by Roman columns cut from coral rock, I look on to the blaze of flowers and foliage that encloses this paradise of Nature. Breakfast is set on a small table where I can hear the cool tinkle of water flowing down the rockery. I have just seated myself, the last of the household to descend to breakfast, when my host comes into the patio.

"Come and listen to the funeral of King George," he says, and, in order that I shall miss nothing of the service being transmitted across the Atlantic, the breakfast table is carried into the drawing-room, where I find my host's family gathered. Thus it was, that at a breakfast table in the drawing-room of a house in Florida, with sunshine and birdsong all about me, I heard as distinctly as if had been present at St. George's Chapel, only a few miles from my English country home, the measured tramp of men, the sad skirl of the pipes playing their lament, the low murmur of a great concourse of mourners, the sound of feet mounting the steps, the majestic swelling of music from the organ within the chapel, and the sweet piercing voices of the choir filling the air with the prefatory anthem. And here we were, one Englishman and five Americans, at half-past 8 of a sunny, June-like morning of January, in a house buried deep in the coconut groves of Southern Florida, listening to the burial of a great King.

I had missed the first part of the procession which had wound its way through London. The commentator had informed us that it had been raining, but now, as the *cortège* approached the Castle gateway, the sun had broken through. Not a detail of the service seemed to be missed by us, sitting in warmth and sunshine, the solemn music of this funeral pageant interrupted only by the singing of the birds in the garden; but at one moment the whole sound was blotted out by the temporary roar of another great hydroplane rising on its flight to Jamaica, Ecuador, Peru, Chile, and Uruguay. The drone died away, again the voice from St. George's Chapel flowed into our still room. It was the voice of the Archbishop of Canterbury, resonant, full toned, "Forasmuch as it hath pleased Almighty God, in his wise providence ... earth to earth, ashes to ashes, dust to dust ... ," and there followed the *ensemble* of voices, "Our Father, which art in Heaven ..." And then, a little later, that heart-stirring loveliness of blended choir, organ, and congregation singing "Abide With Me."

The service ends, a voice breaks in on the grief that we have shared with mourners over 3,000 miles distant, it is an American voice, telling us that we have just heard the funeral service of George the Fifth, a great King. For a few moments we sit there, in the flesh, in a Florida room, in spirit in St. George's Chapel, Windsor. And then, the common day breaking in upon us, we are acutely aware of the miracle of which we have partaken. It is an awareness for me, an Englishman, that has a new and solemn significance. The radio has shattered the sundering power of space, and grief for a revered King has united two great nations in the hour of mourning.

In the West Atlantic, late one night, an announcement chalked up on a board, informing us that the King's life was drawing peacefully to its close, had hushed the festivity of the ship. Two days later in a Florida-bound train, my newspaper devoted 12 pages to the King's death, and, encountering Gene Tunney[1] on my way from the dining-car, he observed, "We shall miss him terribly." That "we" is significant and characteristic. For the next few days I find myself wondering whether the legend of history should not be re-written. One of our Georges lost America, and George the Fifth has won it back again. All flags were at half-mast; on the morning of the funeral, in a church of a suburb of Miami, near where I write these lines, Americans gathered at 8 o'clock, the time of the service in England, to unite in a common tribute. The character of our late King won this general mourning among the people of the United States, a spontaneous, deeply felt grief, and the miracle of radio transmission enabled the members of the two great English-speaking nations to walk side by side through the streets of London, and up the hill to that chapel in Windsor, which many millions on this side of the Atlantic have never seen but where, in spirit, through the miracle of radio, they have unforgettably taken part in the solemn majestic rites of a beloved King's funeral.

I am, Sir, &c.,
CECIL ROBERTS
Coconut Grove, Miami, Florida

[1] The former world champion boxer

One obituary in 1976 of the journalist and novelist Cecil Roberts described his life as often seeming to resemble "a 20th-century grand tour, strewn with places in the sun, grand seigneurs and charming hostesses, in which he was the fastidious literary pilgrim..."

ALL OLD HAT

11 March 1936

SIR, AS AN OLD HATTER I was moved by your leading article on hats. There was a time when a man chose his hat with as much care as he chose his wine. Many famous men have passed through my hands. I had the distinction of fitting Machnow, the Russian giant, with a topper, and I recall his awful majesty when it was placed on his head. The public was spellbound, as well it might be, until that fateful night when a pernickety member of the audience asked, urbanely, if he would have the goodness to remove his hat. Machnow, who understood no English, was unmoved, but his manager's face blanched. He had no choice but to comply with the request; the hat was removed — and the spell broken!

I remember a man, distinguished in the Diplomatic Service, who spent three hours in selecting a hat. I am sure it was longer, but, fearing the incredulity of modern readers, I dare not say so. At the end of this time he declared that he could not settle the matter off-hand but would consult his wife. The next day he came with his wife, who, being a woman of quick decision, made a choice in an hour.

That was a man to stir the artistic soul of a true born hatter.

Just before the war, however, we detected signs of decay; men began to show a strange indifference to the important consequences of an eighth-of-an-inch on or off the brim, and they came less frequently for an "iron-up". After the war came catastrophe; bronzed young men came in casually for a soft felt, threw it carelessly on their heads and walked out without so much as a look in the glass. I realized then that the art of hatting was dead; anyone could clap a hat on a man's head and throw thirty shillings into the till. I looked back to the spacious days of Sir Squire Bancroft, whose hat was famous in Piccadilly, and Arthur Roberts, who set a fashion with his "Gentleman Joe", and sorrowfully sought fresh woods and pastures new. But, I raise my hat to Sir Walter Gilbey (whose hat I know well), and wish him every success in his campaign to restore hat-consciousness to an effete generation.

I am, &c.,
FREDERICK WILLIS

Feodor Machnow visited London in 1905. His height is variously given as having been 7ft 10ins and 9ft 3ins.

HOW THE GOOGLIE GOT ITS BREAK

14 October 1936

SIR, AS SO MANY inaccurate versions of the origin of the "googlie[1]" are appearing, it may be of interest to the public to know how it was evolved.

Many years ago — about 1892 — our billiard table at Claysmore was being re-covered, and we used to "flick" a tennis ball across the bare slates, trying to get the maximum twist on it both ways. My brother, the late B. J. T. Bosanquet, got bitten with the idea of evolving a new sort of "break" on a cricket ball, and he used to practise hard at a game we played with a solid rubber ball and a broomstick. He never said much about it, and, while he was at Eton, no one had any idea of what was then taking a definite shape. His family had no knowledge of anything beyond this, and the first public appearance of the "googlie" was as much a surprise to them as to anyone else. He had very exceptionally strong fingers, which, I think, are essential to a successful "googlie" bowler.

The paralysing effect on the best batsmen of this style of bowling is due, not merely to the off-break with leg-break action, but to the fact that a genuine expert bowls a leg-break, off-break, or no-break ball with the same hand action — or near enough not to be distinguishable. As a matter of fact, I do not think any other bowler has been able to do this efficiently, which would explain why such batsmen as Clem Hill (who was hypnotized by "Bosies") regarded "Bos" as the greatest bowler in history. Certainly R. O. Schwarz, a great friend of my brother, could never do it really well, though he made a great reputation on the strength of the "leg" and "no" breaks, with an occasional effort at the "off". This, in spite of receiving many hours of patient instruction from the inventor, whose only pupil he was.

Unfortunately, my brother certainly developed a form of athlete's heart, which was the main cause of his comparatively early retirement, and which affected him far more than even his friends appreciated, as he never talked about it and would not do anything for it. It was this neglect which undoubtedly caused his untimely death.

Yours faithfully,
NICOLAS BOSANQUET

[1] When a cricketer bowls a googlie (NB), the ball is spun deceptively to make it turn in the opposite direction to that which the batsman is expecting.

"ALCOHOLIC HYENAS"

19 June 1937

SIR, DISTINGUISHED correspondents of yours have lately deprecated the practice of "lecturing" Signor Mussolini.

In an article in the *Popolo d'Italia* (= Signor Mussolini) the leaders of the British Press — including, I suppose, yourself — are described, rather to my surprise, as alcoholic hyenas. I hope that no one need incur the charge of "lecturing" who calls attention to the confusion both of metaphor and zoology involved in this accusation.

"These hyenas in human form," says the Duce or his newspaper, "threw themselves on the pure blood of Italian youth as if it were whisky, without a trace of shame..."

The implication that a hyena is not safe if there is a bottle of whisky about, and is, if anything, disappointed to find that the beverage is, in fact merely blood, will come as a surprise both to distillers and naturalists, and does, I feel, some injustice to a strictly temperate quadruped. The real offence of the hyena is not that it drinks, but that it laughs.

I am, dear hyena, yours, etc.,
CYRIL ASQUITH

PAINTED NAILS

18 August 1937

SIR, THE INTERESTING correspondence which has lately appeared in your columns on the subject of painted finger-nails prompts me to submit the following extract which I have translated from a lecture, "Aberrations esthétiques de notre temps", delivered a couple of years ago by Professor Hulin de Loo to the Class of Beaux-Arts at the Académie Royale de Belgique:

"The mania of painting and varnishing the fingernails comes to us from America. Its origin is simple: the great majority of American women, even of those whose income would be considered lavish by us, are obliged for want of servants, to do their own cooking and household work. Such manual labours thicken the nails and destroy their transparency and natural polish; hence the recourse to coloured varnish."

"It is a fashion of unemployed cooks and chambermaids, and has been propagated by the stars of Hollywood, many of whom have emerged from domestic service or factory employment. That it should be adopted among us in those too quickly elevated classes which we owe to the effects of the War is understandable for the same reasons."

"But here the interests of commerce and fashion papers, who praise the practice and find great profit in it, are involved; and so our poor young well-bred women, even those endowed by nature with the great charm of pretty, polished, and transparent nails, which they should have no difficulty in preserving, follow like the sheep of Panurge. Who would commit the crime of painting rosewood or varnishing marble?"

The Professor is a man so guarded in his statements that I feel sure that his history of the origin of the practice is as sound as his objection to it.

I am, Sir, your obedient servant,
THOMAS BODKIN
The Barber Institute of Fine Arts

BERTIE WOOSTER'S CHIN

30 November 1937

SIR, YOUR CORRESPONDENT Mr. John Hayward is to a great extent right in his statement that Bertie Wooster has a receding chin.

A fishlike face has always been hereditary in the Wooster family. Froissart, speaking of the Sieur de Wooster who did so well in the Crusades — his record of 11 Paynim with 12 whacks of the battleaxe still stands, I believe — mentions that, if he had not had the forethought to conceal himself behind a beard like a burst horsehair sofa, more than one of King Richard's men — who, like all of us, were fond of a good laugh — would have offered him an ant's egg.

On the other hand, everything is relative. Compared with Sir Roderick Glossop, Tuppy Glossop, old Pop Stoker, Mr Blumenfeld, and even Jeeves, Bertie is undoubtedly opisthognathous. But go to the Drones and observe him in the company of Freddie Widgeon, Catsmeat Potter-Pirbright, and — particularly — of Augustus Fink-Nottle, and his chin will seem to stick out like the ram of a battleship.

Your obedient servant,
P. G. WODEHOUSE

TAKE A BOW

7 February 1938

SIR, IN YOUR COLUMNS to-day you refer to the growth of popularity of archery in America, where there are said to be 1,500,000 archers. The Americans are not nit-wits and there must be a reason for this.

There is! The long bow is an intriguing and temperamental weapon — far more intriguing and temperamental than any golf club in the bag. Every bow and every arrow has individual characteristics to be mastered. Part by a hairbreadth from the correct shooting style and the shot is affected: a beginner who once takes a bow in his hand is lost. He may score for his first round a few dozen points where an expert will score 500 or 600. He has a vast field ahead of him for improvement, experiment, and emulation.

And exercise? The principal archery round is the York round, in which 144 arrows are shot at distances varying from 60 yards to 100 yards. Drawing a bow is a strenuous affair, so that only three arrows are shot at a time and after each three a trip to the target is necessary. Consequently the York round takes anything up to three hours to complete — all exercise and walking, the latter some 2½ miles. The bow is drawn 144 times and each time a force corresponding to a weight of perhaps 50lb. has to be borne by the arms and shoulders and held while the aim is completed. This is roughly the same as lifting three tons of packing cases from the floor to a shelf 2ft. high.

During the summer what can a business man of the City of London do between leaving the office and sitting down to dinner? Golf courses are too far away; tennis is too strenuous. Archery provides an ideal solution. He need not change his clothes. He can start as late and stop as early as he wishes. He is in the open, in pleasant company, and taking part in a sport which is good for his health and his soul and one, moreover, which has a longer and more world-wide history than all the rest put together — a history measured not in decades nor in centuries, but in millennia.

Yours faithfully,
CLIVE TEMPERLEY

Just over two years later in France, Major Jack Churchill of the Manchester Regiment would reputedly become the last British soldier to use a longbow in action (although he himself denied the story).

YOU SAY RHINOCERI

17 August 1938

Sɪʀ, Iɴ ʏᴏᴜʀ ɪssᴜᴇ of 30 July you employed *rhinoceri* as the plural of rhinoceros. This is surely a barbarism, although on referring to the *New Oxford Dictionary* I find to my surprise and regret that it is one of the usages cited. This plural has given writers of English considerable trouble. Besides rhinoceros, rhinoceroses, and the above-mentioned rhinoceri, the *N.E.D.* quotes rhinocerons, rhinoceroes, rhinocerotes, and rhinocerontes.

Rhinoceroses would appear to be the least objectionable, but even this still has a pedantic sound. Has not the time come when we can discard our etymological prejudices, accept the usage of the ordinary man, and frankly use "rhinos"? Confusion will not arise, since the slang use of rhino for money is moribund, if not dead.

Zoo for Zoological Gardens has now become accepted usage: I hope we may adopt the same common-sense principle for some of its inmates with embarrassingly long names. In addition to rhino, I would plead for hippo and, with a certain diffidence, for chimp.

Yours faithfully,
JULIAN S. HUXLEY

PEACE FOR OUR TIME

6 October 1938

SIR, A FRIEND OF MINE has received a very interesting card from a distinguished German, dated for last Friday, which runs as follows:

"What a happy night in Munich: I am very happy. ἐπὶ γῆς, εἰρήνη[1]

"We admire Chamberlain. His adversaries must not say he has diminished British prestige. They dare not, for there is no greater authority in the world than a man who is as peaceable and righteous as powerful. Many men in this country did not trust British politicians. But Chamberlain has won the trust. That is the best for the future. God bless you—and our— 'Good Old Chamberlain.'"

I think this will interest some of those who have been listening to the debates in the House of Commons or reading them in your columns.

HENRY S. LUNN

[1] On earth, peace (Luke 2:14)

Ordinary Britons and Germans alike felt much relieved by the agreement at Munich over the future of Czechoslovakia which Neville Chamberlain, and other European leaders, had concluded with Adolf Hitler. War, which had seemed imminent, appeared to have been averted. But Hitler's assurances soon proved worthless.

GERMANY AND THE JEWS

17 November 1938

Sɪʀ, Dʀ. FɪᴛᴢRᴀɴᴅᴏʟᴘʜ[1] has undertaken the task, not less honourable than useful, of serving as the interpreter of German opinion in England. May I therefore ask him to reply, as fully and candidly as his official obligations allow, to one or two questions which are exercising the minds of many English friends of his country? I am thinking of course of the events of the past week[2].

No one denies the competence of a sovereign State to establish degrees of citizenship: to enact that Catholics (to take an example from our own history) may not vote, or that peers may not sit in the House of Commons. These are matters of internal policy; and any foreign criticism of such arrangements must be, or ought to be, subject to the consideration that every country has the right to order its domestic concerns as it deems best in its own interest. Knowing the intensity of family feeling among Jews, and their proficiency in the arts and sciences, I may think it unwise for the German State to say to a Jewish father: "We cannot prevent your son from becoming a famous musician or physicist; we can only see to it that he does not become a famous German musician or physicist." But it is for Germany to discover, not for me as a foreigner to point out, the unwisdom of such a proceeding. So far, I am entirely in agreement with those German statesmen who insist that the treatment of the Jews in Germany is a matter of domestic, and not international, concern.

I will go farther. I know that the Jewish question in Germany to-day has a history of generations or even centuries behind it. I know, too, that in the years of German misery after the war, very many Germans were most harshly dealt with, and suffered the most galling indignities, at the hands of individual Jews, of Jewish firms, and public authorities in which the Jewish element was dominant. I am not prepared to deny, what Germans have often represented to me, that the restoration of Germany to economic health, and therefore national independence, was most grievously impeded by false views urged in London, Paris, and New York by Jews who only saw in the German lands a promising field for international exploitation.

But, I say, those times are past and over. Germany to-day speaks with her own voice: is mistress in her own house. And surely, whatever appetite for revenge on the Jewish people may have subsisted must by now be sated? I ask Dr. FitzRandolph: What are we, the friends in England of the German people, to think? Is the German State verging on bankruptcy, and so compelled, like an Eastern tyranny, to plunder? Is the German Government verging on collapse, and therefore obliged to stimulate its partizans with fresh intoxicants?

Dr. FitzRandolph is an educated man, a member, I take it, of one of those universities which, in the days of their freedom, were the glory of his country. He knows that in these matters recrimination is folly: all great States have great sins on their conscience. But he knows, too, that no major transaction in the thought or practice of one country can be a matter of indifference to all others, because it is by such occurrences that the civilization of a country is assessed, its purposes divined, its strength and honour determined. To-day Germany stands at the bar of human opinion, impeached for hideous cruelty and wrong inflicted on her own subjects, and I ask Dr. FitzRandolph: What defence has he to offer? That Germany is so strong that she can defy the conscience of the world?

And, if so, of what force are her promises? Or that Germany is so feeble that she cannot extend to her subjects impartially the protection which is the elementary right of every inhabitant of a civilized country? And, if so, of what value is her friendship? Of what worth is her civilization?

I am, etc.,
G. M. YOUNG

[1] Attaché at the German embassy in London, who in a recent column in *The Times* had set out his government's policies.
[2] The attacks on Jews and their businesses throughout Germany known, from the quantity of broken shop windows, as "Kristallnacht".

The writer was best known for his superlative evocation of Victorian England, *Portrait of an Age*.

ON JABOTS

15 March 1939

SIR, I AM FREQUENTLY asked when lecturing what would be the correct neckwear which should be worn with an eighteenth-century costume. Historical films and plays have familiarized many people with the costume of the eighteenth century, but in almost all cases the so-called jabot consisting of a bunch of lace hanging over the chest is still believed to be the correct neckwear for this period. This fashion has no foundation of historical fact. It arose in the first half of the nineteenth century when the ruffled shirt went out of vogue. The shirt had sewn on both sides of the breast opening a gathered frill of fine linen or muslin which showed between the unbuttoned waistcoat top, or low cut front of the waistcoat and the coat.

This was the true jabot, and with it was worn a cravat wrapped round the neck several times. Instead of the jabot being attached to the shirt it was sewn to a linen band which fastened behind the neck with the frill hanging over the chest. This type of neckwear was worn as a part of eighteenth-century costume by all actors during the past 100 years. Actually the jabot, consisting of a double frill of lace, lawn, or muslin, was worn on all shirts from the time of Charles II to George IV with a long cravat up to 1728, and a gathered stock after this period to the end of the century. Only three eighteenth-century shirts are known in this country, at Westminster Abbey and at Nottingham and Leeds Art Galleries. The original stocks have also been preserved.

Yours faithfully,
KENNETH W. SANDERSON

PLAIN ENGLISH

2 *August 1939*

SIR, AT THE FOOT of the menu in use in the restaurant cars of our most up-to-date railway we read that: "A supplementary portion of any dish will be served on request." I suppose the first six words mean "second helpings." Why not say so?

I am, &c.,

G. H. PALMER

Replied on 3 August 1939

SIR, YOUR CORRESPONDENT Mr G. H. Palmer should read *Punch*, in which (on March 8, 1939) the official answer to his question was recorded.

A lady wrote to the manager of a railway refreshment department asking as he does, "Why not second helping?" The manager made this disarming answer: — "I... have great respect for the English language but, knowing the public so well, I feel sure, for the few who do not understand the meaning of 'supplementary' there would be many who would accuse us of uneducated crudity if we quoted the phrase in such plain verbiage as you suggest.

"I fully agree we should all be the better for expressing ourselves in simple terms, but in official printed documents it is 'not done,' and I will confess I fear to make myself look odd by being different from others."

It is for the same sweet reason, no doubt, that almost all politicians and papers now say "anticipate" when they mean no more than "expect," "as to whether" instead of "whether," "following" instead of "after," and "emergency" when they mean "war." One might also mention such recent recoils from "plain verbiage" as "deratization," "redecontamination," and "self-evacuating persons."

It is almost unfair to blame a refreshment department when Government Departments set such an example. And, alas, the strong silent Services have been corrupted, too. If Nelson had to repeat his famous signal to-day it would probably run thus:

"England anticipates that as regards the current emergency personnel will face up to the issues and exercise appropriately the functions allocated to their respective occupation-groups."

I am, Sir, your obedient servant,

A. P. HERBERT

EVACUEES

22 *September 1939*

Sir, While from all my friends in the country comes praise of many town-children evacuees—and, without exception, praise of all the secondary schoolchildren—complaints are pouring in about the half-savage, verminous, and wholly illiterate children from some slums who have been billeted on clean homes. Stories with which one cannot but sympathize are told of mattresses and carpets polluted, of wilful despolation and dirt that one would associate only with untrained animals. The authorities, with plenty of time to prepare, seem to have failed both in the physical and psychological examination of the evacuees, although the mechanics of the great trek have been so well ordered.

Now one hears that both women and children of the roughest and uncleanest types are going back to their own "homes." At the present time, when Britain is fighting for liberty, no Briton would suggest dictatorship methods, but surely something short of these can be evolved to prevent these unfortunate children from being allowed to return to the appalling conditions whence they have been rescued. It is not fair that they should disrupt small houses; but is it not possible to cause (to coin a phrase) grass orphanages, under the care of skilled and sympathetic teachers, to come into being? Let the mothers go back if they will. It does not matter so much what happens to adults, but surely children should not be allowed to go back to conditions which shame a nation fighting for civilization.

In the course of my work I have, in the last few years, attended many trials at the Central Criminal Court, and am nearly always horrified by the low physical and mental standards of the accused persons. Stunted, misshapen creatures, only capable of understanding the very simplest language and quite incapable of thought, moved by impulses at the best sentimental, at the worst brutal. During a trial when accused and witnesses are of this sub-human sort, it is as though a flat stone in the garden had been raised and pale, wriggling things, that had never seen the light, were exposed. No one who knows anything of criminal courts would contradict me.

These children, of whom the country residents so reasonably complain, are bound to grow up into just such sub-human savages, unless we seize this opportunity of saving them. I do not, of course, say that all crime is due to the appalling conditions in which most men and women who find their way to our courts live when young—there have been several trials in the last two years which have shown that men, who have had every advantage in youth, can be brutal, treacherous, and base. But I do say that no child, who has not been shown the rudiments of decency, and in whom imagination has not been encouraged, stands a chance of being a good and happy citizen.

War has lifted the flat stone—these disgraces to our educational system have been forced out into the light. Do not let us, even though a certain amount of arbitrary arrangements may be needed, let them creep back beneath their stone. This is, and I repeat it with every emphasis of passion at my command, an opportunity which, if we miss it, we do not deserve to have given to us again.

Yours faithfully,
F. TENNYSON JESSE

Britain had declared war on Germany on 3rd September

THREE LITTLE PIGS

9 October 1939

SIR, I AM ENCLOSING a letter from a Kenya native which you may consider worth publishing. It is a charming — and not unusual example — of loyalty. The letter, which was addressed to the District Commissioner, South Nyeri, was first published in the native paper which we are issuing now in order that the natives shall know exactly what is going on in Europe.

Yours faithfully,
MINNA BARROW-DOWLING

Dear Sir, I beg you to accept me to offer my three pigs to Government, to be used in the war. I have kept three pigs only and I am in wanting them to be in the work of your Crown according my love and power, like other fellows who have given up their lives in order to defend other people's lives. I felt heartedly as I have no knowledge, or experience of any work, except these pigs which I decided that I must give them to Government, exactly as I would give up my life for our Kingdom to remain just to us as it has forever.

In measuring my pigs, they are four feet in length, etc.

Now, sir, I would be very much pleased to hear from you what you have decided for that question of these offerings.

Your obediently servant,
KANOGA S/O NIEGA

CORRECTING DR. GOEBBELS

11 October 1939

SIR, SOME WEEKS before the present war broke out Dr. Goebbels, in a diatribe against Britain addressed to Commander King-Hall, was good enough to drag in my name as a witness to the truth of his accusations.

Dr. Goebbels quotes me as having written: — "Unhappily, side by side with this increasing enlightenment on the part of the governing classes, grew a wish to interfere with all nations possessing a different pigmentation of the skin — purely, of course, for their own good and because Britain had been appointed to this work by Heaven." This quotation is correct: but he omits to say that I was writing of the years that ran between 1833 and 1843.

It is understandable that Dr. Goebbels finds it difficult to believe that a nation can improve, and can become more humane, in 100 years. But it is a fact. All nations have, I am afraid, been guilty of great cruelties and injustices in the past (some of the deeds in the years of which I wrote are indefensible); but I am unable to agree with Dr. Goebbels that this makes it right and advisable that any nation should commit cruelties and injustices in this age.

Dr. Goebbels is shocked, I presume (one can do no more than guess at his meaning, owing to his rather turgid and overemotional style of expression), at the idea that, in the benighted years of which I wrote, the British should have wished to "interfere" with other nations. Let me point out to him that side by side with this "interference" has come a great amelioration of conditions among the people interfered with. Can the German Minister of Propaganda claim that the German "interference" with people of another race, the wretched, stricken Jews, has resulted in any amelioration of their conditions?

It must astonish Dr. Goebbels that when this war was forced upon us, the Indian native rulers, without one exception, made offers of help and of treasure to the King Emperor. It must astonish Dr. Goebbels that the whole of the Empire, and the Dominions, have declared themselves as standing by our side. But this may no doubt be the result of the horrible cruelties and persecutions to which they are subjected by Britain. Just as the rising of the valiant Czecho-Slovak nation against their German "protectors" may be a tribute to one year's experience of the gentle loving kindness of these.

I am, Sir, yours faithfully,
EDITH SITWELL

P.S. This letter will, of course, be represented as part of a new Jewish plot, although I am 100 per cent Aryan; or else as an attempt to encircle Dr. Goebbels and the Beloved Leader.

THE MIND OF HITLER

19 October 1939

Sir, A READING OF Sir Nevile Henderson's "Final Report" fully confirms the conclusions to be drawn from a psychological study of Herr Hitler's character. The following tendencies seem to me to be definite ingredients in his mental make-up:

1. An hysterical tendency, shown in his emotional appeal to crowds, in which his mind seems to undergo temporary dissociation through the very intensity of his concentration upon the matter in hand. With his mind so narrowed down on one point, he may be temporarily oblivious of other considerations, and thus may appear perfidious. There is also a probable hysterical identification, in subconscious phantasy, with Frederick the Great, and a tendency towards a mechanical imitation of the less admirable political manoeuvres of him and of Napoleon, which makes him appear, judged by modern standards, as an atavistic monster.

2. A paranoid tendency, almost amounting to persecutory mania. He is a very aggressive person, and "projects" this aggressiveness upon the world around him, being acutely on guard against aggression from others, with suspicion and possibly delusions that such hostile aggressiveness is active against himself and his nation. This tendency was favoured in its development by the harsh conditions of his early manhood as a lonely outcast in Vienna, although it must have a strong hereditary basis. One important effect of its presence is the fear of encirclement or of being "ringed round with enemies," and where encirclement is already a fact — often the result of the paranoid person's own aggressiveness — there is a great intensification of this fear, with a corresponding intensification of aggressiveness.

3. A growing megalomania, with messianic feelings. This is a further development of his paranoid tendency, making his followers paranoid, and producing a collective paranoia.

4. A compulsive tendency (in his case, a power impulse) towards more and more "bloodless" victories, in which his latest claim to territory or power is called his last — cf., the alcoholic, who claims his latest drink his last.

In the light of above psychological analysis (which I made many months ago) it is possible to explain, at least in part, the strange reversal of policy shown in the Soviet-German Pact. After the events of last March, and the British and French reactions thereto, Herr Hitler's paranoid fear of encirclement became so intense, and his accompanying aggressiveness so magnified, that the unbearable mental tension could only be relieved by a "retreat to Moscow." But by this step he has jettisoned his whole *Weltanschauung*, and made nonsense of "Mein Kampf." He has suffered the most overwhelming defeat in the East that has ever occurred without overt fighting. Only by blind stupidity among his followers is even a temporary continuance of his régime possible. His disappearance from the scene, either by abdication, or in some other way, would clear the ground for the negotiated "peace with justice" which all sane men desire.

Yours faithfully,
WILLIAM BROWN

LOUSY KILTS

22 November 1939

SIR, I HOPE IT WILL not be considered impertinent of a mere southerner to take part in the interesting correspondence in *The Times* about the kilt. I venture to do so because there is another side of the question which should be ventilated, even at the risk of being considered indelicate. May I be personal for a moment?

During the late Great War it was the writer's unique privilege to hold the rank of Rat Officer to the Second Army of the B.E.F. in France. His activities were not however entirely devoted to the theoretical and practical extermination of trench rats. Occasionally other tasks came his way.

One day a large wooden crate arrived from the War Office. On prising open the lid it was discovered to contain a quantity of garments—gents' underwear—and with them emerged a peculiar odour of chemicals. The crate was shortly followed by official instructions. In these it was explained that the vests and pants had been impregnated with certain poisonous chemicals which were thought to be fatal to the body louse—*Pediculus vestimenti*—the scourge of all armies.

It was the interesting duty allotted to the present writer to carry out experiments with these garments. A small camp of bell tents was erected not too near to Poperinghe, and then came the question of obtaining the human subjects for the experiment. First of all 12 volunteers, without lice, were asked for from an infantry battalion in the line. Most of the battalion volunteered, and after some close scrutiny 12 were selected, guaranteed free from infection. Then 12 thoroughly lousy soldiers were indented for, and 12 kilted Highlanders reported themselves at the camp. These heroes in the cause of science, who were to wear the underclothes, had not been selected; they happened to be the first 12 numbered off by the sergeant-major.

The experiment proved interesting if futile, but this is neither the place nor the time to enter into details. The point is that every kilted soldier in the trenches was thoroughly lousy, not, let it be clearly stated, through any fault of his own, but of the pleats of his kilt, which made ideal lurking places for the loathsome parasites, from which safe retreats it was impossible for the unwilling host to evacuate them.

Once again, Sir, I apologize for dwelling on so repellent a subject in the columns of *The Times*, but we all must bravely face what the late Professor A. E. Shipley termed "the Minor Horrors of War."

Yours, &c.,
PHILIP GOSSE

3,000 DOWN, PUZZLINGLY SPOKE IN ANGER

10 October 1939

SIR, RECENTLY WE WERE greeted for our enjoyment with *The Times* Crossword Puzzle No. 3,000. The puzzle was not — as some of us hoped — of a nature specially appropriate to this remarkable anniversary, but I do not think the occasion should be allowed to pass without suitable comment. There must be thousands of readers of *The Times* — especially cricketers and lovers of Shakespeare — who owe an undying debt of gratitude to the author of our daily "food."

At this point, it is interesting to look back and consider which we regard as his cleverest clue. Personally, I still cling to one of his early ones:

Clue. — "It is topping to kiss a monkey." Answer. — Apex.

Bravo! Sir. Kindly carry on through the difficult days that lie ahead.

Yours sincerely,
E. A. C. BUCKMASTER

A LONG WAR IN PROSPECT

1 December 1939

SIR, DR. EDWYN BEVAN, in his thoughtful letter in your issue of November 28, omits one sad but all-important consideration. I am in continuous contact with Germans in this country, many of them of the civilized and liberal-minded type he describes, but one and all agree in saying that it is the young people who are Hitler's most enthusiastic supporters. There are probably some 13,000,000 young Germans between the ages of 16 and 24 to whom Hitler is God, Himmler is his prophet, and the noblest task of a good Nazi is to beat up Jews and anti-Nazis in a concentration camp. Thirteen million young fanatics take a deal of crushing, but until they have learnt their lesson there is no hope of a reasonable Germany. And that is why this war will be long and bitter.

I am, &c.,
GEORGE R. CLERK

THE BEST OF TIMES, THE WORST OF TIMES

1940–49

GRASS IS GOOD FOR YOU

2 May 1940

SIR, IN VIEW OF the publicity you have accorded to Mrs. Barrow's letter, I hope that you will spare me space to say, as an advocate for the consumption of grass-mowings, that I have eaten them regularly for over three years, and off many lawns. The sample I am eating at present comes off a golf green on Mitcham Common. I have never suffered from urticaria or any of the symptoms Mrs. Barrow mentions. Nor did any of the many of my horses to which I have fed grass-mowings, freshly cut and cleaned from stones, &c. For my own consumption I also wash them well.

Yours faithfully,
J. R. B. BRANSON

CHURCHILL'S BROADCASTS

22 June 1940

SIR, I VENTURE TO disagree with Mr. J. A. Gray's suggestion that the B.B.C should be allowed to furnish a record of the Prime Minister's periodical statements to Parliament and so set him free from the "waste of time and energy" involved in broadcasting on the same day. To suggest this is to ignore the mysterious, intimate ties that bind together and the speaker and the audience: the message may be the same but each audience evokes a different method of expressing it.

The incalculable value of Mr. Churchill's broadcasts lies in fact that he seems to be addressing himself to each one of the listening multitudes as though no other human being heard his voice. That is the secret of simple oratory. The response in each individual soul is instant and lasting. Substitute for this a recorded utterance evoked in Parliament by an entirely different audience, and lose for the nation one of the greatest incentives towards winning the war.

Yours faithfully,
GERALDINE MOZLEY

THE B.B.C. AT WAR

22 July 1940

Sir, Major-General Guy Dawnay protests in your columns this morning against "the latest deplorable manifestation" of the B.B.C.'s "standard of taste, feeling, understanding, and imagination" being "surely revolting to all decent citizens." These are grave words, which Major-General Dawnay no doubt weighed very carefully before he felt justified in using them. May I, for the B.B.C., which, subject to the necessary Government sanctions, was responsible for this broadcast, explain that it, too, was earnestly considered before it was included in the news?

This broadcast gave an eye-witness account of an air action, successful without loss of British aircraft, against an enemy attack on a convoy. The business of news broadcasting is to bring home to the whole public what is happening in the world and, at a grim time like this, to play some part in maintaining civilian morale. British fighting men do not wage war with long faces. The high gravity of German troops is alien to them. Theirs is a spirit of cheerful realism, and, in a total war, is it not also the spirit of the British people as a whole? That young men, on a fine July Sunday afternoon, fight to the death over the Channel instead of bathing in it is horrible. But it is, alas, through no fault of our country, a fact. The young men face this fact without loss of their native high spirits. Do civilians want it presented to them in any other way?

People in all walks of life have assured us since this broadcast that they found it heartening and a tonic. One group of 15 listeners voted it "the finest thing the B.B.C. has ever done." Many have suggested that the record should be sold for the Red Cross. Others hoped that it would be relayed to America (as in fact it was), to show the British spirit at this moment. These comments came from all parts of the island. On the other side there were objectors, though not many who thought as ill of us as does Major-General Dawnay.

Broadcasting must face the war, as do individuals in and out of uniform. There is a debatable borderline between gaiety and levity, between cheapness and the cheerfulness that springs from a stout heart. Evidently I shall not persuade some of our critics that we were not guilty of crossing to the wrong side. Other critics, no less detached and reputable, believe us to have been right.

Listeners as a body will, we hope and believe, give us the credit for being aware of that borderline, and, equally, of having no intention of being brow-beaten into a retreat to the safe regions of the colourless. Cheerfulness, even in time of battle, will keep breaking in on the ordinary men and women who, after all, have to win this war, and we mean to keep it in our programmes too. It would be a bad day for listeners—that is, for the great mass of ordinary people in this country, faced at the moment with all the monotony and anxiety of waiting—if the B.B.C. stood, out of deference to the gravity of the situation, with bowed head and arms reversed.

Yours very truly,
F. W. OGILVIE
Director-General of the B.B.C.

———◆———

A DIG AT VICTORY

6 July 1940

SIR, IN THIS VILLAGE yesterday a man remarked, "Oh, well, if the Germans win, at any rate I have my pension, and they can't touch that."

Can nothing be done by the Press, the B.B.C. or the Ministry of Information to bring home to people some of the implications of a German victory?

Yours obediently,
H. A. SMITH

THE SPIRIT THAT KNOWS NOT DEFEAT

27 December 1940

SIR, I AM WRITING THIS letter from my home in the country. My predecessors, who lived here for hundreds of years, experienced war in its various phases, and met it calmly and bravely during the generations that came and went.

Up to a few years ago portions of age-blackened skin which once covered the body of a raiding Dane were nailed to the door of a church in a neighbouring village. The gruesome trophy was removed shortly before the last War by an American collector of "curios." Here in our village there is a tumulus containing the 700-year-old bones of a goodly number of the deceased Dane's countrymen, who in the course of various raids on Essex were so hospitably received by the natives and accorded what may be termed as "decent burial." I believe these raiders were not subjected to the rather drastic process of skinning. But there they lie, giving ocular proof of what happens usually to unwanted invaders.

As I write this evening the air is filled with the ominous sounds of hostile aircraft passing over on their way to and from their objectives in London and other points. The sky is agitated with the flashes of exploding A.A. shells and made weirdly picturesque with the graceful movements of the night-piercing searchlights from various ground points. Our local A.R.P. warden on his bicycle can be heard puffing up the hill, while at intervals he blows his tin whistle to warn us of the alert which we heard from the neighbouring town 20 minutes ago. In the meantime the invaders are over us. The warden, an old friend of mine on the land, stops at times for a little chat. He has a long way to go from farm to farm and cottage to cottage, and by the time he reaches home there will probably be another alarm to whistle for again.

Meanwhile at my gates, while the sky is at war and searchlights search and guns go off in the near distance, while we see the fireworks over London 50 miles away, a little group of six boys are singing Christmas carols. Imagine the scene! They are singing the old carols unperturbed, and not always in tune, as their fathers and forefathers have sung them where they stand, generation after generation. "Hark! the Herald Angels" to the accompaniment of sirens and A.A. guns!

These little carol singers, the future men of England, walking mile after mile in the darkened country lanes, singing their age-old carols, unmindful of the portents above, are proof that, like the rest of the nation, they are of the Spirit that knows not defeat.

Yours &c.,
R. D. BLUMENFELD

Ralph Blumenfeld, who had been born in Wisconsin but lived in Essex, had been for almost 30 years Editor of the *Daily Express*.

OFFICERS AND GENTLEMEN

15 January 1941

Sir, The authorities who govern the Army and, indeed, all senior officers, are rightly and justly worried about one of the aspects of life in our new armies. That aspect is known as man management, and man management is chiefly the responsibility of the junior officers—the company and platoon commanders. The subject embraces not only the physical but the mental and moral welfare of the soldier—and the word moral is not used here in the customary "goodie-goodie" sense.

Two or three weeks ago a Sunday newspaper published an address by the Prime Minister given to Harrow School on the subject of the character training acquired by the boys at the older public schools and completely justifying the human product which cheap music-hall artists have jeered at and labelled the old school tie. Never was the old school tie and the best that it stands for more justified than it is to-day. Our new armies are being officered by classes of society who are new to the job. The middle, lower middle, and working classes are now receiving the King's commission. These classes, unlike the old aristocratic and feudal (almost) classes who led the old Army, have never had "their people" to consider. They have never had anyone to think of but themselves. This aspect of life is completely new to them, and they have very largely fallen down on it in their capacity as Army officers.

It is not that they do not wish to carry out this part of their duties properly, but rather that they do not know how to begin. Man management is not a subject which can be "taught"; it is an attitude of mind, and with the old school tie men this was instinctive and part of the philosophy of life. These new young officers will be just as brave and technically efficient, but they have been reared in an atmosphere in which the State spoon feeds everybody from cradle to grave, and no one feels any responsibility for his fellow men. This, Sir, is a sad reflection on our educational system.

I am, Sir, your obedient servant,
R. C. BINGHAM
Lt-Col R.C. Bingham

SIR, COLONEL BINGHAM's letter on man management, like so many sweeping generalities, contains only half the truth. A very large number of boys, at Eton for instance, have no aristocratic tradition; they are the sons of new men who have made money, who were not at Eton themselves. But the sons of these "new" men absorb at their public schools, and later in their regiments, the old great Army tradition which may be summed up in the words "See to the needs and comforts of your men before you see to your own."

There is, therefore, no reason, if O.C.T.U.s[1] and regiments do their job properly, why the sons of working-class parents should not equally absorb this fine tradition. During the last war I had the privilege of commanding a squadron, and occasionally a regiment, of cavalry. At the beginning all the officers came from the most expensive schools. Towards the end about half the officers came from the ranks. With, of course, some exceptions on either side, the two fused excellently, and there was nothing to choose between them as good officers and good comrades. Anyone who wants to see a very high quality of leadership can look to the Scout Movement, where the officers come largely from the working classes.

I am, &c.,
A. A. BEAMAN
Lt-Col A.A. Beaman

[1] Officer Cadet Training Unit

MUSSOLINI'S METHOD

29 January 1941

Sir, Current events in Milan[1] give some point to the following anecdote told to me by a French friend who was engaged in propaganda in Italy in 1915.

Early in that year he was visited by a young stranger, who gave his name as Benito Mussolini.

"Don't you think," said the young man, "that there are too many Tedeschi [Germans] in Milan?" The Frenchman warmly agreed. "Give me 100,000 francs and I will remove them." "How will you do that?" "You will see." The money was given.

Next morning every important German in Milan was wakened early by three or four young Italians armed with clubs; he was directed to dress quickly and hurry to his train; his luggage would be sent after him.

One recognizes the master's early manner in the treatment of a fine traditional subject. A pity he is no longer interested in it.

Yours,
GILBERT MURRAY

[1] Mussolini had agreed to let German troops enter Italy

The Oxford scholar Gilbert Murray was regarded as the nation's leading authority on Ancient Greece.

FLAK

20 September 1941

SIR, "FLAK" IS THE abbreviation of the German word-monster *Flugzeugabwehr-kanone*, which consists of five parts. *Flug* is our word flight or flying. *Zeug* is stuff, implement, craft, and thus the two words together mean aircraft or flying-machine. *Ab* is our preposition off, and *Wehr* defence, a body of armed men, which makes *Abwehr* mean warding off, fighting off. *Kanone*, of course, is our cannon or gun. No wonder even the Germans, who are somewhat fond of "word sausages," thought it advisable to reduce their word for an A.A. gun to the monosyllabic *flak*.

Another recently adopted German word, *Panzer* (pronounced puntser), is the medieval German word for a coat of mail and now signifies armour and armoured. Thus a German *Panzerkreuzer*, *e.g.*, is an armoured cruiser and a *Panzerauto* an armoured car.

Yours, &c.,
V. GROVE

PER ARDUA AD ASTRA

25 September 1941

SIR, FOR A NUMBER of weeks now I have tried, unsuccessfully, to discover the origin of the phrase "Per ardua ad astra," the motto of the Royal Air Force. I have gone so far as to ask many members of the R.A.F. themselves, but nobody seems to know. It occurs to me that many besides myself would like to know, for the motto is our daily inspiration, as it must be, too, of the R.A.F.

Yours faithfully,
JOHN T. WATSON

Replied on 27 September 1941

SIR, IN ANSWER TO the Rev. John T. Watson's letter, in 1912, when I was raising and commanding the Royal Flying Corps (Military Wing), one of our difficulties was that the officers and men were all joining in different uniforms or in civilian clothes. I was convinced that for practical utility and *esprit de corps* a distinctive uniform was essential. The War Office accordingly approved the double-breasted khaki uniform and folding cap which will be well remembered by all who knew the Royal Flying Corps.

Brigadier-General David Henderson, then Director of Military Training at the War Office, also agreed that a badge for pilots was desirable, and together we sketched upon a War Office blotting pad the "Wings" which were afterwards sanctioned by the King.

I then asked my officers to put forward ideas for a motto, and "Per ardua ad astra" was suggested to me by a young officer of the name of J. N. Fletcher, who had joined the Royal Flying Corps from the Royal Engineers. The motto had been suggested to him by another officer of the Royal Engineers, J. S. Yule, who is now a member of the Historical Section of the War Cabinet Secretariat. It seemed to me the best possible motto, and I referred it to the War Office, where I remember incidentally that one of the pundits, I think it was Harold Baker, then Finance Member, expressed the view that it was bad Latin. However, I pressed the point and the motto was accepted.

Early in 1918 an approved light-blue uniform was introduced, and the khaki double-breasted uniform discarded, as a compromise between the Army and Navy when the Royal Flying Corps and Royal Naval Air Service were amalgamated. The "Wings" (with the letters R.A.F. replacing R.F.C. in the centre) and motto were retained.

I am, Sir, your obedient servant,
FREDERICK H. SYKES

Replied on 29 September 1941

Sir, In your issue of September 25 the Rev. J. T. Watson asks for information as to the origin of the motto of the Royal Air Force.

The following facts, though slight, may be of interest. In the course of the last war — I do not remember the exact date — the late F. H. Rawlins, Lower Master of Eton, asked me to come to see him. I found him with various pieces of paper before him and he said, "I have to choose a motto for the Air Force." The result was what has become perhaps the most famous motto in the world. I remember that the final choice was between that and Virgil's "Sic itur ad astra" and there were other suggestions which I have forgotten.

Your obedient servant,
A. C. RAYNER-WOOD

The words can be translated as "Through Adversity to the Stars"

A WASTE OF PAPER

30 October 1941

SIR, I WRITE TO DEPLORE the present campaign for the indiscriminate destruction of documents and records in the interests of salvage. While it is, of course, important to writers and publishers, as well as to the direct war interests, that every scrap of waste paper should be retrieved, it is even more important to avoid exposing British culture to forms of vandalism comparable to those which have destroyed the culture of Central Europe. This threat is especially alarming when so many valuable books and documents have already been lost through air raids.

History and literature may well be deprived of collections similar in value to the Paston Letters and the Diaries of John Evelyn and Samuel Pepys, if the present injunctions to destroy ledgers, diaries, notebooks, and letters continue unchecked. Had the campaign to save paper between 1914 and 1918 taken this particular form, many lasting records of the Great War could never have been compiled. Cannot something still be done to create a sense of proportion? The appointment of a local librarian or antiquarian to every salvage committee seems to be one expedient worthy of consideration.

Yours, etc.,
VERA BRITTAIN

THE FUTURE OF EDUCATION

27 February 1942

SIR, THERE IS A POINT of view as to the future of our educational system which is of the utmost importance in the present discussions, and yet is hardly represented in them or sufficiently taken account of: that of people who pass through elementary and secondary schools, the vast majority of the nation. It is they who should have the largest say as to the future of education in this country, and we look to *The Times* to give expression to a point of view which was not given consideration in the discussion in the House of Lords.

We do not agree with the Archbishop of Canterbury or Lord Hankey that it will help the nation's education to enable the public schools to play a larger part in it than before. We hold that it is neither practicable nor desirable for any portion of the pupils attending elementary or secondary schools to be taken away to public schools. It is impracticable on financial, still more on social, grounds. Working-class parents will not be prepared to have their children taken away to be educated into a different social stratum, breaking up the unity of their families, when there is a perfectly good day-school system at their doors, which in many cases offers a better education than that at inferior public schools. The proper solution for the difficulties of the public schools, with the decline in the birth-rate and in the incomes of the middle-classes, is not to drain away the pupils from the national schools but for the public schools to concentrate their resources upon the best of their number. The recent amalgamation of Haileybury and the Imperial Service College points the way to the right solution for them.

We want the elementary and secondary schools to develop their own ethos and make their own contribution to the national life. We think that day-school education has its own advantages, and that the education provided at a day-school like Manchester Grammar School, for example, is inferior to none in the country. It is vital that there should not be mere imitations of the public schools. The latter made their great contribution to national life in the nineteenth century; and there are all too evident signs around us that their standards are not wholly adapted to the conditions of the contemporary world. For example, the disproportionate importance they attach to character rather than intelligence: a wrong emphasis for which we are now paying the price in every field of national life, in the conduct of the war, in politics, in administration, in the services, in the Empire. It was not so in the great, creative days of our nation in the age of Elizabeth, of the reign of Anne, of the Pitts, when the Empire was won.

Nor do we agree with the Archbishop that more religious instruction in the schools is going to be our salvation. What we want is more intelligence, putting ability, clear thinking, fore-sight, aggressive energy first — those standards which your Correspondent in his terrible indictment, found so wanting at Singapore.

Yours sincerely,
A. L. ROWSE

Singapore, the gateway to Britain's empire in the Far East, had recently been taken with apparent ease by the invading Japanese.

Replied on 10 March 1942

SIR, MR. ROWSE IS wrong about religious education. Apart from other considerations, he fails to realize how much the study of Christian truth clears the mind and enriches the imagination.

But he is right about character and intelligence. No doubt character is of the first importance to a nation. But it is not in character that we have shown ourselves inferior to our ancestors. Our leaders during the last 20 years have been men of most respectable character. Morally they compare favourably with Cromwell and Queen Elizabeth. But, alas, they have not shown the same penetration in diagnosing a situation, or the same resource in meeting it. It was lack of intelligence, not lack of character, that made the leaders of the Left advocate, in the same breath, resistance to Fascism and reduction of armaments. It was lack of intelligence, not lack of character, that made the leaders of the Right persist, in spite of repeated failures, in believing it was possible to appease Hitler. It was lack of intelligence, not lack of character, that made the majority of the Conservative Party deaf to the warnings of the present Prime Minister.

Nor can the public schools be acquitted of all responsibility for this intellectual decline. It is mortifying to compare the schoolboys of to-day with those of a hundred years back. As schoolboys Pitt, Fox, Peel, and Canning, none of them prigs or freaks, were mentally as advanced as boys of 20 to-day. Already they were talking intelligently about politics and literature and social life; already their interests, transcending the limits of school life, made them citizens of the great world. The human animal does not change so quickly in a hundred years; the change must be due to education. And, indeed, there must be something wrong with an education which spends the larger part of its time teaching boys Latin and sends away 5 per cent at most able to read a Latin book for pleasure. The fact is that public school masters, concentrating on the school rather than the boys, have neglected to encourage curiosity, imagination, mental independence, and enterprise in order to produce "safe" men, steady, loyal, unquestioning supporters of whatever institution fate has seen fit to place them in. It is such "safe" men who land others in danger.

Yours truly,
DAVID CECIL

Leslie Rowse was the son of a china clay worker; Lord David Cecil, his fellow historian at Oxford, was the son of a marquess.

DOGS OF WAR

20 June 1942

Sir, The question of the usefulness of dogs kept in towns merits a little more thought than Mr. G. Wren Howard appears to have given it. Undoubtedly a large proportion of these animals afford protection, companionship, and entertainment not only to many family units but to people forced by present circumstances to live alone.

The dog's value as a vermin killer, too, should be borne in mind. The Ministry of Agriculture, in its "Bulletin on Rats and their Extermination," gives the dog pride of place as a lethal agent. Last year this league organized a rat-killing contest open to domestic dogs and excluding those belonging to professional rat-catchers. The chief winner—a dog living in a large town—scored 960 authenticated kills in five months. The leading 24 (mostly town-dwelling) competitors between them killed 6,210 rats, while the aggregate for all competitors multiplied this figure many times over. It is obvious that these dogs must have saved from destruction an enormous quantity of human food. As for the food consumed by dogs, the giving of foodstuffs fit for human consumption is prohibited by law, and the supply of recognized dog-foods is but a small fraction of what it was in peace-time. The majority live on household scraps, and so the expenditure of money, time, labour, and transport would be just the same whether these scraps were eaten by dogs or not.

Yours faithfully,
CHARLES R. JOHNS
Secretary, National Canine Defence League

SHALLOW BATHS

3 October 1942

SIR, I AM REMINDED by your recent leading article on economy in the use of water that there are certain devices on the market for automatically regulating the quantity of hot water for a bath. The plimsoll-mark on the inside of the bath is a great test of character and the temptation to exceed the ration is great.

One such simple device, installed in a large Midland hospital some years ago, has proved successful in effecting appreciable economy in hot water. It consists of a small cylinder containing a float which turns off the supply when a predetermined quantity of hot water has been delivered. No more hot water is obtainable until the bath is emptied and the operation repeated.

Your obedient servant,
WILLIAM KEAY

MILITARY GENIUS

29 October 1942

SIR, As THE AUTHOR (in 1938) of the first full and consecutive account of Count Belisarius's campaigns published in English for more than a century, I am pleased to learn that Sir Archibald Wavell ranks him with Marlborough at the top of his list of good generals. Personally, I should have put Scipio Africanus in Marlborough's place, because he commanded less dependable troops with equal skill, fought under greater political disadvantages, and succeeded in consolidating his gains.

Scipio and Belisarius were set the same apparently impossible task (which General Wavell himself faced in 1940): that of defeating with inadequate forces a strong and well-posted enemy in North Africa. Belisarius's campaign, fought in AD 532, when he was in his early thirties, is however of more topical interest than Scipio's, because he operated from a distant base against an enemy who held Sicily as well as Africa and was extremely strong at sea, and because this enemy was German, and because later Belisarius had to free the Italians from their German masters, beginning with an invasion of Sicily.

Belisarius was unique among the generals of antiquity in his sensible and humane conduct of war. It was his rule never to terrorize a civil population, always to avoid pitched battles whenever the same advantages could be achieved by forced marches, by the cutting of enemy communications or by digging in, and never to force a defeated enemy to desperation. He was apparently of Slav blood (Beli-Tsar means "White Prince") and had the Slav talent for what your former Military Correspondent, Captain Liddell Hart (by the way, the only modern biographer of Scipio), has named "dynamic defence." One sentence of Belisarius's speech made near Callinikon on the Euphrates on Easter Saturday, 531, in which he tried to restrain his pugnacious army from fighting an unnecessary battle, has often recurred to me during the past three years: "Steady, soldiers! Providence may be counted upon to rescue men from unavoidable dangers, but not from ones that they bring upon themselves needlessly." They threatened to mutiny, and he had to give way; he fought with inadequate forces and supplies, and took the only beating of his career.

Belisarius's declared preference for indirect means of victory is the more remarkable because it was apparently he who invented the prototype of the modern tank — the cataphract, or heavily armoured horse-archer, with whom in his classic defence of Rome he did such terrible execution against Wittich's corps of German lancers.

Yours, &c.,
ROBERT GRAVES

Replied on 30 October 1942

SIR, I AM GLAD TO see that General Wavell does not place Julius Caesar high on his list of great generals. From a careful study of his *De Bello Gallico* it seems clear that the British leader Cassivellaunus (or Cassibelan) soundly defeated him. Unfortunately Cassivellaunus could neither read nor write, so Julius Caesar has had it all his own way with the historians — with the possible exception of Mommsen. Cassivellaunus was undoubtedly our first great national hero.

Yours faithfully,
A. H. BURNE

THE BEVERIDGE REPORT

9 March 1943

SIR, WHAT IS IT IN the Beveridge Report which has gripped the whole nation? It is the expounding of a moral principle. If those who live in Great Britain deserve the place in civilization which they claim to have reached, they should accept the principle that no living soul among them should be compelled to starve so long as any other of them has more than enough to avoid starvation, and starvation means the want of what is necessary to prevent body, mind, and spirit from sinking below a vital standard.

But while we are talking about questions of cost, may we not be jeopardizing the great reaction to the Beveridge exposition, the common bond it made clear to us, the hopes it raised for some, the willingness to sacrifice it engendered in others? The cost will be the amount required to augment the incomes which do not come up to the fixed line. The real question therefore is, how can we arrange that every one may produce goods or perform services which, taken over his whole lifetime, will be not less in value than what is required to keep him above the line? If we can find the answer to this question the cost will be nil. If we cannot find a complete answer the cost will be measured by the extent to which we fail, and it will be borne by those who are able to live above the line. The answer does not depend on governments, political parties, or even Parliament, it depends upon the people. Beveridge has lighted a beacon of faith, faith in our country, in ourselves, and in the triumph of what is good over evil. Are we going to let it die out, or are we going to fan it into flame? Are we a little people or are we a big people? We must all put our shoulders to the wheel, and with new inspiration and renewed faith in our genius and in our tradition we cannot fail to find the answer.

The debates in Parliament suggest a prevailing fear of return to mass unemployment instead of a determination to prevent it. Few are sufficiently well informed to express an opinion about all the recommendations contained in the report, but the setting up of the suggested Ministry of Social Security, not only to deal with the report but also to examine means of making employment reasonably secure, would restore hope to many to whom the debates were a disappointment.

Yours faithfully,
WALTER BENTON JONES

The report had proposed widespread reform to welfare provision and led to the founding of the National Health Service.

THE LANGUAGE OF THE IMAGINATION

9 March 1943

SIR, YOUR CRITIC, commenting on *The Magnificent Ambersons*, is hopeful that "one day film may become an important art." I do not know what is his definition of art, and I admit my own confusion on this elusive topic. But there need surely be no dispute between us in acknowledging the truth of Ruskin's broad assertion that it is the language of the imagination; a language in which the best film directors, actors, and technicians of Britain, America, France, and Russia are often exquisitely fluent. (Fifteen years ago the inclusion of Germany would also have been possible.) The apparent disdain with which your critic dismisses their inspiration and ability, and his condescension towards all that the cinema, in its short history, has achieved aesthetically needs no comment.

His oblique denial of the cinema's importance as an art seems as difficult to follow as to justify. The ubiquity of the film, whether good or bad, assures its affecting the ideas and emotions of a far greater number of people than is at present influenced by any other form of art. To dismiss it, therefore, as unimportant admits a degree of oblivion or partiality which is painful to observe in one who speaks with the authority of a critic.

I remain, Sir, yours truly,
NICOLAS BENTLEY

The Magnificent Ambersons was the second film made by Orson Welles but, unlike *Citizen Kane*, it divided the critics. The illustrator Nicolas Bentley is perhaps best remembered for his drawings for TS Eliot's *Old Possum's Book of Practical Cats*. His middle name was Clerihew, as was that of his father who invented the verse form – see page 200

KNIGHTS ERRANT

30 June 1943

SIR, IN MY CAPACITY as Editor of *Debrett* a great many people turn to me in their family troubles and I have become deeply concerned lately at the increasing number of cases of fraudulent assumption of titles. Cases which have come under my notice during these past few months have been chiefly in connexion with matrimony. Troubled parents have come to me saying that their daughters have married "baronets" or "knights" whose names they cannot find in *Debrett*, or any other work of reference, and in two cases notices of the marriages have actually been inserted in leading London daily newspapers. In one such instance the man concerned was subsequently sentenced to imprisonment for double bigamy.

Occasionally parents are wise enough to consult me beforehand; as has happened in the case of the man serving in the Air Force and posing as a baronet, who had been endeavouring to gain the affections of a member of the W.A.A.F. In most instances, however, the parents do not come to me until after the event, when it is too late to take any action. No doubt the increase in this contemptible type of fraud is largely due to the war and the fact that young people meet away from their homes in abnormal surroundings, which makes it much more easy to avoid detection, and I can only hope the publication of this letter may serve to draw attention to the scandal.

Unfortunately there seems to be no remedy at law, as in itself it is not a crime to assume a title, neither can a marriage be dissolved because one of the parties is proved to be an imposter, and a parent who wrote to me "Thank goodness, the marriage can now be annulled," was, of course, quite in error.

Yours faithfully,
C. P. J. HANKINSON

THE BOMBING OF ROME

22 July 1943

SIR, IN YOUR ARTICLE of July 20 on the bombing of Rome[1] the military principle behind it was clearly expressed:—"Unconditional concentration upon the ruin of the armed forces and war potential of the enemy"; and the significance of "unconditional" was revealed in the last sentence: "It must not be diverted by fear of the unintended damage incidental to the main necessity."

An important part of every country's war potential, especially when threatened with invasion, is its morale: and that, apart from individual courage, depends upon the conviction that one's own country stands for the right, for desirable life, for civilization, which is enormously intensified by evidence that the enemy, on the contrary, cares for none of these things. In the worst days nothing steeled us more than proofs, at home and abroad, that the strategy of the Nazis was "unconditional." It is possible, then, that bombing Rome has been good for Italian morale and bad for ours.

This possibility should be weighed against any temporary military advantage of dislocating railway traffic. How many times have the marshalling yards of Hamm been bombed? True, the war is going so well that we hardly feel for the moment the need of morale; but the war is not yet over.

Yours, &c.,
DESMOND MacCARTHY

[1] On July 19, US aircraft had bombed marshalling yards in Rome to disrupt German troop movements reacting to the Allied invasion of Sicily. Attacking the Eternal City was controversial but most correspondents welcomed the raid.

Replied on 24 July 1943

Sir, l should like to reassure Mr. Desmond MacCarthy. If the Italian compares the precautions taken by the allies before and during the bombing of Rome with the precautions taken by the Axis before and during the bombing of Guernica, Rotterdam, Belgrade, London, Coventry, Exeter, and Abyssinia, his morale will hardly be fortified by the thought that he stands for all the holy things and his enemy for all the unholy things. And the morale of Russia, of our soldiers who are hazarding their lives, and of all the tortured and enslaved peoples of the occupied countries will be strengthened by the knowledge that we are really engaged on a war of liberation, not on a sentimental pilgrimage.

Yours, &c.,
A. A. MILNE

———◆———

JET AIRCRAFT

14 January 1944

Sir, The successful development of a jet-propelled aircraft emphasizes how few are the really new ideas and how long it takes to realize some of the old ones.

Hero of Alexandria described about AD 50 a machine demonstrating the principle of propulsion by the reaction of jets (of steam) and the Abbé Miolan attempted in 1784 to apply it to the navigation of a hot-air balloon. The project was dismissed as having "no aviating merit," but this did not deter J. W. Butler and E. Edwards from patenting in 1867 (36 years before the Wright brothers flew) a design for an aeroplane which envisaged propulsion by the reaction of jets of compressed air or gas, or by "the explosion of a mixture of inflammable gas or air" emitted through jets.

Your obedient servant,
M. J. B. DAVY

EQUAL PAY FOR WOMEN

31 March 1944

Sir, If the favour shown by the House of Commons to equal pay on 28 March reflects national opinion, no doubt that principle will sooner or later be adopted not only by the Government but also in due course in all sections of industry, trade and finance, where the two sexes do similar work. In drawing attention to an important corollary, I do not wish to add to the distractions of the authorities in the hour of supreme endeavour, but rather to give food for thought to the friends of equal pay.

The majority of active women are engaged on the tasks of motherhood. Even under the old system these have had an unfair deal, and we have recently been thinking of family allowances as a method of redressing the balance in their favour. But the most generous proposals so far suggested would barely cover out-of-pocket expenses incurred on behalf of the children. If the remuneration for women's work outside the home is to be improved, we shall have to go farther and think in terms of the endowment of motherhood as such. The work of bringing up children is probably harder and certainly more valuable to the community and more skilled than any work done in factory or schoolroom. No woman should be allowed to suffer financially for choosing the better path.

So long as woman are paid considerably less than men in their occupations, it is arguable that a woman may not lose very much by giving up her work on marriage, since a married couple can live on less than twice what is required for a single person. Where equal pay operates women will inevitably lose on renouncing their outside work.

To ask whether we could afford to endow motherhood is to misconceive the issue. It is not a question of supplying something extra, but of redistributing what we already have. That is also true of equal pay. For some time — namely until our industrial efficiency had increased in proportion to the increase in total pay-roll involved — equal pay would mean reducing (through higher prices and taxes) the spending power available for men, married or single, for married women employed on their domestic duties and for children, and it would mean reducing the relative amounts going to these classes permanently. Thus by itself it would be a retrograde measure. But if it were accompanied by a proportionate endowment of motherhood, the burden would be shifted off the families on to bachelors, unoccupied spinsters, and married people without dependent children where the wife was unoccupied. Thus equal pay and the endowment of motherhood should be indissolubly linked in projects of reform.

But the matter is not simple. For example, the injustice to mothers would not be removed by offering the same endowment for an ex-school mistress as for an ex-waitress. And how would those who marry before taking up any settled occupation be graded? It is easier to legislate for equal pay than for an adequate endowment of motherhood: before returning to the charge it is incumbent on those who urge the former to offer proposals for giving simultaneous effect to the latter.

I am, &c.,
R. F. HARROD

The economist Roy Harrod would become best known as the biographer of his friend John Maynard Keynes.

DOWN THE HATCH

5 April 1944

SIR, THE INTERESTING correspondence on "treating" has more than two sides to it, I think. Logically, the demand for a non-treating order is fair enough. Treating has been proved to increase drinking expenditure, especially among the young and alcoholically inexperienced. People in groups also drink about 10 per cent. faster than solo drinkers.

Sociologically, the demand is less firmly based. The pub is above all else a fundamental British social organization—the only simple, public, informal, communal unit still freely available to anybody every day. It serves alcohol among many other things. The biggest other thing is company, comradeship, and good cheer. Treating and toasting are the symbols of public friendliness. It has been so for centuries, and bans on those customs —always unsuccessful— go back to Charles II, Pope Innocent III, and the 1356 Council of Cologne. A new attempt, in these democratic days, would probably lead to mass evasion, unless there were a complete new inspectorate to ensure enforcement. But if successfully applied, would such an order not knock one more nail into the coffin of private liberties and of positive social groups?

Moreover, while the solitary drinker goes more slowly and quietly, there is much to suggest that he or she is the one who, chatterless, anchorless, private, carries on into the area of extremism— drunkenness. Whereas the friendly, noisy, treating group go off to the dance or the whist drive, at least keeping each other on the rails.

These are at least points worthy of consideration. So often in the past our social habits have been altered by sincere but one-sided legislative action which has inhibited traditions integral in our way of living.

Yours, &c.,
TOM HARRISSON

Among his many accomplishments, which included wartime service in the jungles of Borneo, the anthropologist Tom Harrisson was a co-founder of Mass Observation, the project to study the habits of ordinary people.

THE DEATH OF
PRESIDENT ROOSEVELT

14 April 1945

SIR, SOME AMERICANS may be asking how the man in the street in this country feels about the death of Mr Roosevelt.

The old paper-seller who has a pitch near my home handed me my copy and pointed, mutely, to the headlines. We stood looking at one another for several moments and neither could speak. Then he said: "The man next door heard it on the wireless, in the midnight news, and came and knocked me up. The missus and I were so upset that we couldn't sleep and were glad when it was time to get up."

I think that describes, as well as they can be described, the feelings of most British people.

Yours truly,
CHARLES J. SEYMOUR

CONCENTRATION CAMP CHILDREN

7 May 1945

SIR, THE MOST SHOCKING discovery made after the liberation of the concentration camps is the large number of children found in these "cities of sorrow." These, mostly orphans of parents who died fighting Hitlerism, were regarded by the Nazis as hereditary unreliables and potential rebels.

The story of "re-education" in the Third Reich as practised in the *Erziehungslager* (educational camps for children) has yet to be written. If children after having passed through such a place still showed signs of moral or mental integrity, they were outlawed by being pronounced *wehrunwuerdig* (unworthy of serving in the army) and were assigned to penal battalions or thrown into concentration camps for the most trifling offences.

What is to be done with these children? The final answer to this question lies with the future administration of Germany. Allied Military Government cannot be more than a stop-gap. No doubt, here is a task for Unrra and for the Economic and Social Council, the enlargement of whose authority is understood to be among the British suggestions at San Francisco. Rehabilitation for the victims of Hitlerism is not a case for charity. These men, women, and children hold title to help as of right. That principle must be clearly established and observed; but some time must elapse before the necessary machinery can be set up.

In the meanwhile something must be done. I suggest the opening of a national fund for the purpose of removing a group of these children (for instance, the juvenile inmates of Buchenwald) to suitable surroundings to give them a new start in life. They may — for the beginning at least — be more a task for the doctor and psychologist than for the teacher. But the chances are that under normal conditions they will recover quickly and be fit to become the first unit to benefit from what we understand by education. If we succeed the victims of to-day will be the vanguard of the free world to-morrow and could play a proper part in the so much talked of — and so little thought out — re-education of the German people.

I am, Sir, your obedient servant,
ALFRED EDWARDS
Member of Parliament for Middlesbrough East

THE FUTURE OF GERMANY

8 May 1945

SIR, IT IS BECOMING clear that the "re-education" of Germany by the allies will not be a pious aspiration, but an unavoidable duty. To administer an entirely shattered nation involves educating it, whether one likes it or not. If so, it is surely necessary to think out carefully what is meant by the term.

There are certain lines of policy about Germany on which all are agreed, *e.g.* that the criminals should be punished and the nation completely disarmed. Would it not be well to consider this problem of re-education, on which there seems to be little agreement, except on the fact that it will take a long time, and especially to decide what kind of country we expect a "re-educated" Germany to be? It is in the hope of raising this issue that I make these three suggestions, which do not pretend to cover more than a part of the field.

First, although the German people certainly did know about the horrors of the concentration camps, their real crime was not that they failed to stop them when all power was in the hands of the Nazis, for this would have been practically impossible, but that they ever allowed the Nazis, whom they knew to be villains, to rise to power at all. They allowed this because they were politically irresponsible. For a century they have been fatally ready to accept any government which would save them from having to make decisions for themselves. The first task is to teach the Germans to face responsibility. In planning their education this is even more important than the provision of the right text-books or broadcast information. It will mean that the proof that Germany is being successfully re-educated will not be that she is submissive to the allies, but that she is found capable of producing a stable democratic government.

Secondly, it is no use hoping to build anything except on some foundation of national tradition. Germany will not be a *tabula rasa*. Every means should be taken to persuade the Germans that they themselves have such a tradition, however completely forgotten now, on which a decent society can be based. There was once a Germany of Goethe, a country which the young Meredith visited because it was a land of liberal thinkers, one with universities which inspired Americans like George Bancroft. "It was in part the influence of American scholars who had caught the flame in Germany that made Harvard, as early as the 1830"s, a steadfast defender of the scholar's freedom from political and religious pressure." (Morrison and Commager: *The Growth of the American Republic* – I, 412.) Germany will not be truly re-educated until she is once more proud of that tradition.

Thirdly, the Germans must learn to respect the Slavs. In Western Europe it is not generally recognized that one of the main traditions in German history, and the most sinister, is that of the conquest and colonization of Slav lands. As a result the ordinary German has come to regard the Slav as an inferior being and he has never begun to adapt himself to the Slav renaissance of the last 100 years. The victory of Russia is probably the most valuable, as it is the hardest, lesson the Germans have learnt in this war. Perhaps the acid test of German re-education will be their readiness to accept the Czechs and the Poles as people with cultures and traditions of their own.

Yours faithfully,
R. BIRLEY

Robert Birley was shortly to become educational adviser to the Control Commission of Germany, and later Head Master of Eton.

A KHAKI ELECTION

14 August 1945

SIR, THE FOLLOWING description of the general election of 1710 provides an interesting historical parallel:

"Two hundred and seventy Members lost their seats. In the new Parliament the Whigs were not a third of the House of Commons ... Thus was ended ..., as it now appeared, by the will of the electorate, the ever-famous administration of Marlborough and Godolphin, which for eight years had led the league of European nations to victory against the exorbitant power of France, which had made the British Island one United Kingdom, and had raised Great Britain from despondency and weakness to the summit of world affairs."

The quotation is from *Marlborough, his Life and Times*, fourth volume, page 329, by Mr Winston Churchill.

Yours, &c.,
MERRIMAN

Lord Merriman was a former Solicitor General. The General Election the month before had, to the surprise of many, resulted in a victory for Labour rather than for the Conservatives and the wartime premier, Churchill.

THE ATOMIC BOMB

16 August 1945

SIR, THE SCIENTIST WORSHIPS truth as the Christian holiness. To ask him to desist from seeking knowledge is as unreasonable as to ask the saint to cease from sanctity. The Christian should be the last to make such a demand since his God is the Way, the Truth and the Life.

If Mr Churchill and his advisers had withheld support from scientists who were researching into atomic energy, our enemies, Nazi and Japanese, would have been before us. They would then have destroyed the bodies of those who opposed them and the souls of those who yielded. In short they would have destroyed humanity itself, for the Nazi-conditioned human being is not human; he is a specialist being whose nature is decided by his master, the State.

The destruction of our bodies is a ghastly thing: the destruction of our souls is the end of man. It is said that the use of the atomic bomb is the destruction of our souls. Why? Because it involves frightful suffering, is indiscriminate, and is used against "innocent civilians". In what sense are civilians innocent and soldiers guilty? In none. If we could see to it that only soldiers suffered for our common guilt, would that be more moral, more acceptable, more just? I do not think so. But those who ask for the disuse of the atomic bomb are asking for a longer war.

I believe that if those who protest would think again they would see that the bomb shocks us all, not because it is cruel, indiscriminate, or frightful, but because it is new. The final truth is that we are becoming masters of terrifying power. As never before, we are compelled to make choices "— perhaps the last we shall be allowed to make. Nazism means evil: their choice is made. Ours is not yet; and to assume that it will be evil is, to quote Sir Lawrence Bragg, "a craven point of view".

Yours,
MAUDE ROYDEN SHAW

Maude Royden Shaw was known for her work on social and religious issues. It was she who in 1917 described the Church of England as "the Conservative Party at prayer".

HITLER'S OBITUARY

7 May 1945

SIR, TWO SHORT FOOTNOTES to your obituary of the Führer. The often alleged change of name by Hitler's father amounts to this:—Austrian peasants have regularly two names, one derived from the name of their freehold —the "house name" (*Hausname*)—transmitted from owner to owner in case of inheritance or sale of the property, the other the family name a man signs on documents (*Schreibname*). A man is "called" (*heisst*) by his house-name as long as he dwells there and owns his place; he signs himself (*schreibt sich*) with his family name. The change from the one to the other is evidence of the sale or cession of property-rights to a new owner. "*Hitler*" (from *Hütte, Hitten*, diminutive *Hittel*) means "small cottager" or "little cotman," and is originally an expression of contempt on the part of the bigger landowners in the neighbourhood. So is *Schicklgruber*, "the owner," "the man of the chequered pit"—*i.e.*, a low-lying patch of land, piebald with sandy patches and dark scrub.

Hitler "drank in the pan-Germanism of" Georg von Schoenerer, not "of Luege." Dr. Karl Lueger was the great leader of the Christian-Socialist Party, a fervent Austrian, and an enemy of Pan-Germanism.

I am, Sir, your obedient servant,
ROBERT EISLER

The writer was a German Jewish art historian — an expert, among other things, on werewolves — who had been interned in Dachau and Buchenwald before finding refuge in Britain. Adolf Hitler's father, who was illegitimate, had been born Alois Schicklgruber but when he was almost 40 changed his surname to that of his stepfather (who may have been his father), Hiedler, though this was registered as Hitler. His son Adolf was born in 1889, when Alois was 52.

THE FUTURE OF EUROPE

16 May 1946

SIR, THERE IS AN alternative policy for Germany to that put forward in your leading article of 9 May, and by Mr Stokes. It is to bring the British, French, and American zones into a Western European Federation. And it has the merit of being based upon the realities of the present situation, and not merely upon wishful thinking.

What is done cannot be undone. At Teheran, at Yalta, and at Potsdam we accepted solutions of the frontier problems of eastern Europe which had no geographical or ethnical justification, and took no account of economic facts. Further, we acquiesced in the policy of forcible mass deportations as the only method of implementing the arrangements that were then made. To-day the eastern zone of Germany has been, for all practical purposes, incorporated in the Soviet Union. Russia has already imposed upon the German territories under her control her own political system, and brought them within her closed economy. Indeed, we may well be told, when the Peace Conference comes eventually to be held — and with considerable justification — that the population of eastern Germany is now predominantly Slav; and we shall not seek to probe too deeply into the events which have brought about this remarkable transformation.

In such a situation, phrases in Mr Stokes's letter such as "Germans must be allowed to form their own political parties independent of zones," and "Elections should be held as soon as possible," are perfectly meaningless. If Mr Stokes seriously believes that Russia will now hand back Eastern Germany to social democracy and free capitalist multilateral trade, he is the victim of an illusion. On the other hand, he is quite right in emphasizing the incredible folly of limiting German industrial production in the west.

The truth of the matter is that, flanked by the tremendous aggregations of political and economic strength represented by a federated Soviet Union and a federated United States, the countries of Western Europe cannot hope to survive as separate and isolated units in the modern world. Unless they get together in pursuit of common policies, based on social justice, individual freedom, and a deliberately planned economic expansion, social democracy on the continent of Europe is doomed. And the inclusion of Western and Southern Germany is absolutely vital to the security and economic strength of any Western regional *bloc*.

The first essential is an agreement between Great Britain and France. We are separated by only 20 miles of water. But for the last two years we might have been inhabiting different planets. The French demand that the industries of the Ruhr should not be returned to German control is justified. They should be administered by an international authority; and co-ordinated with the heavy industries not only of Belgium, Luxemburg, the Saar, and Lorraine, but also of this country. This was Rathenau's vision 25 years ago. Its realization now is a necessary condition of the renaissance of Western Europe. As Mr Walter Lippmann recently observed: "The security and the power of the Empire based on the British Isles cannot be divorced from the countries across the English Channel. Nor can the reconstruction of British industry be planned intelligently without a clear understanding of how far it will collaborate with, how far it must compete with, Western European industry."

We must face the fact that any practical policy designed to create a western *bloc* in Europe will meet with some initial opposition both from the Americans and the Russians — from the former because they are making a final attempt to revive the *laissez-faire* economic system of the nineteenth century, based on promiscuous unplanned international trade, within the framework of fixed exchanges; and from the latter because it would set a limit to their westward expansion. The United States would, however, very soon find that a stable and unified Western European economy could provide far better markets for her export surplus than a number of small, weak, poverty-stricken, and conflicting national units. And the Kremlin well knows that the main purposes of such a federation would be economic rather than strategic. It could in no sense be a coalition directed against the Soviet Union. Moreover, they have done precisely the same thing themselves in Eastern Europe; and imitation is the sincerest form of flattery.

What is the alternative? For the continental democracies of Europe, a gradual absorption by the Communist *bloc*. For us, a gradual absorption by the American *bloc*. We should cease to be a world Power, and become a bastion — a kind of Aden — of the American strategic and economic system. The emergence of two *blocs*, based on diametrically opposed political and economic systems, and culminating in a struggle for world power, is a terrifying prospect. The case for a third *bloc*, subject to the over-riding authority of the Security Council, which would steer a middle course between the extremes of collectivism and individualism, is, in my submission, overwhelming.

Your obedient servant,
ROBERT BOOTHBY

PALESTINE AND THE JEWS

31 May 1946

Sir, Mr. Crossman, in his reply to the letter of Major Beaumont and his co-signatories, gives the impression that they are able to see only one side of the case and that the policy they are urging is one of complete surrender to the Arabs, while the policy suggested in the Anglo-American report was based upon a full consideration of both points of view and a deliberate if reluctant choice of the lesser injustice.

The issue in Palestine is not between two parties on the same level as one another, each claiming more than it deserves, unwilling to see the other side of the case and unable to agree with the other without the kind offices of a third party. The issue is between an indigenous population which claims the ordinary and inalienable democratic right of deciding for itself such question of general interest as immigration, and an immigrant minority which is trying to turn itself into a majority and to establish a State, and which is relying upon the help of external Powers to hold down the indigenous inhabitants until it can accomplish its ends.

Surely there can be no doubt where the path of wise statesmanship lies? The paramount practical consideration is lasting peace in Palestine, and there can be no possibility of this until the Zionists realize that, whether they like it or not, they do need Arab consent and good will.

Moreover is it human kindness, on a deeper view, to take the Jews from Europe to a place where their coming will be bitterly resented by the majority of the existing population, with a risk of arousing grave civil disturbances or even war throughout the Middle East and of jeopardizing the position of the Jews in a region of the world where they have always been well treated?

I am, Sir, your obedient servant,
ALBERT HOURANI

The State of Israel came into being in 1948 at the expiration of Britain's mandate over Palestine. Albert Hourani would go on to write, among other works, *A History of the Arab Peoples* (1991).

DYED KIPPERS

25 February 1949

Sir, I was glad to see Mr Evans's letter in *The Times* of February 22, in which he exposed the dyed kipper.

If my memory is not at fault, it began with the control of fish prices during the first world war. Kippers, which till then had always been sold by the pair, were now to be sold by weight.

The curers, except a gallant few, were not slow to take advantage of a very simple way of increasing their profits by selling at kipper price the water which is removed by the kippering process. The old established process of kippering, which can be, but seldom is, applied to other fish than herring – a properly kippered mackerel is very good – consists in curing the fish with salt and wood smoke – oak, if I remember rightly, preferred.

It should be illegal to sell kippers otherwise prepared.

In process of kippering the fish steadily lose moisture: in the process of dyeing they probably acquire a little more than they originally contained. The perfunctory whiff of smoke given them after they have been dyed is of little or no account.

A fishmonger with whom I discussed the subject a good many years ago assured me that housewives preferred the dyed article because they liked a "bright" kipper. It is in fact the dye that leaves the brighter polish to the skin than one finds on that of a real kipper. But I doubt whether the British housewife is really lured from the path of common sense by this tinsel effect.

A remedy for the present mischief would be to make it illegal to sell as a kipper a fish cured otherwise than by kippering; to require kippers to be sold by number, fixing, if need be, a maximum price; and to require dyed herrings to be marked as such – or better still, as "bogus kippers".

I have the honour to be, Sir, your obedient servant
HENRY G. MAURICE

The writer was a former Fisheries Secretary at the Ministry of Agriculture and latterly President of the Zoological Society of London.

BRITISH MANNERS ABROAD

6 August 1949

Sir, I HAVE JUST RETURNED from five weeks in France, Italy, and Switzerland. Along with a universal concern in these countries over Britain's parlous financial position and the febrile handling of the recent dock strike by His Majesty's Government, there is a growing distress with the manners of British tourists on the Continent. At an exclusive country club outside Rome I watched British guests taking part in a bear-garden tumble which consisted of throwing each other into the swimming-pool, cannonading into Italian hosts trying to swim, and sousing Roman matrons and débutantes whose tables flanked the pool. At Lugano I watched British visitors appropriate all the boats belonging to a large hotel for all the afternoon, indulging in a regatta which involved ramming each other just off-shore. When tired of this sport, they handed their boats to other British visitors. The 80 per cent of the hotel guests who were Swiss had the alternative of watching this unedifying water-gala or of risking a bat over the head with a paddle if they ventured into the water. At two other places in Switzerland I heard complaints of British tourists who jostled, elbowed, and stomach-charged their way through hotels and restaurants.

These are no isolated incidents. Obviously the bulk of British visitors to the Continent travel in order to enjoy themselves and do so with the tact and good manners which have formerly made them the most welcome of all foreign guests. But an increasing number of Britons are giving grounds for criticism and complaint, particularly from their habit of moving about in gangs which, if by no means so lethal as those of Chicago and the Bowery, are superficially far more offensive. This is a serious matter. I am convinced that Englishmen are becoming less welcome abroad than ever before — not because austerity has reduced the size of their purses, but because they are failing to behave with their habitual restraint, good breeding, and understanding.

I am your, &c.,
TERENCE PRITTIE

CHANGING TIMES

1950–59

TURNED-UP TROUSERS

19 April 1952

SIR, FORGIVE THIS aside in troubled times; but even in such times justice should be done. It was at Oxford, in the early nineties, that I first beheld, as a small boy, the astonishing spectacle of a host of god-like young men, all of whom were wearing — on a fine summer's day — the ends of their trousers turned up. Did this fashion originate at Oxford, and is the originator known? I feel that he must be by somebody. Yet if so, why is it not general knowledge? No philosopher, dictator, hero, or statesman – indeed, nobody else in the history of mankind — can ever have set an example so long and so fervently followed by so many millions of the human species. Is he alive in an ignoring world? If he is dead, why does he lack a monument?

Yours, etc.,

H. H. BASHFORD

Bashford, a prominent physician, was also the author of the satirical memoir of the odiously sanctimonious *Augustus Carp*.

Replied on 21 April 1952

Sir, INDEED JUSTICE should be done, as your correspondent suggests. Our records show that the first big change in the styling of men's trousers came in 1898 when some Cambridge undergraduates turned up the bottoms of their trousers to show their brightly coloured socks. A great controversy raged around the new style, and shortly afterwards "turn-ups" became popular. But I believe the originator is still unknown. The fashion of creasing the trousers down the front was started by King Edward VII, creases being at the sides before this. Now the trend is to abandon "turn-ups" on trousers in a return to Edwardian styling.

Yours faithfully,

CHARLES E. CLARK
Assistant Editor, *The Outfitter*

Changing Times

Replied on 22 April 1952

SIR, AT CAMBRIDGE in the middle nineties some of us turned up our trouser-ends, but the practice must have been regarded by the authorities as faintly raffish, for a man presenting himself for a degree in the Senate House was always required to turn them down. When I took my degree in 1897 I was in the same bunch as my friend the late H. H. Thomas, F.R.S. Being a man of originality he had turned his ends up. But he was quickly spotted by the Proctor (or was it the Esquire Bedell?) and was hustled into the wings (so to speak), whence he emerged demurely, ends down, to kneel before the Vice-Chancellor.

Your obedient servant,
G. MCFARLANE

Replied on 22 April 1952

SIR, COULD THE FASHION of turned-up trousers have originated at Eton? When I went there in May 1892, wc wore all our trousers turned up, whether they were those which were worn with tailcoats and Eton jackets, "fives bags," or change suits; and of course the bottom buttons of waistcoats were left undone. I do not know how long before this date these fashions had started, but they were well established then.

Yours, &c.,
C. E. PYM

Replied on 23 April 1952

SIR, TIMID BY NATURE, I am shy of questioning the pronouncements of the *Outfitter*, pontifical in its domain. But 60 years ago the *jeunesse dorée* (chiefly Civil Servants and lawyers) of Pretoria, then the capital of the Transvaal Republic, were fastidious about the frontal crease in their trousers. And Jerome K. Jerome, in his celebrated *Idle Thoughts of an Idle Fellow* (published in 1889), advised his contemporaries who could not afford a valet to put their trousers under the bed when they retired for the night. This obliged him to explain to a youth who had taken the advice literally and been disappointed with the result that "under the mattress" obviously was intended. It was only at a later date that King Edward VII started the fashion of the crease down the side, but it never became popular and did not endure. In other words, the frontal crease preceded the side crease, and has long survived it.

I have the honour to be, Sir, your most obedient servant,
RODERICK JONES

Replied on 23 April 1952

Sir, THE TROUSERS of Dr. Grace
Were not folded at the base,
But surely those of Mr. Burnup
Had a turn-up.

Yours faithfully,
E. V. KNOX

A rare example of a successful clerihew, as one might expect from the former editor of *Punch*. Cuthbert Burnup of Kent topped the first-class batting averages in 1906, two years before cricket's greatest name, WG Grace, retired from the game, aged 60.

Replied on 23 April 1952

Sir, THE LEGEND, whether true or not, current at Oxford at the turn of the century, was that the practice of turning up trousers, then a peculiarity at Oxford, was originated by Wilde and the aesthetes to display the highly embroidered socks which they affected in their parades down "the High".

Yours faithfully,
J. B. OLDHAM

Replied on 24 April 1952

SIR, ON THE SUBJECT of fashions in dress in his undergraduate days the late Dr. T. G. Bonney, who went up to St John's College, Cambridge, in the Michaelmas term of 1852, wrote in his *Memories of a Long Life*: "We did not go about, except on wet days, with our trousers turned up, and to have had them stitched into that position would have evoked merciless chaff, and deservedly, for the custom is only surpassed in folly by that of a woman who totters about on narrowing heels two inches high."

I am, Sir, your obedient servant,
J. H. H. SUTCLIFFE

Replied on 24 April 1952

SIR, I WOULD BE loth to enter a controversy between Cambridge and Eton over turned-up trousers: may I, however, give a French reason for this fashion? In the days of my youth I was told that one fine June day Edward VII, then Prince of Wales, after attending the races at Auteuil prepared to cross the large sandy square opposite the exit, noticed that it had been too well watered, and turned his grey trousers up. The smart young men of the day copied what they thought to be a new royal fashion.

Yours faithfully,
MAURICE VIGNON

Replied on 25 April 1952

SIR, I AM PRETTY sure it was an Eton tailor who introduced "turn-ups" to trousers, his dictum being that the extra weight of the "turn-up" gave a better setting to the trousers and prevented bagging at the knees. All upper boys wore turned-up trousers when I left in 1891. Further, I think the Eleven at Lord's had their trousers turned up to show their immaculate white boots. Eton set other sartorial fashions, to wit, the bottom button of waistcoat unbuttoned, and the watchchain across the chest and not across the tummy.

Yours faithfully,
M. C. COLLIER

Replied on 25 April 1952

SIR, THE FACT that
Mr. Burnup's Trousers had "turn-ups"
Underlined Dr. Grace's
Need for braces.

Yours, &c.,
GUY NOTT-BOWER

Replied on 26 April 1952

SIR, THE LATE HORACE de Vere Cole used to claim that it was he who first started the fashion of turned-up trousers when an undergraduate at Cambridge.

Yours faithfully,
AUGUSTUS JOHN

De Vere Cole — the brother-in-law of Neville Chamberlain — was a celebrated prankster. His greatest hoax was convincing the Royal Navy to give a tour of their latest Dreadnought warship to the "Emperor of Abyssinia" and his party — a group of De Vere Cole's friends in disguise, among them Virginia Woolf. The Abyssinians greeted descriptions of the ship's firepower with shouts of "Bunga! Bunga!" which, when the jape was revealed, became a music-hall catchphrase long before Silvio Berlusconi thought of it. Augustus John had, and was reputed to be the father of De Vere Cole's son.

Replied on 29 April 1952

SIR, MAY I TRY to suggest a date? I was at Eton from 1883 to 1889. In the eighties, if I remember rightly, the only people who wore turned-up trousers were boys who were members of "Pop" — the Eton Society. In any case, could not the date be settled by photographs?

Yours faithfully,
ERIC PARKER

Replied on 29 April 1952

SIR, IN THE EARLY nineties men were prohibited by the casino authorities in Monte Carlo from entering the gaming rooms with turned-up trousers. This was not on account of any sartorial objection, but it appeared that it was easy to flick a coin off the tables into the "turn-up." At least that was the reason given to me by an attendant.

Yours faithfully,
C. F. SIMOND

Replied on 30 April 1952

SIR, IF FURTHER DATA are required in the matter of trouser-ends, I recall that, in 1905, at the British Embassy in Paris, a junior attaché, who had been invited to luncheon, made his appearance with trouser-ends turned up. His chief, Sir Francis Bertie, after a look at the young man, directed a glance at the ceiling, as though to see if it was raining, and then, after a closer inspection of the floor, asked his guest whether he considered the drawing-room carpet so muddy as to require him to turn up his trouser-ends.

Yours faithfully,
CLAUD RUSSELL

Replied on 2 May 1952

SIR, IN THE ETON MESS photograph, taken in 1889, in which Mr. Eric Parker is one of the fag masters and I hold a kettle, no one has his trousers turned up. The same holds true for the college photograph of 1889; not even the wearers of white flannels were thus distinguished. In the college photograph of 1893, on the other hand, both the wearers of white flannels had them turned up, as also had a few of the other 68.

Your obedient servant,
R. E. MARTIN

Replied on 3 May 1952

SIR, WILL YOU ALLOW ME to thank the correspondents who have tried to identify the originator of turned-up trousers as a world-wide custom? King Edward VII, Oscar Wilde, Mr. Horace de Vere Cole, and some past presidents of "Pop" have all been suggested, and Oxford, Cambridge, Eton, and Auteuil as possible places of origin — but none, I fear, with the conviction of certainty. The display of socks, the prevention of bagginess, and an intra-school distinction have been put forward as motives. But even if these were the first motives, they could not, I think, account for a response so almost immediate, so international, and, for more than two generations of mankind, so pertinaciously clung to. Some far deeper and more universal aesthetic need must have been diagnosed by somebody — though perhaps unwittingly — and, by this simple device, satisfied. What this was, and why it became manifest when it did, could hardly be dealt with in the scope of a letter. But a clue to the latter can, I think, be found in the minor change that took place, almost concurrently, in the threading of boot and shoes laces. The former involves the mystery underlying all that is embraced in the word "art."

Yours, etc.,
H. H. BASHFORD

Replied on 5 May 1952

SIR, YOUR CORRESPONDENCE concerning the original date and derivation of trouser turn-ups has become so prolonged, and so many factions are now involved, that I feel it my public duty to settle the dispute. In the year 1858 a Mr. Aloysius Bredloser (a highly successful kitchen-range manufacturer of the period) attended for a final fitting at his tailor's in Albemarle Street only to find that the trousers were too long. To mark the alteration his tailor turned the bottoms up to the required length.

Casually inquiring the price of the suit, Mr Bredloser was startled to find it somewhat beyond his sartorial budget, and taking advantage of his tailor's temporary absence (he had gone for a piece of chalk) Bredloser hot-footed it for home leaving his old suit in part exchange. As the trouser alteration had never been effected, Bredloser was compelled to retain the turned up portions — swearing that he preferred them that way. The apparent idiosyncrasy caught on among his friends and finally became a fashion.

The day of Mr Bredloser's fitting (research discloses) was 1 April 1858; and the time at which he silently pulled the door to behind him and launched himself upon Albemarle Street and society with his trousers turned up was 3.46 p.m.

I trust that you will now close this correspondence and oblige
Yours faithfully,
JOHN TAYLOR
Editor, *The Tailor and Cutter*

A leg-pull, perhaps

REAL SKIING

13 February 1950

Sir, I paid my first visit to Switzerland 47 years ago. I first began to ski in 1925, and in my opinion the general standard of skiing was far higher in those days than it is to-day. By "skiing" I mean, of course, real skiing, and not rattling down prepared pistes.

In 1925 a man was regarded as a good skier if he could find his way about the mountains and if he could run fast and steadily on all kinds of snow — soft snow, breakable crust, and unbreakable crust. To-day, the one standard of excellence appears to be speed down a prepared course from which every vestige of natural snow has been removed: the result is that modern skiers are for the most part incompetent in soft snow and, therefore, inferior to their predecessors. What are the main reasons for this decline? In my opinion they are commercial. A ski teacher would waste his time hunting for soft snow: he can teach more people and earn more money by sticking to the practice slopes. The kind of worthless badge given for speed down pistes, "Cresta skiing," is easy to obtain; and as hotel keepers like their clients to be happy, badges which increase the sum total of happy clients are encouraged by Kurvereins.

Against this decadence the Ski Club of Great Britain and the Kandahar are fighting a desperate rearguard action. The Ski Club of Great Britain still includes soft snow in its tests and still demands a list of expeditions from candidates for the higher tests. The Kandahar Ski Club, which originated the modern downhill racing movement (the slalom is a British invention worked out at Mürren), still insists that its candidates shall pass a test in soft snow. It is no credit to the leaders of the various Alpine schools (and I am assured that there is no difference in this respect between any of them) that they should acquiesce in the degeneration of skiing into a kind of glorified tobogganing on wood. I know that many teachers still teach soft snow skiing, but no determined and organized effort is made by those in control of the Alpine schools to stress the infinite superiority of mountain skiing.

Recently I saw the Inferno Race in Mürren: I also saw it in 1949. This race, like all modern innovations in ski racing, originated with the Kandahar. The Inferno is a test of real skiing. Most other races, including world championships, are only a test of piste skiing, a debased and impoverished variant of the real thing. The Inferno Race starts from the summit of the Schilthorn and finishes at Lauterbrunnen, 7,000ft. below: the course from start to finish is on natural snow as shaped by sun, wind, and frost. As a soldier, this type of race appeals to me immensely; it calls for quick decisions; these have to be taken almost instinctively, and this can be done only against a background of knowledge which is acquired only by hard work and study of snow conditions. We want more races like the Inferno and more badges like those of the Ski Club of Great Britain and Kandahar, which still stand for real skiing as opposed to "Cresta skiing." I appeal to the leaders of the Alpine schools to do something to arrest the decadence of a noble sport.

Yours faithfully,
MONTGOMERY OF ALAMEIN

From 1952, a trophy named for the Field Marshal was presented to the top-placed Briton in the annual Inferno race. Monty viewed the competition as ideal training for soldiers. The cup subsequently required considerable repair work after being used as a ball in an informal game of mess rugger by the inaugural winner, Captain Henry Irvine-Fortescue.

A CURE FOR INSOMNIA

2 January 1951

SIR, THE FASCINATING if somewhat frightening article of your Special Correspondent on high-speed flying and the new means devised to combat blackouts and unconsciousness may make the sleepless wonder wistfully whether the scientists at the R.A.F. Farnborough Research Station have yet applied their ingenious minds to the possibility of inducing these very conditions, gently, harmlessly, and helpfully, to the relief of the unwillingly wakeful. It is commonly held that sleep is encouraged if blood can be enticed away from the over-busy brain by the lure of a hot water bottle at the feet or by food demanding attention in the stomach, but traditional folk charms are too often merely mocked at by a really resolute and up-to-date bout of insomnia.

Could not cause and effect be now fruitfully studied in reverse, and the jet pilot's peril be tamed and domesticated to become the bed-borne sufferer's friend? I could, for example, see myself being given immense confidence about falling quickly and soundly to sleep if my bed were pivoted at the head and were free to rotate, silently, smoothly, and at the prescribed optimum speed, until such time as my hand, lightly holding the spring switch, relaxed and the little motor ceased its purring and my soothing gyrations.

The delicately suspended bed might well have a snug, well-ventilated hood complete with reading light so that the occupant would be comfortably unaware of his otherwise seemingly spinning bedroom. A further refinement might be a device for reversing the centrifugal effect, whereby, at a pre-selected time, the sleeper might be automatically and thoroughly roused by being swung around by his heels, his blood being sent coursing to his head, where it would now be welcome again to stimulate the brain.

Again, by means or a sliding pivot, you could, of course, adjust things so that, at will, you rotated about your middle as gaily or as gravely as matched your mood, with the blood pull between head and heels thus nicely balanced. That, I imagine, could at present have no clinical pretext and would frankly be just for the fun of twirling, yet it might well make for serenity of mind, and – who knows? – perhaps be most subtly comforting to the body. Has it been tried?

Yours, &c.,
CLOUGH WILLIAMS-ELLIS

The author was the creator of the village of Portmeirion, in Wales.

ORIGIN OF THE BLAZER

15 May 1951

SIR, THE OXFORD DICTIONARY and the author of your leading article have by no means traced the blazer back to its origin. The earliest reference I have been able to locate — see the *Cambridge Review* of 8 June 1950 — is in *The Cambridge University Almanack and Register*. The first issue, referring to the season 1851–2, gives the uniform of the Lady Margaret Boat Club alone as consisting of "a red guernsey or 'blazer'." The fact that the word is in inverted commas shows that it was still slang, while its red colour gives the origin of the word. We still do not know how early it originated, and another problem is set. What was the garment like? For a guernsey should be knitted, while Walter Wren, who was at Christ's College, Cambridge, in 1852, said in a letter to the *Daily News* in 1889 that, in his time, the blazer was the "red flannel boating jacket" of the Lady Margaret Boat Club.

I am, Sir, your obedient servant,
H. M. STEWART

———◆———

VIDEO NASTY

16 June 1952

SIR, THE APPALLING volume and rapid increase of juvenile crime call for preventive action. There appear to be two main causes: relaxation of parental (and perhaps school) discipline, and the influence of films and so-called comic papers. It is well known to teachers, of whom I have been one, that the influence of pictures on the young mind is far more powerful than that of the written or spoken word. Many of the films and "comics" which children see are nothing but visual aids to crime, and the results of the continued suggestion made by these are revealed in the criminal statistics and the chief constables' reports. Surely it is time that a determined effort be made to get at the root of the evil.

I am, Sir, yours, &c.,
MINNIE DOUGLAS OF BARLOCH

STRIKERS' VOTES

16 March 1953

Sir, The strike of Austin motor-car workers is kept alive by the daily votes by a show of hands. Men hesitate to vote against striking while their comrades can see how their hands indicate their decision. I had experience of this matter years ago. It was my duty to ask about a hundred printers in Manchester to work on Saturday to produce a special edition of a newspaper because a railway strike prevented copies coming from London. They asked for a meeting and a vote. It was taken by a show of hands. Two men voted to work; all the others voted to refuse. The two secretaries made new speeches and asked for a vote by secret ballot. Two men voted to refuse work; all the others voted to work. So the newspaper was produced without any bother.

Our rulers might consider whether it would be possible to enact that secret ballots should be the rule for trade unions. I believe it is the fear of criticism by their fellow workers which induces so many men to vote for strike or no work in the show of hands. Let them have the secret ballot as a right.

Yours faithfully,
ANDREW CAIRD

Unions were not compelled to hold secret ballots until 1984.

U.S. ATTITUDE TO BRITAIN

9 April 1953

SIR, LIKE YOUR OTHER correspondents, I too have just been in the United States. I was there for several weeks on a lecture tour sponsored by the Foreign Office; I spent most of my time in the western half of the country. I agree strongly that the curve of Anglo-American friendship has reached an alarmingly low level — a lower point, in fact, than is generally recognized here in Britain. When doing my best to present our case on various aspects of foreign and economic policy, I found myself constantly thanked with real warmth for what I had said, by no means necessarily because people agreed with my views but because they were pleasantly surprised to find that I had such vigorous ones. Much of the misunderstanding is certainly due to sheer lack of knowledge about happenings and conditions in Britain.

It would be wrong, however, to believe that this is the whole cause. The American people are going through a period of intense frustration. Having become the strongest Power in the world, and having leapt into the active leadership of the free community of nations within a decade, they are beginning to feel their own muscles. It irks them very deeply, therefore, to feel that they have always been made to dance to the Communist tune, that the men in the Kremlin always seem to make the first moves, to which the free world must then reply. They are consequently searching, both consciously and, even more, subconsciously, for a way out of this impasse.

As a result, two constant dangers exist: first, that America will seek to act alone in an emergency — there have been examples of this already; secondly, that it will place the main blame on its biggest ally, Britain, if, as we seem to, we always try to put the brake on its policy. Professor Brogan recently made the first point admirably in writing of America's basic tendency no longer being towards isolationism but to an "illusion of omnipotence." The second point emphasizes the fact that irritation with Britain has been endemic as a result of the apparent insolubility of so many present international problems. And if, as seemed likely until the present *volte-face* in Russian policy, the new Administration were still to be confronted in a few months time with most of the same difficulties as it is to-day, the dashing of many high hopes now placed in it by the American public would risk putting Britain more than ever in the position of a scapegoat.

Perhaps we cannot do much about this except to take much more care than we do to explain the reasons for our point of view as fully as possible on all and every occasion. But we do fall into a trap which we could and should avoid. We are quite mistaken if we imagine, as many British people do, that this country stands on a special pedestal in America. President Eisenhower is trying to get the view generally accepted in Washington that Britain is America's "most valuable ally." The fact that he is doing so emphasizes the fact that it needs doing. If that is true in Washington, how infinitely greater is the need in the rest of the country. It is absolutely no use our blandly assuming either that all we do is immediately seen to be right and proper just because we do it; or that Americans necessarily understand and appreciate our motives; or that most of them think of us as special allies apart from the rest of Europe; or that the United States will ever consequently underwrite Britain and British policy just because we are us. Unless we learn to act on these truths I fear that the dangerous decline in Anglo-American friendship will continue. That in the long run spells disaster not only for us but for the whole free world.

I am, Sir, your obedient servant,
RICHARD GOOLD-ADAMS

SI MONUMENTUM REQUIRIS

29 May 1953

Sir, The comments in the Press have shown the strength of feeling which exists against the prevalent tendency to permit great blocks of offices in the heart of London to rise in ever increasing height and bulk. The size of the proposed new building hard by the east end of St. Paul's had already increased our fears that worse is in store for us and that the City we love is about to be engulfed in a tidal-wave of brick and stone. If what we now hear is true, these fears have been alarmingly justified, and we shall be faced with a gigantic block of 14 storeys and of a height of no less than 170ft. in the very middle of the City barely 500 yards from the cathedral.

The London Society is second to none in wishing to see the devastated areas of the City rebuilt at the earliest possible date, but its members, and surely all true lovers of London, both here and throughout the world, will be shocked beyond measure if the rebuilding takes the form of a faint imitation of the skyline of New York when we already have our own incomparable skyline dominated by the dome of St. Paul's Cathedral and Wren's exquisite spires.

Yours, &c.,
ESHER

Viscount Esher was chairman both of the National Trust and of the Society for the Protection of Ancient Buildings.

TIBETAN NAMES

16 June 1953

SIR, – NOW THAT MOUNT Everest has been conquered and important records are being made, may I suggest that care is taken in spelling of Tibetan names? Each name that a child bears is given him by a lama, and has a meaning, so that it is necessary that the translation of names into another language should convey the same significance. The word "Sherpa" signifies an inhabitant of the eastern or southern part of Tibet, and is written in Tibetan as "Shar" – "east," "pa" – "inhabitant of." "Tensing" is "Stan-Dzin," "a supporter of the Doctrine": "Norkey" is "Nor-Skyid" "Wealth and Happiness"; and "Ang Nima" is "Wang-Nyima," "Powerful Sun."

It is very difficult to discern the correct pronunciation of names as spoken by the central or southern Tibetan without a knowledge of the written language. The consonants are sounded so softly that a European ear cannot detect them. It is necessary, therefore, to look at the written word to be correct. The Tibetan language was written down in its own script about the eighth or ninth century, and the first dictionary intended for European students was published in India in 1826. The Tibetans are very proud of their classical language and will accept or read nothing that is printed in a provincial dialect.

It would be a pity, therefore, if our records of the fine achievement of climbing Tibet's highest peak should be spoilt by the incorrect spelling of Tibetan names. Our old Tibetan teacher still writes to us in almost faultless English.

Yours sincerely,
ADA BURROUGHS

PUNCH AND JUDY SHOWS

25 July 1953

Sɪʀ, Tʜʀᴏᴜɢʜᴏᴜᴛ Gʀᴇᴀᴛ Britain daily during the summer months a conservative estimate indicates that 12,700 children between the ages of one and a half and four and a half years witness Punch and Judy shows at approximately 85 seaside resorts, and 18 to 25 inland watering places or gala-decked villages and towns.

A general survey shows that each performance offers for the delight of the children a hanging, an attempted hanging, an undertaker (complete with coffin), hand smashing by sledge-hammer (with small hammer variations), ghost-walking and its attendant convulsions and collapse of the frightened puppet, manhandling of a uniformed police officer, threats of imprisonment, a man-eating crocodile, and an invariable boxing match where the Negro opponent is beaten to the ground (with variations – *e.g.* an occasional draw between contestants). A small proportion of showmen refuse to include the hanging and coffin scenes, but, nevertheless, the basis of the Punch and Judy show still remains one of violence, cruelty, and delight in deception.

I am, Sir, yours very truly,
GEOFFREY HANDLEY-TAYLOR
Arts Theatre Club

ON LEADERSHIP

22 February 1954

SIR, IN HIS LETTER TO you published in *The Times* of 17 February Sir Pelham Warner mentions my name. But I am not clear as to the point of his reasoning, whether it is applied to Caesar or to any British commander. A commander-in-chief will certainly encourage the troops under his command. But he cannot count on public opinion in the home country, or in the Press, to help him in giving confidence to his armies; he would like such help, but as to whether he gets it will depend on himself and on no one else. The greatest single factor making for success in war is morale; and the surest road to high morale is success in battle.

A general is meant to win battles. And if he does so with a minimum loss of life he will have the complete confidence of his soldiers and also of the public in the home country. But once a general begins to lose his battles he must expect to be replaced in command. It is of no avail to plead bad luck, or inefficient subordinates, or bad weather, or that events were too much for him. He is given the best possible resources; if he succeeds he gets the credit and the honour; if he fails he probably gets another chance; if he continues to fail he goes. This may be hard; but it is what happens in life and I reckon it is about right. Do not the same principles apply in cricket, in political life, and in fact in every sphere where leadership is required?

When all is said and done the true leader must be able to dominate, and finally master, the events that surround him. Once he lets events get the better of him those under him, and the public, will lose confidence and he will cease to be of value as a leader. If you are Captain of England you must win your battles; if you do not you must expect criticism, and will most certainly get it. The team you lead must be good and disciplined. It must also have that infectious optimism and offensive eagerness that comes from physical well-being. It is then up to you, the leader.

In the end no leader can long continue unless he wins victories. The supreme example of a British leader who was always able to dominate, and finally master, the events that surrounded him, is Sir Winston Churchill — and he is still doing so, thank God.

I am sure that my friend "Plum" Warner will not mind my suggesting to him that the principles outlined above are equally applicable in cricket.

Yours sincerely,
MONTGOMERY OF ALAMEIN

At 17, playing for the cricket team of St Paul's School, the future field marshal took the chief part in a last wicket stand of more than 100 when defeat seemed certain.

———◆———

THE DISAPPEARANCE OF THE NANNY

4 January 1955

SIR, I SHOULD LIKE to put on record that one of the greatest losses to English society since the Second World War is the ever-increasing disappearance of the nanny who used to reign supreme in the nurseries of our childhood.

Her code of manners and morals, of good and bad behaviour, of respect due to parents and visitors — many of these foundations of well-bred society are nearly gone. Also her traditions and folk-lore, and her knowledge of family history and genealogy, for often she came of villagers who in various capacities had for generations served "the Quality" of her neighbourhood. The cult of the old-fashioned nanny occupies much space in the delightful novels of Mrs. Angela Thirkell.

Visiting our friends' houses we realize this loss: we have to see and hear too much of their very young children. They used to be kept under "Nanny's" control in the nursery, but nowadays they are generally with their parents, and are often a nuisance to everybody, even to people "fond of children." One result is that the parents are far less free than they used to be to pay visits and calls and to get away on holiday. Nowadays, too, the mothers, having to act as nanny, and often also as cook and house-parlourmaid, have no leisure for culture, and so families and homes that were formerly the best-cultured are losing more and more that high standard. The communistic "wireless" is taking its place, and minds are being lowered to the same dull level.

Another result is that "the Quality" that ought to breed larger families than "the Quantity" is — "prudently" — breeding, and will continue to breed, smaller. In short, the disappearance of "Nanny" is affecting the social life of the nation adversely in several different ways. *Sic transit* ...

I have the honour to be, Sir, your obedient servant,
CHARLES PARTRIDGE

GIANT LEAP NEEDED

6 January 1956

Sir, I am surprised that, according to your report of 3 January, our new Astronomer Royal has stated that the prospect of interplanetary travel is "utter bilge," although he apparently admits both that it is technically possible and that he has no idea how much it would cost.

Surely it is unwise for him to prophesy that nobody will ever put up enough money to do such a thing, when he himself can exert little or no influence on the persons who seem most likely to have to decide whether or not to finance the first expedition — namely, the next two or three Presidents of the United States, or the corresponding wielders of power in the Kremlin? While it is obvious that the next war could not be won by the first man — or even the first regiment — getting to the moon, the cold war might well be decisively influenced. The propaganda value is obvious: a landing on the moon would unquestionably be man's greatest material achievement, and would no doubt be claimed to demonstrate its technical superiority by the nation concerned. It is hardly necessary for the expedition to be a financial success, any more than it is for the present Trans-Antarctic Expedition.

There are many fields of human endeavour which are more worthy of support — cancer research is an example which springs immediately to one's mind. Nevertheless we cannot confine our activities to one or two narrow branches of knowledge. We now seem to be approaching the stage at which we both need to colonize the other planets (where suitable), and have the means to do so. Interest in and research into space travel are not confined to this country but are world-wide. When the moment of history arrives no doubt some organizations will be prepared to play the part of Queen Isabella. Perhaps the real question facing us in this country so far as space travel is concerned is for us to decide whether we are content that it should come about under the spur of national rivalry or whether to press for its being undertaken under the aegis of the United Nations.

I am, Sir, &c.,
G. V. E. THOMPSON

PROPER PAY FOR SECRETARIES

21 January 1956

Sir, By all means let salaries for secretarial staff be stabilized at an economic level; but in this process let us not lose sight of economic justice.

A financial distinction should surely be made between the great majority of unskilled and semi-skilled typewriter punchers of little or no education, and the women of genuine education and background who bring a professional skill, sense of responsibility and capacity for initiative to bear on their work.

For women of this calibre a minimum salary in the region of £600 would not be excessive, and in any case that salary is below what a man of comparable attainments would expect, or receive. Your issue, of to-day, for example, carries an advertisement for a young male private secretary "at a four-figure commencing salary, together with bonus and non-contributory pension scheme." I entirely agree with Mr Nesbitt, whose letter you print this morning, that £9 and over, plus "perks," is excessively generous remuneration for the "half-baked flibbertigibbets."

An adequate type of skilled secretarial assistant could be ensured by certain responsible bodies— the Institute of Management and the Federation of British Industries, for example — holding examinations for executive secretaries/ personal assistants (as opposed to company secretaries), such examination to be taken after the usual training and some years of general office experience, the passing of which would rank as a professional qualification.

Such a qualification would ensure that the secretary: (1) was capable of relieving her employer of the burden of correspondence, other than that relating to technical or policy matters; (2) was able to collate material for and draft reports; (3) was experienced in committee/board work, the taking of minutes, &c.; (4) could, in her employer's absence, conduct responsible interviews on his behalf, as opposed to receptionist duties; and (5) was capable of administering her office efficiently. If the present somewhat nebulous term and status of "secretary" were defined by such an examination, a different type of young woman would surely come forward, thus ensuring an adequate supply of candidates for what would then rank as a profession.

My feelings on this subject are strong, for I am of the secretary as opposed to the "sekketary" class, as many young women now call themselves. My own experience is that employers are aghast at the idea of paying women like myself a salary genuinely commensurate with our abilities: they often employ two flibbertigibbets when one woman of proven capacity would, in spite of a higher individual salary, ultimately prove the more advantageous proposition.

I am, Sir, yours faithfully,
MARIE TREVETT

◆

THE YETI

16 July 1956

SIR, YOUR SCIENCE Correspondent's recent article about the "Abominable Snowman" mystery leaves many questions unanswered. Furthermore, the learned theories by Swami Pranavananda as to the Tibetan origins of the creature's name may well be correct academically but they ignore some of the basic evidence of people who have seen this creature or its footprints.

Of particular importance are its bipedal and prominent big toe characteristics. Red bear will undoubtedly stand on their hind legs for short periods, to climb a tree or attack a rival, but they will never walk long distances or descend steep snow slopes in this fashion.

During seven seasons in the Himalaya I have repeatedly heard tales of the *yeti* and its habits. Many have come from native hillmen in widely separated districts who have been illiterate and quite incapable of "comparing notes." Yet their stories have nearly tallied to a marked degree.

Last summer I was a member of the Royal Air Force Expedition to Lahoul, in the central Himalaya. While walking up the snow-filled glacial valley of the Kulti, I came across some extraordinary large footprints which had not been there the previous afternoon, the tracks of what undoubtedly had been a very large two-legged beast. Nowhere had it walked on all fours, even descending steep gradients. Its stride was about twice that of a man and on very steep sloes it had slid on its rump, using its fists to retard its descent.

I took numerous still and coloured cine shots of the tracks and my photographs have since been studied by zoologists and anthropologists. None has been able to identify them and several have likened the prints to *yeti* photographs taken by Mr. Eric Shipton and Sir John Hunt.

Yours faithfully,
L. W. DAVIES
Squadron Leader LW Davies

SUEZ AND HUNGARY

6 November 1956

SIR, I AM ONE OF millions who watching the martyrdom of Hungary and listening yesterday to the transmissions of her agonized appeals for help (immediately followed by the description of our "successful bombing" of Egyptian "targets") have felt a humiliation, shame, and anger which are beyond expression. At a moment when our moral authority and leadership are most direly needed to meet this brutal assault on freedom we find ourselves bereft of both by our own Government's action. For the first time in our history our country has been reduced to moral impotence.

We cannot order Soviet Russia to obey the edict of the United Nations which we ourselves have defied, nor to withdraw her tanks and guns from Hungary while we are bombing and invading Egypt. To-day we are standing in the dock with Russia. Like us she claims to be conducting a "police action." We have coined a phrase which has already become part of the currency of aggression.

Never in my life-time has our name stood so low in the eyes of the world. Never have we stood so ingloriously alone. Our proud tradition has been tragically tarnished. We can restore it only by repudiating as a nation that which has been done in our name but without our consent — by changing our Government or its leadership.

Yours faithfully,
VIOLET BONHAM CARTER

Lady Violet was the daughter of Herbert Asquith, the former prime minister, and a formidable public speaker. The Soviet Union moved to suppress the anti-Communist rising in Hungary just as Britain and France attacked Egypt following its nationalization of the Suez Canal.

HELL IN A HANDCART

11 January 1957

SIR, THERE IS A DEEP and wide malaise, akin to despair, among us. All who regularly move among all social groupings are struck by it. It is in the news: a sixfold increase in applications to emigrate, the increasing loss of expensively trained young scientists and other skilled men, exasperation of the middle class shown by abstention from voting in by-elections, a state of affairs among the doctors unimaginable up to 1948, senseless unofficial "strikes against redundancy" (the worst moment for them), and disbelief (in all political quarters) in short-term and "short-time" palliatives like "sharing the work." These items tell much more on a natively shrewd people than synthetic pep-talking.

Everyone knows things are badly wrong here, and will take a lot of imagination, courage, and work to put right.

In these columns you, Sir, have allowed many authorities in the past decade to say, time and again, that uninterrupted inflation would produce such a disordered society. But — in spite of the Government's exercises over the past two years — total public expenditure goes on rising, along with borrowing from the banking system (and colonies); so taxes cannot be reduced (in real terms, *i.e.*, more than the rise in the cost of living); so that, in turn, no material incentives can be given to persons paying the full rate of income tax and/ or surtax.

The trade unionist has more than kept pace with the cost of living since the war (on Socialist economists" showing, he is the only element in the population to have raised his and his family's real consumption, by an average of 20 per cent, since 1939). But the professional men, Judges, senior Civil servants, technologists, managers, and others on whom our national future depends for productive and constructive leadership, have steadily lost ground. Resignation and exasperation are rife among them. Many of our younger trained, talented folk take a look at their lot — at the apex of our pyramid of earned rewards — and emigrate. Many of those who stay do not blench at the vision of a static, managed society — a "social engineer's paradise."

Sir, I was a student in Germany in the 1920s when the inflation knocked out an upright, austere, hardworking, public-spirited (if dull) middle class. I saw lack of belief in any worthwhile future lead to despair; and despair to the destruction of moral fibre in what was the backbone of Germany. Europe has not recovered from that. Yet we persist in policies which wrecked central

European societies. I may be thought tasteless to breathe this in a British context. But however peculiar our nature, we British are human. Driven far, fast, and unfairly enough, any society — or group of it — will rebel, even if the prospect be as grim as in Hungary. And ways of revolt to-day allow minorities more power to paralyze the State. Much more despair, sense of inequity, and feeling of penalization among the necessary minority of responsible, skilled, and trained leaders in Britain, will, I think, quickly produce a bigger loss to us (and gain to foreigners) of talents, a not necessarily deliberate going-slow in management and administration, and a decline in the whole nation's standards of living.

But I also think that our present hopelessness, disbelief, and *malaise* could instantly be turned to creative account, if only Tories and Socialists — to start with, the thinkers among them — revised their ends, ways, and means. (Physicians and psychiatrists know that responses are often energetic when stimuli are applied to patients in a "low" state.) Any Government has to run the State for all of us — not for the majority that have made no material sacrifices since the war, nor for the better-off minority who have. Why should the latter, the most productive and constructive group of earners, make all material sacrifices only for their own extinction through inflation? That is poor social building, and poor cement.

I am, Sir, your obedient servant,
GRAHAM HUTTON

CLASHES IN THE STREETS

5 September 1958

Sir, The widespread attention given to the sadly misnamed "race riots" in Nottingham and Notting Hill, and the utterance of MPs and public men, have all apparently misconstrued the really significant issues at stake.

The solitary solution proposed is for some sort of restriction of immigration to this country — as if the coloured people were in some sense responsible for the disturbances. All the evidence suggests that this is not the case. What value can there be to a measure which would undoubtedly discomfort immigrants already here by stigmatizing them and giving the appearance of justification to the riotous white elements; which would make excellent propaganda material for those who would choose to see such a measure as essentially Fascist, and which would provide retrospective vindication for the racial politicians of South Africa, Southern Rhodesia, and the southern states of the United States for their own more pernicious legislation?

The real factors demanding attention in these disturbances (and in some of them coloured people have been involved, if at all, only as defenceless victims of aggression) are the social causes of the mob behaviour of the white population. The usual explanations of racial tensions — employment anxiety or sexual jealousy — are surely appropriate to only a limited extent in these sudden outbursts. The real causes appear to be principally in the boredom and frustrations experienced by our own Teddy boys, who are, to-day, a very sizable proportion of British youth. Coloured people are simply a convenient, and often defenceless, target for the aggression arising from mass-frustration of this kind.

Clearly the causes of frustration cannot be stated *a priori*, and sound sociological research should be directed to this problem. One might, however, suggest that the following factors play a part:

(a) The development of a high wage economy for unskilled, untrained, socially illiterate youths, too young to have acquired social responsibilities to absorb the money they earn, and whose "big money" cannot effectively buy the social importance which is craved. An alternative is to gain self-importance and prestige within the peer-group by acts of bravado.

(b) The development of an American-type "youth culture" in which parental discipline has grown lax, and in any case is undermined by social and economic changes which have steadily destroyed the traditional basis of social respect by giving young people too much independence before they are properly equipped for it.

(c) The glorification of high-powered violence and alien acts of daring by the Press and the mass-entertainment industry, whose products are increasingly available to the new moneyed adolescent class; and which provide the basis of their standards of behaviour.

(d) The absence of creative purpose, and of the need for real effort in the lives of young people to whom society has promised full economic security, and for whom it has, perhaps, succeeded in producing ennui. (This is not necessarily to condemn the welfare state, but rather to suggest that our educational system has not yet effectively come to grips with the release of energy, once used in the struggle for existence, and with the mass-culture which has replaced our traditional way of life.)

What needs to be clearly set on record, for the benefit of the citizens of Bulawayo, Pretoria, and Little Rock — whose comment has already been forthcoming — is that there is no widespread hostility towards coloured people in Britain: that they are not our basic problem, but rather an ill-disciplined, over-paid, frustrated youth, whose life chances have been vastly improved moneywise without commensurate social adjustment either to preserve our traditional values, or to effectively forge for them a new way of life.

Yours, &c.,
B. R. WILSON

MEN ONLY

27 December 1958

Sɪʀ, Bᴜsɪɴᴇss ᴍᴇɴ living within a 50-mile radius of London are becoming exasperated by the fact that their daily rail journey to London on trains leaving their stations between the hours of 8.30 and 9.30 a.m. has become an ordeal. The coaches are invaded by ladies, with the result that business men holding season tickets are crowded out and forced to stand in the corridors. Which is the more important — that the regular workers should be able to read their newspapers and keep abreast of world affairs and arrive fresh for their business or that the seats should be filled by women travelling to London to have their hair permed and to shop?

The time has come when a certain number, perhaps 25 per cent., should be reserved "for men only." The real solution would, of course, be for the railways to provide sufficient accommodation for everybody.

Yours faithfully,
E. W. D. TENNANT

———◆———

A LESSON FROM THE FRENCH

1 January 1959

Sɪʀ, Yᴏᴜʀ ʟᴇᴀᴅɪɴɢ ᴀʀᴛɪᴄʟᴇ of 27 December on "The Thread of Honour"[1] provides food for thought for all those who are interested on the difficulties which beset would-be undergraduates and which you state so admirably in an adjacent column under the title "Too Much Cramming."

If young Frenchmen and young students of French can proclaim the influence of St-Exupéry, Corneille, and Camus on their lives — precisely these three authors, as you point out — it is because they have read and thought about enough books to make the confession of such an influence possible. Too many schoolboys in this country have no time for this sort of reading. They cannot read books; they must study them. Books are a necessary obstacle on the road to examination success and, together with the notes and commentaries which accompany them, something to be learnt, written down, and, very frequently, forgotten.

Under modern conditions of specialization the cramming of the two set books for Eng. Lit. is often the only contact which the prospective scientist has with the literature and thought of his own or any other country. It is the good fortune of the French schoolboy that he does not have to spend time in mastering the intricacies of sterling money sums, or in learning the fractional identities of rods, poles, and perches. His syllabus, too, gives him far greater encouragement to read widely at the lower levels. As a result the French schoolboy can be given at least an introduction to disciplined thought, as distinct from the mere acquisition of fact, before he enters a university.

The need for students who can think analytically or speculatively is no less urgent in the Sciences than in the Arts. Those who can only memorize are not likely to become more than expert technicians, and for them the technical college, from which an equalitarian society will surely not long withhold parity of esteem with the universities, would provide a more suitable training. By limiting admission to the universities to those who have shown that they can think the present pressure would almost certainly be relieved and the universities would be able to fulfil their proper function.

For this to become a practical reality three things are needed. First, a syllabus for schools which encourages wide reading and intellectual initiative. Secondly, an effective recognition by the universities of the value of objective thought and idea in candidates for admission. Thirdly, teachers who are not content with an equipment of facts learnt long ago and added to haphazardly with the passing years, but who are willing and capable guides, stimulating by their own thought and the thought of their pupils.

I am, Sir, your obedient servant,
CEDRIC BURTON

[1] French students had been asked to write about their favourite author

KEEPING UP WITH
THE TIMES

1960–69

SOUTH AFRICA

11 April 1960

Sɪʀ, Iᴛ ɪs wɪᴛʜ ᴍᴜᴄʜ regret that I am compelled to ask you to dissociate me from the advertisement you published on behalf of Christian Action on March 25, to which my attention has only just been drawn, and to which my name was added without my consent. I was not consulted and I have not given permission for my name to be used by Christian Action save for two specific ends: to raise money for the Treason Trial Fund and the subsequent Defence Aid Fund.

I, myself, have been an opponent of *apartheid* ever since it was adopted as policy by the Nationalist Government, and also opposed its forerunner, General Hertzog's policy of segregation. In fact, ever since I was a boy I have fought with every positive means at my disposal against colour prejudice and racial discrimination in Africa. But no matter how much I deplore the handling of this tragic situation by the Government of South Africa, no matter how fully I sympathize with the object of the advertised appeal, I cannot identify myself with its mood and wording of unqualified condemnation of "the whites."

To-day the situation in Africa in general, and South Africa in particular, is so grave that the need for the utmost precision in our thinking, feeling, and example is imperative. In my opinion in this country the lack of this precision is doing irreparable damage and adding to the confusion in the minds of my countrymen of all races. One example of it, as illustrated by the boycott, is the increasing inability in this country to distinguish between the Government of South Africa and its people. General Smuts, who was born a Boer as I was (unlike Dr. Verwoerd, who is a Hollander and studied at a university in early Nazi Germany), once said to me: "Outsiders will never understand South African politics unless they realize that they are essentially a battle between Afrikaner and Afrikaner over the role the British should play in our country."

I would amend this to-day by saying that no one can understand our politics unless they realize that they are increasingly a struggle between white and white over the emancipation into full citizenship of our black countrymen.

As an example of the injury done by this lack of precision let me give you the reaction of a Boer on reading the Christian Action advertisement. He has been a gallant opponent of colour prejudice all his life and was involved in the first tragic riot near Vereeniging. "Last week," he writes, "was a bitter week for us Afrikaners. There was not one of us, and very few among the Nationalists, who did not deplore such a tragic loss of life. But there is not one of us who was not shocked also by the denial in the outside world of our right to defend our lives against violence. Imagine, 150 police find 20,000 angry Africans advancing on them. They realize they are outnumbered by 130 to one. Only a few weeks before eight of their colleagues had been stoned to death by 'unarmed' Africans. The police try to telephone for reinforcements and find the telephone wires cut. Not until three shots have been fired at them by the 'unarmed' mob do they open fire. Had they allowed themselves to be overpowered they would have lost their lives. Even worse for the community that it was their duty to protect, their arms would have been snatched from them. I myself have no doubt that a massacre of the whites would have followed. What seems so strange is that, in the world, European blood in South Africa apparently is cheap, and African blood alone is sacred. Apparently Christian Action, judging by its advertisement in *The Times*, condones in the African the violence it deplores in the whites."

May I myself make one personal appeal to the people of this country? Remember that under the South African system of voting it was possible for Dr. Verwoerd's Government to have a majority in Parliament although it polled less votes than the Opposition. Be positively for the good rather than merely against the evil in South Africa, resisting violence without yourselves becoming violent in spirit. Finally, keep open the bridges, whatever they are, between yourselves and the creative forces struggling for expression in all races in my country. Like the Pharisee, it is never enough to pass by on the opposite side of the road.

Yours sincerely,
LAURENS VAN DER POST

LADY CHATTERLEY'S LOVER

20 August 1960

Sir, Report and rumour would seem to indicate that the Penguin editions of *Lady Chatterley's Lover* lies in some danger of official attention. At this late stage is it possible to appeal for the preservation of perspective and common sense in an approach to this matter?

Reputable publishers possessing a sense of responsibility and vocation find themselves in these days in a situation almost intolerable. Most of us find ourselves from time to time declining novels obviously destined for commercial success which are in our view contrary to public interest but on which no subsequent official action seems ever to be contemplated. I have recently read for the first time the unexpurgated edition of *Lady Chatterley's Lover* and would like at this juncture to proclaim my conviction that Messrs. Penguin have shown the utmost wisdom in arranging for its publication under their admired imprint at the present time.

It is difficult to compare the honesty of this novel with tawdry perversions which now appear to escape official notice and if action is contemplated against this book we shall be rightly branded as a nation of puritanical ostriches unable to distinguish between honest integrity and the explosion of human depravities.

Yours faithfully,
ROBERT LUSTY
Chairman, Hutchinson Publishing Group

When Penguin was prosecuted later in the year for publishing DH Lawrence's novel, a jury found that the book was not obscene. The verdict marked a watershed change in attitudes which helped to usher in a more permissive society.

INDEXES

16 October 1961

Sir, You say in your leading article today, "No one has ever suggested that novels should have indexes."

I possess a translation of Tolstoy's *Resurrection*, published by Messrs. Grosset and Dunlap of New York and "illustrated from the photoplay produced by Inspiration Pictures Inc.", which has a particularly felicitous index. The first entry is: "Adultery, 13, 53, 68, 70"; the last is "Why do people punish? 358." Between them occurs such items as: Cannibalism, Dogs, Good breeding, Justification of one's position, Seduction, Smoking, Spies, and Vegetarianism.

I am, Sir, your obedient servant,
EVELYN WAUGH

BY DEGREES

9 December 1961

SIR, THE NEWS THAT the Meteorological Office proposes to adopt for its published forecasts the scale of temperature preferred by all scientists and most technologists and used internationally is most welcome. On reaching your fourth leader of 6 December, I was amused until I noted that you also had a fifth leader and that the fourth was presumably to be taken seriously.

The population of the countries using the international scale vastly outnumbers our own and it is high time that our 50 million should be "put out" slightly for the greater convenience not only of our numerous technologists but also of 500 million people in other lands.

In 1934 irresponsible attacks deprived us of the 24-hour clock. It is indeed shocking that so serious a paper as *The Times* should fail at this present time warmly to support the move away from our archaic Fahrenheit scale, which not only causes international confusion but also hampers technology at home.

If, Sir, you do not wish the body-temperature of all right-thinking people rapidly to rise above 36·9°C please treat this long overdue reform in a less insular manner.

Yours faithfully,
E. J. LE FEVRE

Replied on 18 December 1961

SIR, MR. LE FEVRE's letter in your issue of 9 December draws attention to yet another example of our wicked insularity. When one thinks of all those poor Germans and Italians wearing themselves out trying to translate the probable midday temperature in East Anglia into their own centigrade, just because the selfish English expect the weather service, for which they pay, to use a scale they understand, it makes the heart bleed.

But Mr. Le Fevre and his friends at the Meteorological Office have overlooked a worse scandal. Not only are the forecast temperatures given in the Fahrenheit scale, which is not used outside the Commonwealth and the United States, but the forecasts are written in English, a language also only used in the Commonwealth and the United States. It is time we gave up this "confusing" habit of insisting upon English and had our forecasts in German (or is it French?) with perhaps the regional bits in Flemish, Dutch and Walloon.

Everybody knows that the only people who matter are the Western Europeans; or have the Common Marketeers been overplaying their hands?

Yours, &c.,
P. L. C. RICHARDS

MEMBERS ONLY

10 January 1962

SIR, AS AN OLD clubman (20 years a member of The Savage Club and more than 40 years a member of The Press Club) I was alarmed by your Correspondent's report (January 2) on the growing menace of women invading men's clubs, even to the point of becoming associate members.

We all know they are now allowed to enter club premises on special occasions such as cocktail parties, not because we want them but because men are inclined to show off in front of women and spend more money at the bar — the only institution that keeps most clubs solvent.

But those who contemplate making them members, associate or not, seem to have forgotten that most men join clubs to avoid women. After all, you can meet women anywhere without paying a subscription for the privilege.

Members regard their clubs as male sanctuaries, not because they hate women, but because women are never happy on mixed social occasions unless a man is dancing attendance on them. They are too tired to light their own cigarettes (if they have any), too weak to open doors, and too fragile to stand if there is a man to offer his chair or bar stool.

If women become members of our clubs shall we be expected to leap about like a jack-in-the-box, giving up our seats, opening doors, lighting cigarettes, and, yes, buying all the drinks, if only to stop them fumbling in their handbags?

If this happens most men will resign from their clubs and that will be the end of clubland.

Yours faithfully,
NATHANIEL GUBBINS

READING IN BED

10 January 1962

SIR, I AM SURPRISED that none of your correspondents has proposed the obvious solution — the provision of a series of slits in the bedclothes through which the hands may be projected in the manner of the old-fashioned Turkish bath box. When not in use the slits may be closed by zips or buttons, or even by a handful of straw, barley for preference, as being softer than wheat or oats. It should, however, come from the binder, as the combine generally breaks it up and makes it rather untidy for indoor use.

I am, Sir, faithfully yours,
H. MALCOLM CARTER

POETRY PLEASE

30 March 1962

SIR, AT THE RISK of offending my friend Cecil Day-Lewis, let me offer "Ignore the Poet!" as more salutary advice to public spirited organizations than "Don't Forget the Poet!"

A true poet writes because he must, not because he hopes to make a living from his poems. Obsession with principle keeps him out of literary gang-warfare, commerce and patronage. He never considers himself affronted by neglect, and treats whatever money comes from the sale of his poems as laughably irrelevant to their making. If neglected enough and obsessed enough, he buys a hand-press and publishes his own work, despising any form of whipped-up public charity. He knows that "who pays the piper, calls the tune." How to reconcile poetic principle with earning a livelihood is for him to settle, and no one else.

A pretended poet with nothing urgent to say, joins a movement, studies fashion, courts publishers, badgers elder poets for testimonials and expects the nation to support him. I beg the directors of all public-spirited organizations to ignore him. He is one of many idle thousands. There are never more than four or five poets in any country at the same time who are worth reading, and all tend to be fanatically independent. It is far better for a poet to starve than to be pampered. If he remains true to his obsession, then the older he is when fashions change and money suddenly pours in (often with a rush that would have made Alfred Lord Tennyson gasp) the less self-reproach will he feel, and laugh the louder.

Yours, &c.,
ROBERT GRAVES

DEATH, THE INFALLIBLE FRIEND

28 May 1962

Sɪʀ, Bᴇꜰᴏʀᴇ ᴡᴇ ᴛʀʏ to make up our minds about dying, we should clear our ideas about death. At present, the whole of secular and political thinking assumes death to be the great enemy. Hence, the unquestioned aim to live as long as possible at all costs. To this end it has been suggested (with religious support very often) that tobacco, drink, sweets, butter, scooters, boxing, among other things, should be banned.

Soon cancer and coronary disease will yield and we shall all look forward to a useless, miserable, unwanted nine score years and ten. The problem of the aging population is the most serious of our time. The fact of the matter is that death is the infallible, unfailing friend, and until we make up our minds about this, the truly awful problems of resuscitation cannot be solved.

Yours obediently,
R. W. COCKSHUT

The writer was a doctor and noted proponent of male circumcision.

THE ASSASSINATION OF
PRESIDENT KENNEDY

28 November 1963

SIR, OTHERS WILL speak officially of this but as one American family living in Britain, my wife and I and our children want to say how much the love and brotherhood of the British people mean to us and all Americans in these terrible days.

The assassination of a President is the end of the world for Americans, for so much of our national identity is found in him, who in our way of life is so much more than merely the chief executive. And in our stunned grief, the brotherliness, the prayers, the shared pain, the support, the plain companionship of so many —known and unknown—meant more to us than any of us could possibly say. I wish I could take every British friend by the hand and say thank you.

Faithfully yours,
STEPHEN BAYNE

DIPSTICK

24 November 1964

SIR, I MAKE SO BOLD as to address you upon a subject which I am sure will raise an echo in the heart of every motorist. When, Sir, will some enlightened manufacturer deliver us from the incubus of the *dipstick*? Every year our cars improve in sophistication of finish and performance and nothing is done about this prehistoric contrivance. It remains the only way of making an oil-reading: dirty, unreliable and foolish.

I seem to remember that as a child the very primitive models of cars used to have an oil gauge on the dashboard which enabled one to know the oil situation at a glance. What has happened to this instrument, and why is it no longer in use?

Yours faithfully,
LAWRENCE DURRELL

COMPREHENSIVE SCHOOLS:
AN AMERICAN VIEW

18 January 1965

SIR, MAY AN AMERICAN who has now taught in an English school for two years comment on one of your current educational controversies?

For the sake of your schools, England, please examine thoroughly the American experience with comprehensive schools. After years of teaching in American state and independent schools I have no doubt that schooling is less effective for the bright in a comprehensive school, if the goal is to provide a rigorous academic education. The bright who are stable and motivated will work well almost anywhere; but the bright who are weak and/or lazy and/or who come from homes where learning is not greatly valued often suffer in a comprehensive school, where a high intellectual tone simply cannot be maintained and where the anti-school elements among the less able often include colourful youths who can exert great influence over the weaker of their bright peers.

My two years here have confirmed my opinion that the British as a whole are the soundest people on earth, in education and other fields. But I am most disappointed to see a strong movement afoot to destroy the supreme grammar school aspect of your school system in favour of a barely tested (in England) comprehensive plan. Why the haste? Have the advocates of comprehensivism clearly examined America's disappointments? And why have not national leaders pointed out more clearly that strict internal selectivity will be necessary in comprehensive schools if academic excellence is even to be attempted? Most American schools have learnt this lesson now, after 30 years of experience with non-selectivity, and its most unhappy results (the tide turned in the late 1950s). And even at that a student in an ordinary English grammar school is well ahead of a selected student of the same age in an ordinary American comprehensive school. You have something good here, worth being very proud of; do not throw it away.

This whole situation is a bit tragic, as an educational issue becomes lost in the swift, changing currents of politics and social reform (and, more specifically, there will be the personal tragedies of those many bright youngsters from all classes — the nation's future leaders — who will not develop as well in a comprehensive as in a grammar school). That the major public schools — those inbred bastions of class consciousness — might be attacked can be understood; that the excellent direct grant or maintained grammar schools, based on selection by merit, should be attacked is not understandable to this American.

My faith is in that standard that has so often guided the English: the common sense of the calm, balanced, intelligent, educated, experienced man. And I think all such men would agree that the selection of youngsters having the most ability, in a pretty reliable way, without regard to class, for the purpose of providing them with the fullest possible schooling, is in the finest traditions of democratic belief. I hope that British common sense will determine that a rush to comprehensive schools is not to the advantage of the English people.

Most sincerely,
L. R. STERLING

MOLTO RUMORE PER NULLA

18 February 1965

SIR, FIRST OF ALL, let me say, that the idea that the sound of the production[1] should be Italianate, as well as the look, the feeling, and the atmosphere of it, was one that I most strongly encouraged and I promised the director that I would take full responsibility for it if it was brought into question.

What your critic has to say brings into the open a question which has been vexing me, and I am sure many of us in the theatre business, for some years. How should the peasant class speak in a Shakespeare play? What also vexes us is how these people should sound in English adaptations in foreign plays of all periods. These two questions are not unrelated, and I feel we can take them together to some extent.

We do not know, we cannot guess, how Shakespeare would like his plays to be interpreted in this day and age, any more than we know how Cervantes would like Sancho Panza to speak in an English version. We can only hazard that both would like the interpretation to be made so that the work can be appreciated by the greatest number of people, including intellects both high and low.

In general practice, and in the general way of vaguely localized Shakespearian presentation, our peasant can get away with regional, Mummerset, or a vaguely "off" accent, or has done so up to now. Nobody has required Bottom the Weaver to have Athenian characteristics, and the Fourth Citizen in *Coriolanus* has not been reproached for coming straight from Salford, but I can't believe that Shakespeare intended an English atmosphere to pervade all his plays, much as I feel some people would wish it to be so.

There are times when his specified choice of place and character-naming brings this very much into question and invites exploration and expedition into further fields. I think that most would agree that *Romeo and Juliet* invites an Italian atmosphere, *Macbeth* a Scottish one, and *Antony and Cleopatra* largely an Egyptian one. The porter in *Macbeth* has been presented with a native accent with impunity on countless occasions.

For some mysterious reason the Cockney accent is very seldom welcome in Shakespeare except in the Eastcheap scenes in the histories.

On the very "First Night of Twelfth Night" (January 6, 1601, according to Leslie Hotson), the most daring jape lay in the fact that a distinguished member of the audience was a Duke Orsino, Italian Ambassador to the English Court, and popularly supposed to have a béguin for the Queen. Did the first actor playing Orsino speak with an Italian accent by any chance? I'm only asking.

Now every producer has the right to express a point of view on any play, in fact that is one of the main things required of him and if the point of view taken is one that requires strong local characteristics, then this promotes a problem that has yet to be solved somehow or other.

In his production of *Much Ado About Nothing*, Mr Zeffirelli has been inspired by the tradition created by the Teatro San Carlino in Naples. This tradition has ceased to exist in Naples for some years but still survives in Sicily. This influence, being applied to this production, must bring with it a strong atmosphere, redolence and impression of Sicilian character and characteristics in the behaviour of the people concerned, and consistency requires that it sounds as well as it seems.

What would the captious find preferable in these circumstances? Cockney? Mummerset? English regional? I think not.

Proper logic is not by any means always to be applied to the stage which owes far more to the instinctive, the intuitive, the inexpressible, even to clown's logic. (Grock's way of getting down from a high piano stool.)

True logic will dictate to us that if a play is translated into the English language it must therefore be translated into English custom and characteristic, but do we really believe it is more fulfilling to Shakespeare to have Don Pedro behave like a gentleman from the Marlborough Club, than to suggest the kind of blood and ésprit that made Shakespeare choose his name and station.

Is Dogberry worse and less real as a low down carabiniero or a Warwickshire buffoon? The question I say is a vexed one and it cannot be answered by the bigoted or the severe logician. The answer can only lie in the mysterious impulse of stage logic.

Yours faithfully,
LAURENCE OLIVIER

[1] Laurence Olivier's National Theatre company was then staging *Much Ado About Nothing*. *The Times*'s drama critic had observed of Franco Zeffirelli's production (which starred Maggie Smith, Robert Stephens, Albert Finney, Ian McKellan and Derek Jacobi) that "one of the most Italianate figures is Dogberry" — played by Frank Finlay — "a wrong-headed reading if ever there was one."

TRAVEL BY RAIL

19 January 1966

SIR, WHAT CAN BE done about British Railways? I had occasion to go to Paddington last Friday. The heating of the train on the way up was barely adequate; on the way down it hardly existed. The ticket-collector told us "the boiler had gone", but that "the engine would be changed at Swindon".

Either it wasn't, or that boiler had "gone" too, for the carriage was, if possible, colder from then on. This is the third long winter journey in two years on which I have had this experience.

Of course the train was late, in both directions, though less than the hour or more late that I experienced not so long ago on three journeys out of four. No one can now rely on the help of British Railways in keeping important engagements.

Of course, too, we came into a longish and unexplained stop, in the middle of a remote and snow-bound countryside. Cannot British Railways in some way broadcast information on such occasions? Or do they think, like the more old-fashioned doctors, that the less the sufferer knows the better?

Yours faithfully,
GLYN LANDAV:
Glyn Simon, Bishop of Llandaff

DESERT ISLAND DISC

18 June 1966

SIR, I REALLY MUST rise to the defence of my old friend, Mr. Roy Plomley, whose radio programme *Desert Island Discs* is attacked today by your Correspondent, Mr. Oliver Edwards. "It never seems to have occurred to the B.B.C.", he writes, "that the least practical and most perishable commodity on a desert island would be a gramophone record."

Now it so happens that for nine months or so I lived on a desert island (or at least the desert part of an island) with a gramophone and about four dozen records and can disprove this allegation completely.

The island was Ramree in the Bay of Bengal, and the gramophone had already survived two years in jungle and a year of the Burma campaign. Later on it survived the disasters of the Morib Beach landing in Malaya and another period in the jungle, and when I sold it in 1949 was still working perfectly.

Of course the sand got in, but all one had to do was tip it out again. The white ants got in too, but for some reason they find gramophones indigestible. As your Correspondent remarks, records warp in the heat; but one only has to put them between two boards and sleep on them to render them perfectly playable again. Also, as I found, an old sock moistened with hair oil is very effective for getting sand out of the grooves.

Finally, your correspondent asks: "Where is the electricity to come from?" Is he too young to have heard of wind-up gramophones? From my experience on Ramree and elsewhere I consider a gramophone a *must* for any desert island.

Mr. Roy Plomley's instinct as always is right.

Yours faithfully,
ARTHUR SWINSON

KNIGHT WATCHMAN

14 June 1967

SIR, I AM NOT IN the class of the famous literary names that have been so far mentioned in this discussion regarding the distribution of Honours. But, speaking for my humble self, I'd like publicly to state that I accepted my particular award for two reasons: (1) because I was pretty certain I'd enjoy being a knight, and (2) because it is not for the likes of me to go counter to the pleasure of Her Majesty the Queen and (to adapt the language of Doctor Samuel Johnson) indirectly "bandy civilities with my Sovereign".

Yours truly,
NEVILLE CARDUS

Cardus's knighthood was thought to have been awarded for his writing about music, but he was better known still for his writing on cricket, the reporting of which he transformed. Years before, Thomas Beecham, the conductor, had advised him to accept a knighthood were he to be offered the honour — "It makes booking a table at The Savoy so much easier."

———◆———

ORBITING THE SUN

15 May 1967

SIR, IS IT NOT TIME that the Governments of great nations ceased to brag about their astronauts orbiting the earth? I have myself circled round the sun eighty times, without any publicity; a far greater achievement. I am in fact, just starting on my eighty-first orbit. And although am an old man (I was born on May 10, 1887) I have been circling regularly from the day of my birth; if not before; and have suffered no ill effects.
Everyone does it.

Yours faithfully,
FRANK TOWNSHEND

THE WAY AHEAD

12 January 1968

SIR, IN TIMES OF CRISIS the tendency of those in charge, having exhausted all convincing abuse of their political opponents, is to put the blame firmly on the shoulders of the public.

This is by no means a recent development; keen students of the Old Testament will readily recall that the unfortunate results of Moses' frequent navigational bloomers were invariably attributed to the hard-heartedness and backsliding of the Children of Israel. Now, as then, such charges are always the prelude to general exhortation, in which leader writers, Archbishops and even Poets Laureate enthusiastically join, and we are all urged to pull up our socks without, however, being offered any very solid inducement to discontinue wearing them comfortably at half mast.

Provided the public maintains its usual healthy cynicism no great harm is done, but once a mood of uncritical self-abasement is induced danger looms. "Backing Britain" with a contrite heart is all very well provided one has clear idea of the sort of Britain one is backing. But the experience of other, less sceptical, countries has often demonstrated that those who cry *"Mea Culpa!"* loudest today are frequently among the first to cry *"Sieg Heil!"* tomorrow.

I remain, your obedient servant,
OSBERT LANCASTER

———◆———

CASTING ASPERGES

16 February 1968

SIR, YOUR COOKERY EDITOR, with all the authority of *The Times* behind her, advises us to make cream of asparagus soup by opening a tin.

No wonder, Sir, that General de Gaulle considers that we are not yet ripe to enter Europe.

Yours faithfully,
W. R. SELLAR

REASONS FOR DECLINE IN NATIONAL MORALE

12 December 1968

SIR, YOUR LEADING article The Danger to Britain makes an unanswerable case — at least to all those who care primarily for the well-being of this country and community. I meet a great many people in different walks of life, and it is some time since I spoke to anyone who is not disturbed or even disgusted at the present mismanagement and low morale.

Among the most sensitive points are:

(1) The endless inflation in which a minority is maintaining or improving its standard of living at the expense of the rest of the community;

(2) The growing indiscipline which enables small, selfish minorities to hold the majority to ransom in industry, to disrupt education and damage property and amenities with impunity;

(3) The failure of the Government to communicate clearly with the people;

(4) The wasteful element in public spending which often does not relieve genuine hardship but transfers money to categories of people who neither need nor deserve it; and

(5) The manner in which political debate is debased from serious discussion to a kind of fourth-form defence of frozen attitudes.

In 1948 I had the privilege of being a member of the small Allied team which introduced the German currency reform, which created the conditions for the German economic miracle. This was done quite simply by making it worth while for an honest man to do an honest job of work. Things had reached a point at which a skilled worker earned less in a month than his teenage son could make in a couple of hours by black market deals on street corners. We have not yet reached that point, but we are overdue for a mental or moral currency reform.

I believe there would be very wide support in the country for a Government of the kind you envisage, drawn from any or every party which would undertake to tackle our malaise in a practical way and re-infuse a spirit of purpose and a climate of responsibility. I also believe there are enough Members of the present Parliament willing to call a truce to the party vendetta and provide support for a Government pledged to a programme of sane, practical and humane administration. Such a move would do more than anything to restore confidence in this country and its currency, pending the negotiation of a more rational international monetary system.

Yours faithfully,
GEORGE GRETTON

DYING FOR LAUGHTER

8 February 1969

SIR, HAVING JUST READ the wonderful article in your paper, I feel that perhaps a little more could be said concerning the profession, the environment, the very existence of a comedian.

The big difference between a dramatic actor and a comedian is basically one of "sound". They both thrive in creating emotions in their audience, but it is the lot of the comedian also to create a sound — laughter. It is not enough for him to feel the moment is amusing, he must *hear* the audience feel it. This can, and quite often does, cause deep anxiety to the man whose task it is to make an audience forget their anxieties.

Throughout the theatrical profession you will find it is the funny man who is the worrier, the crier, the creator of difficulties. He dreads the day his timing goes; he fears his audience; he thrives on laughs and dies with silence.

The comedian is never off stage. He has to prove 25 hours a day that he still has control over his listeners. He always has new material to test. He has his act which he protects like a tigress guards her young. He lives in constant fear that his "gems" will be stolen, and they often are.

It is said that when the end of a comedian is at hand, he "dies from the eyes". Sit in an audience long enough and you have to see it at least once in your life. He stares transfixed. You will feel his animosity with every line. He loved you once, but now you frighten him. He knows you will never laugh for him again.

Such a comedian is not unlike Manolete[1]. He faces the same dangers, he is tortured into risking all to please his audience and, alas, as in the case of the great Tony Hancock, he comes to the same end for the same reason.

Yours,
TOMMY STEELE

[1] The celebrated bullfighter

The entertainer had been reading an article about the life of the comedian Tony Hancock.

OVER THE MOON

25 July 1969

SIR, WHILE THOUSANDS are viewing the august spectacle of the gallant astronauts reaching the moon and gathering further data to launch a new era more astounding than the industrial revolution, I am one of the few old-fashioned content to say, "Dear, the busky moon that's rising, seems so unbelievably near".

Cheers to the intrepid adventurers of the twentieth century scaling the stars and touching the moon. To me, however, the moon's still a mystery, a presence to be felt, a divine pulsation. I'm not out to analyse the moon but to enjoy it. Let scientists analyse the hive. I'm content to sip the honey; let them probe this "mysterious universe". I'm mystified by the magic, the indefinable charm, the calm, the peace, the radiance of it all. That is enough for me.

And we, back to Peshwa politics in a rich and resonant world full of possibilities. How strange.

Yours, &c.,
R. J. COOPER
Poona, India

THE TOP PEOPLE'S PAPER

PAPER

1970–79

MARMALADE AT BREAKFAST

11 July 1973

SIR, WHAT A dangerous omission. A loyal English knight defends and extols the excellence of the English breakfast without a mention of English *marmalade* (Sir Dingle Foot, special article, 30 June).

Yours faithfully,
EDMUND S. HAVILAND

Replied on 13 July 1973

SIR, DESPITE THE strictures of the Rev. E. S. Haviland, Sir Dingle Foot is undoubtedly correct in omitting marmalade from an English breakfast. Marmalade, like many other inventions, which other nations have sought to appropriate, is of Scottish origin, since it took a canny Scot to see value in the peel that others threw away.

Yours faithfully,
PETER B. MACDONALD

Replied on 16 July 1973

SIR, SURELY THE Rev. E. S. Haviland is correct, and by what right does Peter Macdonald claim English marmalade to be Scottish? These are vital matters of national prestige and I put forward as my authority a certain Gervase Markham (1568–1637) who published a recipe for Marmalade of Oranges in, please note, his *English Huswife*.

Scottish indeed! Let Peter Macdonald substantiate his prior claim!

Yours faithfully,
COLIN S. DENCE

SIR, IN REFERENCE to certain letters on the subject of marmalade, I have heard that it was derived from a confection prepared by the chef for Mary Queen of Scots when she was married to the Dauphin of France and was indisposed. The word "marmalade" is a corruption of the phrase *Marie est malade*. This may be a little far-fetched but it has the ring of truth.

Yours faithfully,
JOHN ORR

SIR, ALAS, I DO NOT think Mr John Orr can be correct in suggesting that marmalade was first prepared for Mary Queen of Scots. I too had been brought up to believe in the story of the chef in the French royal kitchens, hearing of the illness of the child Queen, and muttering frenziedly "Marie est malade, Marie est malade" over and over again as he stirred a confection of oranges, until they turned by mistake into a delicious golden mixture.

On inspection, this proved to be yet another example of those legends which surely *ought* to be true because they are so appealing — but unfortunately are not. The *Oxford English Dictionary* gives a 1480 date for the word marmalade, deriving from the Portuguese *marmelo* — a quince. A Portuguese origin for marmalade?

Yours faithfully,
ANTONIA FRASER
© Antonia Fraser

SIR, I SHOULD LIKE to know the nationality of the people who were enjoying bitter oranges for their afters when Mr Peter Macdonald's canny Scot saw them throw the peel away.

Yours faithfully,
GEORGE PAZZI-AXWORTHY

Replied on 20 July 1973

SIR, I HAVE READ that the Duke of Wellington in the Peninsular Wars much enjoyed the conserves of our ally Portugal and asked his aide-de-camp to send home to England a crate of quince preserve (*marmelada*) and another of orange jam. But the aide-de-camp made a mistake with labelling the crates and Portuguese orange jam was henceforth known in England as marmalade. Before this time marmalade had a broader meaning, referring to conserves made of quinces, oranges and other similar fruits.

This I think is Lady Antonia Fraser's Portuguese origin for marmalade.

Yours faithfully,
JOAN RICHARDS

Replied on 20 July 1973

SIR, IT WOULD BE interesting to know why and when orange marmalade became standard for breakfast here, for abroad one never knows until one sees it on the tray of what fruit the breakfast conserve will be made.

Yours faithfully,
MORLEY KENNERLEY

Replied on 23 July 1973

SIR, LADY ANTONIA FRASER is on the right track when she suggests that our marmalade had its origin in the Portuguese *marmelo* — quince. But surely we got the word from the Spanish *mermelada*? In the Spanish Academy Dictionary the derivation of *mermelada* is given as from the Latin *melimelum*, quince. In Spanish *mermelada* means quince jam or jam made from other fruits; so orange marmalade in Spanish is *mermelada de naranja*.

It seems likely that since our marmalade is traditionally made from Seville oranges then it was from Spain that we got the name marmalade for orange jam.

Yours faithfully,
HELEN F. GRANT

Replied on 23 July 1973

SIR, I TOO HEARD that the name of marmalade derived from a confection prepared for Mary Queen of Scots. But my story told that she was prone to seasickness and found this preparation effective for "Mer Malade".

Yours very sincerely,
ELIZABETH INMAN

Replied on 23 July 1973

SIR, THIS WHOLE matter, including the answer to the question put by Mr. Pazzi-Axworthy, is dealt with in a poem by Hilaire Belloc who wrote:

The haughty nobles of Seville
Could find no use for orange peel

Yours etc.,
JOHN CARSWELL

Replied on 24 July 1973

SIR, THE DUKE OF Wellington was by no means the first Englishman to use marmalade. It is mentioned as "marmaled" in the English translation of Renodaeus' *Dispensatory* published in 1657 by the London apothecary Richard Tomlinson. An earlier reference is in the inventory of Thomas Baskerville, apothecary of Exeter, who died in 1596. This lists "marmalade 11 lbs, 10 shillings". Another item, apparently an early form of our biscuits, reads "biskye bred, 8 lbs 5s. 4d.".

Yours faithfully,
G. E. TREASE

SIR, I HAVE READ the correspondence about marmalade with considerable interest, but can only conclude that some of your correspondents have not adequately considered the implications of their information.

Lady Antonia Fraser is correct in quoting the date 1480 for the use of the word, as given in the *Oxford Dictionary*, but the *Oxford Dictionary* gives no information about the context in which the word is used.

Professor Trease quotes Renodaeus's *Dispensatory*, but although a reference is given to *Marmaled* in the index as p. 171, I have been unable to find any reference to the word in the book itself. This is not uncommon with books of this period and it would appear that Renodaeus expects his readers to know that marmaled is the same thing as marzipan. He makes no reference to marmalade under either lemon or orange.

My Spanish dictionary makes no mention of oranges being used for marmalade, but describes it as a "preserve of fruits". Larousse's large French dictionary devotes some space to *marmalade* as a confection of fruits, which have been reduced to the form of a gruel. The only recipe given is for apple *marmalade*, and at the end the apples are passed through a sieve to smash them up.

I have not had the advantage of seeing Gervase Markham's recipe (16 July), but in 1767 A Lady in *The Art of Cookery Made Plain and Easy* gives recipes for both orange and quince marmalade which would produce a sweet, smooth confection not at all like the marmalade we know.

In spite of Mr Dence's scorn (16 July) it was in 1797 that an extra large shipload of Seville oranges became available at Dundee and the enterprising Mrs Keiller bought them and converted them into marmalade. She was so successful that the firm prospered and her younger son invented a cutting machine to slice the oranges instead of grating them. For many years Keillers marketed their marmalade in white porcelain jars with black print on the front "James Keiller and Sons Ltd. The Original Dundee Marmalade", and this claim has never been challenged. Orange marmalade, as we know it, is essentially British and comparatively modern.

Yours faithfully,
THOMAS MCLACHLAN

LIFE IS NOT FAIR

7 September 1970

Sir, You have had a lot of letters about people being bloody-minded. You have not had any that I have seen about why people like me are what you would call bloody-minded.

I read your paper in the public library — I can't afford to purchase it every day. It is the same for a lot of ordinary working people like me. So you don't get much of what we think.

I am 50 years of age. I started work at 15 years of age. I will work, if I am lucky, until I am 65 years of age. I might live to 70, but I will be lucky if I can work to 70 because, even if I am able, and willing, the bosses don't want us. So I shall have the old-age pension. I have not been able to save. In all my working life the money I have got will amount to about £60,000. That is the highest it could be.

I saw in your paper that the Chairman of Bowring's insurance gets £57,000 a year. And of course he gets a free car, free drinks, trips abroad with his wife, etc. He gets in a year as much as I get in all my working life. The differential is a bit wrong somewhere. Or what about your reports about wills.

Often you see someone, a stockbroker, for example, leaving £500,000. That is his savings, not what he lived on. It would take me 500 years to earn that little lot. Something wrong with the differential there too.

The Tory Party goes on about competition. How much competition was there when Brooke Bond put up their prices and all the others did the same. They didn't want to, they said. But they did it. Beer, petrol, milk, it all goes up the same ... what price competition?

Then we get a lot of talk about the law of supply and demand. Well, this affluent society produces a lot of effluent. So dustmen are in short supply. So they ask for more money. What a howl from the papers, T.V., radio, the lot. No howls about Brooke Bond or the others. Why? If you ask 99 people out of a hundred they can manage all right without stockbrokers. But they don't like being without dustmen. The law of supply and demand is fine for some, but not for others. Why?

We get lectured about our duty to the country through exports. Well, more and more we work for international firms. What country are they loyal to? Dividends and profits is the answer. The people who lecture us spend a lot of time, with the help of newspapers like yours, finding out how to miss paying taxes. We help to earn the money they should be paying taxes on ... but we can't dodge by insurances or going abroad to live.

You talk about equality of opportunity. What was the first thing Mrs Thatcher did but help those with money to stay at grammar schools? And what about B.O.A.C. having some of its routes taken away to give them to a private company, private shareholders and bankers. It was some of my money through the taxes that built up B.O.A.C. Nice social justice this is.

I am not a communist or an anarchist. I believe there must be differentials. But the trouble is the differentials are all wrong, and there's too much fiddling at the top. Where I work there are lavatories for bosses ... you can only get in with a key, hot and cold, air conditioning, nice soap, individual towels. Then there are lavatories for senior staff ... hot and cold, not so good soap, a few individual towels, but good rollers. Then there is ours ... no hot and cold, rough towels, cheesecake soap. And no splash plates in the urinals. How do you think we feel about things like that in the twentieth century? Waving Union Jacks doesn't help.

Well, if ever we get a government in this country that will pay and play fair, you will get an end of strikes. When profits matter more than people you will get trouble. It didn't need Barbara Castle to tell us that power lies on the shop floor, in the drawing-room and the typing pool. We know that power is what matters. The Government is going to change the rules of the game to try to beat us down. That won't work either. Starving our wives and kids if we strike is just going to get what it deserves. But give us a deal that we can see is fair, and the trouble will end.

It's no good economists and financial experts preaching. You can use the telly, radio, papers the lot to try to convince us that we have got to be the first to suffer. That's useless. We know the papers and the telly and radio give one side of the story. We know the other. You don't. Or you don't want to. So there will be a fight. We might lose a round or two. But we will win in the end. And if we have to fight to win instead of being sensible on both sides, the losers are going to suffer a lot.

You can call this bloody-minded. Try bringing up three kids on my pay and see how you like it. There's plenty for everybody if it's shared reasonably. And if, as my mate says, we want to try to have the bridge and beaujolais as well as beer and bingo, what's wrong with that?

Yours faithfully,
JAMES THOMSON

FROSTPROOF PAPER

15 January 1970

SIR, HAVE YOU ever considered the insulation qualities of your newspaper? I am filming "A Day in the Life of Ivan Denisovitch" here in Norway and I find *The Times*, well crinkled and pushed into the sole of a boot, can help keep out up to 40 deg. of frost.

Yours faithfully,
ERIC THOMPSON

Eric Thompson was perhaps best known as the presenter of the children's programme *Play Away* and as the narrator of *The Magic Roundabout*.

Replied on 19 January 1970

SIR, ERIC THOMPSON claims a crinkled copy of *The Times* inside his boot resisted 40 degrees of frost. I have done better.

World War II, scene, winter in Italy, conditions freezing, the mail arrives, with it three copies of *The Times*. After reading I removed my battledress then page by page wrapped the three editions around my body, before re-donning my uniform. From then on, for the next three weeks, I never felt the cold.

We were withdrawn from the line to do a refit. I removed all the pages from around my person, reassembled them and they were still all readable.

Yours &c.,
SPIKE MILLIGAN

DEATH AND TAXIS

10 *February 1970*

SIR, MY HUSBAND, T. S. Eliot, loved to recount how late one evening he stopped a taxi. As he got in, the driver said: "You're T. S. Eliot." When asked how he knew, he replied: "Ah, I've got an eye for a celebrity. Only the other evening I picked up Bertrand Russell, and I said to him: 'Well, Lord Russell, what's it all about,' and, do you know, he couldn't tell me."

Yours faithfully,
VALERIE ELIOT

The philosopher had died the previous week, aged 97.

KEEP THE COUNTRY IN LONDON

17 *February 1971*

SIR, LONDON IS STILL livable, lovable and sane. Today we can no longer take these essentials for granted. We must ask ourselves the questions "why" and "how" and implement the answers.

London is a city penetrated by the English countryside, by the trees and hedges, the flowers and shrubs, the animals which love and breathe the English air. They belong together and to us, as we belong to them. We thus remain sane by remaining lovable to and livable with each other. There is no other way. After all we cannot embrace a slab of poured concrete, but we can embrace a tree, and we can feel tender about a flower, the deer grazing in Richmond Park, the sheep in Hyde Park, or the return of the nightingale to Hampstead Heath.

It is time that we stringently defend the perimeters of and the approach to our heaths and parks as an essential measure of protecting our balance of mind. If we allow these irreplaceable rural incursions to shrivel, to be nibbled by greedy teeth at their circumference, London — perhaps the only city in the world to be accepted by her countryside — will no longer be penetrated by it.

It was only a few years ago that Parliament Fields including the Highgate ponds were saved for the nation from a similar fate. The owner fancied himself equally the owner of the grass, the birds, the trees, the air and the light of these beneficent spaces, just because his legal title to the land presupposed his right to sell and to build, or, as we euphemistically say, to develop. Public monies and private collections were mobilized and the spaces were saved for our own joy and for that of future generations.

This year is the 100th anniversary of the declaration of Hampstead Heath as an open space, representing as it does the accumulation of acts of public and private farsightedness and generosity. Witanhurst is the last great property belonging to this same green expanse; it belongs in concept to the Heath, as do the various green spaces adjoining it. These frontier spaces cannot be interpreted as empty and useless so long as they remain in their natural state, but rather as the property of that threatened Goddess of Nature, whose death humanity will never survive. This year must see our recurrent act of reverence renewed. More than ever today must we make amends for human follies and depredations; for only by defending our heritage of air, space, grass and earthworms can we or our children hope to avoid spiritual and physical suffocation and degradation.

Yours sincerely,
YEHUDI MENUHIN

After Buckingham Palace, Witanhurst is the largest private house in London, boasting some 25 bedrooms. Built for a soap magnate a century ago, it has been owned by the Assad family and used as a location for the BBC's *Fame Academy* television series. It is now reputed to belong to a Russian industrialist.

FIRST FOOTER

28 May 1971

SIR, YOUR CORRESPONDENT Mr. Milner-Gulland is correct in thinking Mary Queen of Scots whiled away her captivity at Carlisle Castle in 1568 by watching a form of football match. But it can hardly have been the first of the England–Scotland international matches, as he suggests, since it appears that all the players were Scots. The comment of Mary's jailer Sir Francis Knollys that there was "no-foul play" was in fact prompted by his own surprise that the Scots were capable of playing themselves without it.

However it is pleasant to think that the captivity of Mary Queen of Scots had at least one good effect: unfortunate prejudice concerning an aspect of the Scottish national character was eradicated from the mind of a prominent Englishman. It all goes to show what an important part the royal patronage of sport (even if involuntary) can play in the sphere of international relations.

Yours faithfully,
ANTONIA FRASER
© Antonia Fraser

———◆———

BRITAIN'S SOVEREIGNTY AND THE EEC

27 July 1971

SIR, IS IT FOR FEAR of driving undecided Tories into the pro-Market lobby that the left in this country has thus far soft-pedalled the strongest single argument against our joining the EEC — namely, that entry will do enormous and possibly irreparable harm to the chances of socialism in Britain? (I mean, of course, genuine socialism, and not the sort of coalition-caretaker-capitalism which your editorials have been holding out as bait for hesitant leftists.) Sir Tufton Beamish is one of the few Tories who have openly admitted that the tremendous threat it poses to the left is among the Market's most enticing features.

The EEC is a capitalist power-block dedicated to the perpetuation of the post-war schism of Europe. Its face is set firmly against the Warsaw Pact countries, so much so that Dubcek's Czechoslovakia — the finest flower of European socialism since the war — would have stood no chance at all of being considered for admission to the EEC. The Market is essentially the economic arm of NATO, and it deplores any backsliding towards neutralism, let alone socialism and its dread concomitants, the public ownership of land and the means of production.

One sees why the Labour right are so eager for entry: it would mean that they would never again have to worry overmuch about placating their left. Yet it is sad that a wing of the party so rich in historians should not have reflected that the Common Market in its fullest state of development will be the most blatant historical vulgarity since the Thousand Year Reich. Hitler's blueprint for the salvation of Europe was a vision in which the western powers — Germany, Britain, France, Italy, Spain and the Low Countries — led the world in a crusade against communism. He failed to realise his dream. The Market could come close to fulfilling it for him.

Not long ago the Swedes, after careful thought, withdrew their application on the grounds that it would be incompatible with their tradition of political neutrality. They are quite content with associate membership, which has all the economic advantages and none of the political fetters of full membership. Perhaps we should learn from their example. Recent history has spelled out a message we would be foolish to ignore. It is that small countries are flexible and capable of change, while large power groups (the USA, the USSR) are musclebound dinosaurs, inherently conservative and equipped with enough repressive strength to resist any internal pressures for change.

A politically and economically unified Western Europe would be a capitalist fortress in which this country would have lost its manoeuvrability and above all its freedom to choose the socialist path.

Yours sincerely,
KENNETH TYNAN

CLEOPATRA AS THE DARK LADY

3 February 1973

SIR, I HAVE READ with great interest the article written by Dr A. L. Rowse and published by you on 29 January, on his discovery of the identity of Shakespeare's Dark Lady of the Sonnets. She has always had a peculiar fascination for me, particularly in connexion with Shakespeare's *Antony and Cleopatra*.

I have no pretension to be in any way a historian — but I am one of those who claim to belong to the group for whom Shakespeare wrote. I have gone to plays from an early age and am a great believer that that is the way one should approach Shakespeare. He wrote to entertain and he wrote for playgoers.

I took my daughter and some friends to Stratford when she was twelve years old and later my grandson at about the same age and also some nephews. One young schoolboy gave an immediate criticism after seeing *Macbeth* — "I never would have believed that was Shakespeare. It was wonderful, all about gangsters, so exciting and so real." Shakespeare was clearly associated in the boy's mind with a school-room lesson of extreme boredom, but the real thing thrilled him. He also murmured after seeing *Julius Caesar* — "What a wonderful speech. That Mark Antony was a clever man."

To me Cleopatra has always been a most interesting problem. Is *Antony and Cleopatra* a great love story? I do not think so. Shakespeare in his Sonnets shows clearly two opposing emotions. One, an overwhelming sexual bondage to a woman who clearly enjoyed torturing him. The other was an equally passionate hatred. She was to him a personification of evil. His description of her physical attributes — such as "hair like black wire" — was all he could do at that time (1593–4) to express his rancour.

I think, perhaps, that as writers do he pondered and planned a play to be written some day in the future; a study of an evil woman who would be a gorgeous courtesan and who would bring about the ruin of a great soldier who loved her.

Is not that the real story of *Antony and Cleopatra*? Did Cleopatra kill herself by means of an asp for love of Antony? Did she not, after Antony's defeat at the battle of Actium, almost at once make approaches to the conqueror Octavian so as to enslave him with her charms and so retain her power and her kingdom? She was possibly by then tired of Antony, anxious to become instead the mistress of the most powerful leader of the time. But Octavian, the Augustus of the future, rebuffed her. And she — what would be her future? To be taken in chains to Rome? That humiliation for the great Cleopatra — never! Never would she submit; better call for Charmian to bring the fatal asp.

Oh! how I have longed to see a production of *Antony and Cleopatra* where a great actress shall play the part of Cleopatra as an evil destroyer who brings about the ruin of Antony, the great warrior. She has finished with Antony.

Dr Rowse has shown in his article that Emilia Bassano, the Dark Lady, described by one of her lovers as an incuba — an evil spirit — became the mistress of the elderly Lord Chamberlain, the first Lord Hunsdon who had control of the Burbage Players. Presumably she abandoned the gifted playwright for a rich and power-wielding admirer. Unlike Octavian he did not rebuff her. In his mind Shakespeare kept that memory until the day that he wrote, with enjoyment and a pleasurable feeling of revenge, the first words of *Antony and Cleopatra*.

Shakespeare was probably not a good actor, though one feels that is what he originally wanted to be. All his works show a passion for the stage and for comparisons with actors.

How odd is it that a first disappointment in his ambition forced him to a second choice — the writing of plays — and so gave to England a great poet and a great genius. Let us admit that his Dark Lady, his incuba, played her part in his career. Who but she taught him suffering and all the different aspects of jealousy, including the "green-eyed monster"?

Yours faithfully,
AGATHA CHRISTIE

AL Rowse's identification of Emilia Bassano as the inspiration for many of Shakespeare's sonnets has since been doubted, but she remains probably the first Englishwoman to have identified herself as a professional poet.

ENGLISH ATTITUDES TO IRISH CRISIS

9 February 1972

Sir, The real tragedy of the Ulster problem is not, hard though it may be for the relatives and friends of those involved to understand, the dead and injured, whether in Londonderry or elsewhere, but the real and deep division between the people of Great Britain and those of Ireland which neither side seems prepared to understand, or if they do, unable to admit.

It is difficult for any Englishman, though probably less so for the Scots and Welsh, to understand the almost appalling depth of irrational feeling the Irish have about their country. If the International Court of Justice was to find unanimously that every person killed in Londonderry had been shot in the back by the IRA there would still be three million Irishmen who would believe, and ensure that their children and grandchildren believed, that the British were responsible, and that Ireland had gained another 13 martyrs to oppression.

The English are not great brooders on martyrdom. Ask any hundred people in London who was Nurse Cavell and it is doubtful if 10 could answer. Ask any hundred people in Dublin who was Kevin Barry and it is doubtful if fewer than 90 would tell you, and at great length.

This is not to decry the temperament of the Irish, that is their way of life. It is simply to point out that it is almost impossible for the English to come to terms with a people that, for example, insist on holding illegal marches, on which they have in the past demanded a ban, to express a political feeling, which they refuse to express by constitutional means, that the British Government should take "Political Initiatives", which they refuse to discuss except on their own terms.

I am afraid, therefore, that just as we are incapable of understanding this type of logic, there will be a backlash in Britain by people who will no longer be willing to see their soldiers shot, or their policemen injured, in the interests of a turbulent and seemingly irrational people who rely on us for their economic existence, whether in Ulster or Eire, whose citizens have free access to our country, and liberty of expression here, and who are treated by our laws better than our relatives in Australia or New Zealand or Canada.

There are as many solutions to the Irish problem as there are Irishmen, and many of these — a revision of the border, economic sanctions, withdrawal of troops, etc. — have been ably aired in your columns. Any of these are possible, and all would be unpopular in some quarters, but what is essential, if the Irish people are to be preserved from a British backlash that could destroy them, is that the British Government should lay down a long-term policy for the country, and insist, under the threat of the many sanctions available to it, that it will implement these policies within two years. If the Irish, whether from the North or South, wish to have these policies modified, then we should accept these modifications if they are mutually agreed. If not, we should go ahead and carry them out.

If nothing else, such a policy would lead to talks of some sort.

Yours faithfully,
P. G. B. WILLS

Edith Cavell, a British nurse, helped more than 200 Allied troops to escape from German-occupied Belgium during the First World War. She was shot by a firing squad in Brussels in 1915. Kevin Barry, an 18-year old member of the IRA, was captured after taking part in an attack in 1920 on British troops in Dublin which led to the deaths of three soldiers. Barry was subsequently hanged. Both executions generated widespread international protests.

"LITTLE BLACK SAMBO"

1 May 1972

SIR, THE EXISTENCE of *Little Black Sambo* for 73 years leads one to think that it might well have contributed (along with other things) to the prejudice that many white British have against non-whites, rather than detracted from it.

Mr Laycock no doubt found him lovable but then most white people find black babies also lovable, as one white lady said to me recently, when admiring a black baby, "It's a pity they have to grow up". It is a pity that we have to grow up because the love and admiration is not transferred to us when we are black adults, particularly when seeking employment, accommodation and leisure facilities.

It is doubtful if the story of *Little White Squibba* gave any British child a feeling of inferiority; after all the British were, until recently, ruling nearly a quarter of the earth's land mass and a quarter of its population, most of them black. The white child might of course have felt different if *Little White Squibba* had been presented to him/her in a class in which he was the only white pupil, or one of a few, and in a country which, according to Rose in *Colour and Citizenship* (1969), only 17 per cent of the population were not racially prejudiced.

The days have gone when the British could talk of Sambos, greasers, wogs, niggers and Chinks, and not find one of them behind him, refusing to accept his description and demanding to be treated with dignity.

We now have to take note that we live in a multiracial society, and need to consider not whether the white children so find *LBS* lovable, or the white teachers think it "a good repetitive tale", but whether the black child and teacher feel the same way.

As a black Briton, born and educated in this country, I detested *LBS* as much as I did the other textbooks which presented non-white people as living entirely in primitive conditions and having no culture. I did not relate to him, but the white children in my class identified me with him.

Helen Bannerman was a typical product of the age in which she lived: then the blacks were treated with at the most contempt and at the least paternalism. She may not have been malicious but she certainly was condescending.

Little Black Sambo along with many other such books must be removed from the classrooms if *all* our children, black and white, are to grow up with an understanding and respect for each other regardless of differences of colour, creed or religion. I would not suggest we burn the books, but rather put them in a permanent exhibition along with some of the jokes of *The Comedians*, the exhibition could be titled "Echoes of Britannia's Rule" — subtitled — "Information that made the British think they were great".

Yours faithfully,
DOROTHY KUYA

The Scottish author Helen Bannerman wrote *Little Black Sambo* in 1899, drawing on her experience of southern India where she had lived for many years. Sambo, drawn as a Tamil child, outwits four tigers who want to eat him; they end up as piles of ghee, or clarified butter, which his mother makes into pancakes for his supper. The book was long a favourite of British children but from the 1960s began to draw accusations of racial stereotyping. Bannerman died in 1946, but in 1965, based on a draft, her family had published a new version of the story, *Little White Squibba*, with a white girl as the protagonist. *The Comedians* was a popular television series of the period which showcased the humour, and attitudes, of entertainers and audiences in working men's clubs.

Replied on 2 May 1972

SIR, ALL LOVERS OF the tiger and conservationists in general must deplore a work (*Little Black Sambo*) in which a great number of man's noblest and rarest eaters is wantonly oleaginated without rebuke.

Nor, as parents, should we tolerate the encouragement it gives our children, at an age when eating patterns are established for a life time, to over-indulgence in pancakes (obesity forming carbohydrate), cooked in saturated fat (cholesterol — prime suspect in the fight against heart disease).

In the face of these arguments for the book's suppression the racist aspect must pale into insignificance. At the time when I was first exposed to it (*circa* 1927), my personal reaction was one of interest that the Blackamoor could figure in literature as a heroic child like myself and not solely as the bloodthirsty cannibal I had previously supposed him to be.

Yours faithfully,
MICHAEL FLANDERS

Michael Flanders was, with Donald Swann, the author and performer of such wry musical masterpieces as *The Gas Man Cometh* and *The Hippopotamus (Mud, Mud, Glorious Mud)*.

WHY THE CROW IS BRAN

24 February 1973

Sir, The article on British dialect bird-names in your issue of 17 February raised a host of questions and problems, in answer to which I propose to make only a few points.

Some local names reveal the complex linguistic history of a given area. Thus the answer to the query as to why the crow is called "bran" in Cornwall is that this name is, not surprisingly, of Celtic origin.

Some bird-names, e.g. of the falcons, were introduced with the Norman Conquest. The name "kestrel" clearly derives from French *cresserelle*, but what of "windhover" and "flutterer"? Such names, clearly descriptive, are unlikely to be older, Anglo-Saxon, ones; they are probably of comparatively recent origin, replacing perhaps an older name which has become "opaque".

Chaffinches never stop calling themselves "pinks", "spinks" or "twinks" ... "wincs" in Wales. Such names, apparently pure onomatopoeias, are probably deformations of an older opaque name. It is not difficult to trace these names back to the basic English name "finch", Old English *finc*, compare German *fink*, Old High German *fincho*. This last name is related to French *pinson*, which seems to derive from a Gallo-roman *pincio/pincionem*. It is interesting to note that French dialects show a common variant of this name which changes the initial *p* to *k*, e.g. *quinson* in the east and south-east. There also occur sporadic variants especially in the border zones between *pinson* and *quinson* regions, e.g. the monosyllabic *tuin* and *tchui* and numerous reduplicative types, e.g. *tuintuin*, *kuikui*, *puipui*, *pinpin*, for reduplication is common in onomatopoeic reformations.

The giving of proper names to birds is an ancient usage and the explanations are complex, linguistic opacity and lexical confusion being two main causes. It is familiar birds that most frequently receive these appellations. The Londoner's "Philip" for the sparrow has its parallel in the French *Pierrot*, of Parisian origin, which has here and there replaced *moineau*, i.e. "little monk", itself a lively substitution for the earlier *passe/paisse* from the Latin *passer*.

Popular descriptive names in English dialects often have their parallels in the popular names found in France. The wagtails (incidentally often termed *hoche-queue*, etc., in French dialects) bearing the English names "cow-bird", "dish-washer" and "washer-woman", referring to their fondness for following farm animals and for frequenting water, are called in French and Provençal *bergeronnette*, *bergère* and *pastourela* "shepherdess", *louraire* "ploughman", *vatseirouna* "cow-girl", and *lapandière* "washer-woman",

Yours,
DAFYDD EVANS

WORKING-CLASS CULTURE AND SCHOOLS

6 March 1973

SIR, MOST CHILDREN come from working-class homes and inherit a distinctly working-class culture. Most of the education budget is funded by working-class taxes.

Nevertheless, school overwhelmingly matches the social needs of middle-class parents. So it was inevitable that we should see pressures for reform — such as the end of eleven plus and the collapse of the streaming system; together with pilot ventures such as the Open University and the Education Priority Area programme.

In my article in *The Times*, which has drawn such a strong response, I am trying to raise the next question. It is not enough to achieve structural reform if we wish schools to offer equal opportunities to all children. There is also a cultural challenge.

Most schools do not know what working-class culture is, or if they do, dislike it. It is as if the children came to school with nothing behind them. Inevitably, school cannot then convince many pupils that it offers a genuine educational dialogue. Inevitably it still breeds elites who are not so much hostile or friendly, but who are uncomprehending when they meet working-class life in action. Leaving aside rights and wrongs, observe the quality of bewilderment in the face of trade union firmness.

The traditional culture of the British working-class is something of which an educated nation should be proud. Consider the part it has played in the rise of Nonconformism, of the Co-operative movement, of trade unions, of sport, of brass and choral music. Look at the rich soil it provided for artists like Henry Moore, D. H. Lawrence, L. S. Lowry. Simply listen to the vitality of so much working-class speech. But above all note how, over so many generations, it has bred a habit of asking questions, of opening perspectives that are relevant for most people — but unusual for teachers.

Now visit a characteristic school. Depressingly often, it offers a social and intellectual entry into Janet and Johnland. School ultimately fails because it does not ordinarily recognize the validity of any other life style than that of the lower middle class — whose officers staff the institution.

None of this suggests that middle-class life styles are bad. I don't think that. Nor that children should be denied Shakespeare, Mozart or Newtonian physics. Nothing I have written implies that, or is likely to.

What I do insist on is that — if you observe the day-to-day reality of schools — it is clear that much of it is fundamentally irrelevant. School, instead of acting as a critical centre in society, is usually a *pax scholastica*: a buffer state defending the labour market.

If we want school to play some part in creating a multi-cultural society, then not only do we have to learn to see, accept and creatively deploy the cultures of the 3.3 per cent of immigrant pupils. We have to accept that of the 70 per cent working-class pupils.

Yours faithfully,
BRIAN JACKSON

OARSWOMEN'S DRESS

19 March 1973

SIR, I DO NOT KNOW where Mr Philip Howard got his information about women's rowing in Oxford in 1927 (article, 13 March), but I can assure him that "long skirts with elastic at the bottoms to prevent their ankles being exposed" were not worn. Apart from the impossibility of rowing on sliding seats in such garments, women's dresses at this time, both for day and evening, were up to and even above the knee, and ankles had long been "exposed".

As a member of the Oxford crew until a few days before the race with Cambridge — which I was forbidden to take part in by the Principal of my college — I wore navy-blue shorts, woollen ankle-socks and suitable shoes, a short-sleeved open-necked cotton blouse, and a heavy white woollen polo-necked pull-over which could quickly be discarded when necessary.

And it was not "to avoid shocking the men" that we rowed before breakfast, but because it was the most convenient time, the river being comparatively empty then and our days already overfull from 9 a.m. onwards. We certainly rowed also in the afternoons as soon as we had achieved a certain degree of competence, as I remember to my shame that on one occasion while coxing the women's boat I inadvertently committed the heinous crime of holding up the university eight.

Yours sincerely,
PHYLLIS HARTNOLL

Replied on 21 March 1973

SIR, I GO BACK further than Miss Phyllis Hartnoll in rowing at Oxford. In 1919, at St Hilda's College, we wore our ordinary skirts and slipped a loop of black elastic over them just above the knee. This had nothing to do with showing ankles (which were visible anyhow under mid-shin-length skirts). The elastic was to keep the skirt from catching in the sliding seat, throwing the boat into confusion and causing someone to catch a crab. We did not use elastic for fixed-seats training crews.

The elastic was a perfect pest, and made for hard work when you came forward and opened your knees to pull. So annoying was it that in 1920 it was abandoned. I was one who advocated shorts: but they were thought too "forward", and were not allowed. So we graduated into short "divided skirts", which were the next best thing and did not catch in the slide. We wore long black stockings and white sailor blouses with regulation square collars and black scarves.

Yours sincerely,
ROSAMUND ESSEX

Replied on 21 March 1973

SIR, IN LONDON not all of us were so up-to-date as Oxford in 1927. I sculled for Bedford College on Regent's Park lake in that year, wearing a white cotton blouse, black shoes, black woollen stockings, and navy blue bloomers beneath a short navy blue skirt, which, to prevent it catching in the sliding seat, was held together between the thighs by a large safety pin.

Yours truly,
ISABEL S. JACOBS

Replied on 22 March 1973

SIR, TO CORRECT THE statements of Mr Philip Howard (13 March) and of Miss Phyllis Hartnoll (19 March) I brave the potential sneers of Radio 4 to write that it was Newnham College, not Cambridge against which Oxford rowed in the twenties. I was No. 5 in that VIII in 1929 wearing dark brown shorts, stockings to match and a blazer of the same colour with mustard facings. Girton rowed in skiffs only. We had a competition in style and speed for one mile on the Thames and were judged equal.

My pale-blue blazer was awarded for swimming for members of both colleges were included in that team.

Yours faithfully,
MARY KING

SIR, MISS HARTNOLL MAY have rowed in shorts at Oxford in 1927 but at Cambridge in 1918 we rowed in gym tunics. I stroked the first women's eight on the Cam, a very amateurish affair as we had no proper coaching. There were four oars from Newnham (my college) and four from Girton, and Newnham provided the cox.

Our tunics came just over our knees, and to prevent them catching in the slide we did have a piece of elastic, which we buttoned, not round our ankles of course, but round our thighs. The college authorities insisted on our wearing skirts to bicycle down to the boathouse, and a dressing-room had to be provided where we could take these off before getting in the boat. I went down in 1918 so I do not know when shorts were first permitted.

Yours faithfully,
ELEANOR PRICE (née Marshall)

FLOWERS FOR THE QUEEN

31 March 1973

Sir, I would be most grateful if I could pass on the following to you and your readers before the bloom goes from it.

I have just stepped out of a cab in which I travelled through London with a starry-eyed taxi driver. I had hardly got into the cab when he looked at me and said: "D'you mind guvnor if I tell you something? I have just been at the airport at Heathrow and there, suddenly, this Frenchman comes up to me carrying a magnificent bunch of flowers in his hand. Gosh, you should have seen it guvnor, and he hands it to me and says 'Taxi, if I pay you double fare, will you take these flowers and give them to your Queen?' And I looks at him as if he was mad and he says to me: 'Now look taxi, I am serious; are you on or are you not?' And what do you think I did?"

"What did you do?" I asked him.

"Cor, I couldn't let 'im and 'er down, so I just come from the bleeding Palace."

Yours truly,
LAURENS VAN DER POST

ADAM AND EVIL

14 August 1973

Sir, During the course of some researches into the causes of violence in our modern society, I have had my attention drawn to what would appear to be yet another instance of the sort of mindless thuggery with which in recent times we have become, alas, all too familiar.

In this case, a young man, pleasant, likeable and totally inoffensive, known to those around him simply as Abel, is attacked in a field by a psychopathic elder brother by the name of Cain, and receives injuries from which he subsequently dies.

One is loath indeed to draw overhasty conclusions from insufficient data, but one cannot but be forcibly reminded of scenes in *A Clockwork Orange*, where I believe similar muggings result, likewise, in the deaths of the victims concerned.

It is, of course, a matter for speculation whether it was this or some other film or television programme that in fact triggered off this abominable crime, but, bearing in mind that it had the effect of reducing the total world population at that time by no less than 25 per cent at a single stroke, it seems to me that the makers of films and television programmes, together with the writers of the books on which films and television programmes seem so often to be based, have a good deal to answer for.

Even though, as my assistant now somewhat belatedly tells me, the crime was committed some time before a good many of them were made, the principle remains the same, and the lesson is crystal clear to those not too wilfully blind to see it.

Yours in anger,
N. F. SIMPSON

HOW TO HAVE A HAPPY LIFE

12 December 1973

Sir, The scholar is not higher than the craftsman, he *is* a craftsman — *of words*. My father was a classical scholar and a life-long teacher of the classics who could never knock a nail into a piece of wood without damaging his thumb and the wood. For more than 30 years I have been a sculptor in wood and stone, and I could never construct the simplest Latin sentence without committing at least three major howlers. Yet both of us were sufficiently adroit in our own spheres to realize that our paths were exactly parallel, and that the semblance of perfection which he loved and pursued all his life was the same beacon as mine.

The greatest happiness that life can afford is to be found in the pursuit of these paths, and their number is almost without count but the goal is one. The chief aim of our educators should be to direct our young people into one path *or another* and not to insist on the priority of academic learning.

Yours faithfully,
PETER WATTS

JUNIOR CHOICE

23 February 1974

Sir, Conversation overheard on my station platform:
Small boy: "I hope Harold Wilson wins."
Commuter: "Why?"
Small boy: "cos my dad says we're going to Australia if he does."

Yours faithfully,
R. S. LEVY

Harold Wilson and Labour did indeed win the General Election, albeit they were able to form only a minority Government.

MINERS' WAGES: PAY FOR CASUAL WORK

22 January 1974

SIR, MY WORK HAS been entirely in schools within a mining community for twenty years. During that time, I cannot recall a single entrant into the mining industry from my schools. In the early part of that period when apprenticeships were offered only to grammar school boys and for the whole of the time when good students might have taken up mining engineering, no pupils from my schools took up mining as an occupation or a career.

The reason is that all our fathers and grandfathers said to their sons with emphasis that they would never go down the pits. The unemployment and short time, the massive injuries and frequent tragedies, the dust and the water and the danger have stamped themselves on the race mind in South Wales. You don't have to argue that the miners are a special case; you feel it in the blood.

The miners up to this moment in the present crisis have broken no law and no agreement. They have simply ceased to work overtime and they draw for a week's work their basic £29.80.

Many of my sixth formers in the interval between A levels and university take casual jobs in local industry. They are untrained, unskilled and inexperienced. Several of them earned up to £28 a week. One of these because his birthday happened to fall in his work period, received a rise of £10 in his final month's pay. One fine young man netted £50 in one week as a teaboy (admittedly with overtime).

They told me of a man working in the same place who regularly took his bed to work with him. A boy earned £29 a week for cycling six times a day a distance of three-quarters of a mile with a sample of the furnace's melt to the laboratory. These boys tell me of even higher wages earned on building sites and motor-road construction. I am also familiar with some caretakers who earn £30 (with a house) for only and quite literally locking and unlocking premises.

The present government is intent upon inflicting defeat on the miners and thereby a psychological blow at every union who might push as far. The Prime Minister rejects appeasement. This might have been good psychology in the sixties. But in the present world crisis and in the economic state of the country, who is going to rally the nation, urge us to tighten our belts, face austerity and work harder?

It will be good for us all to do so. But what fool's paradise are we living in when, faced with the frightening problems of the day, we respond by working less? We deserve what faces us. Those of us who have clamoured against the permissive society and the throw-away life style are at last vindicated. "We have told you so!" But we are also as a result becoming ungovernable.

Yours sincerely,
JOHN HERBERT

SELECTION PRINCIPLE IN EDUCATION

19 April 1974

SIR, I HEAR ON my radio Mr Reg Prentice, of the party which I support, saying to a gathering on education the following: "The eleven plus must go, so must selection at twelve plus, at sixteen plus, and any other age." What can this mean? How are universities to continue? Are we to have engineers without selection of those who understand mathematics, linguists without selection of those who understand grammar?

To many teachers such declarations of policy must seem obscure and astonishing, and to imply the adoption of some quite new philosophy of education which has not, so far as I know, been in this context discussed. It is certainly odd that the Labour Party should wish to promote a process of natural unplanned sorting which will favour the children of the rich and educated people, leaving other children at a disadvantage.

I thought socialism was concerned with the removal of unfair disadvantages. Surely what we need is a careful reconsideration of how to select, not the radical and dangerous abandonment of the principle of selection.

Yours faithfully,
IRIS MURDOCH

THE WELSH TRADITION

27 April 1974

SIR, IN THE Welsh tradition of referring to people by the names of their jobs, as Jones the Post or Davis the Bread, would it not be in order to speak of the Rt. Hon. Member for Ebbw Vale as Foot the Bill?

Yours faithfully,
CELIA FLEMING

Michael Foot was then Secretary of State for Employment, while Celia Fleming (the wife of Peter Fleming) was also known as Johnson the Actress.

THE GREEK TRIREME

6 September 1975

SIR, I SHOULD BE glad if you would allow me to comment briefly on Mr Eric Leach's article in your issue of August 30 as one of those classical scholars whose conclusions about Greek trireme he regards as "unconvincing", and as an, albeit newly appointed, Trustee of the National Maritime Museum to whose Chief Archaeologist, Mr Sean McGrail, he refers.

Mr Leach says: "Our knowledge of Greek triremes comes from conflicting descriptions, vase paintings, sculpture and coins", which "rely heavily on artistic licence", although there is enough consistency to hint that we have underestimated the sophistication of these vessels. In fact the evidence from the representatives he mentioned, though very scanty, is not conflicting, and is almost all so accurate that a three-dimensional projection can be made from them which is not only inherently plausible but satisfies the structural evidence from other sources. The Greek artist had a very accurate eye.

Furthermore, no one who has read the recent publications on these ships could regard the reconstructed vessel as "an unlikely hull" (his phrase) or as anything less than a highly sophisticated affair. Triremes were plainly, as an ancient author says, "a complicated kind of mill", a rowing-machine designed for high speed and manoeuvrability in the sheltered waters invariably chosen for sea battles, in which the ships were used as rams. When the sea became choppy action was broken off. Thucydides says that the Corinthians in these conditions were more likely than the Athenians to catch crabs. Thucydides and Xenophon tell us incontrovertibly that main-sails were left ashore before battle. Indeed, on two occasions they were captured by the enemy, Conon captured Lysander's after Aegospotami.

Mr Leach finds all this "unconvincing" and prefers to believe that triremes, being highly sophisticated sailing ships, must have used sail in battle "to secure the tactically valuable windward position". I am afraid that if he can believe that he can believe anything. Sail was used in transit, when the wind was favourable; and when the wind was unfavourable they did not normally attempt to row instead, though we do hear exceptionally of long voyages under oar, on one occasion for training. On another, a trireme under oar covered 140 miles in a long day i.e., if that is 12 hours, at nearly 12 knots. Presumably the wind was favourable but not strong enough for sail, and the oarsmen rowed one or possibly two of the three divisions at a time. Much higher speeds would have been possible in short spurts in battle.

There is evidence that the trireme's square sail was braced round when the wind was on the quarter or abeam, but we only hear of small boats tacking into the wind. The area of sail could be varied by use of brailing ropes. These facts suggest a degree of sophistication in sailing as well as rowing techniques. The Athenians of Pericles' day were outstandingly fine oarsmen and fine sailors; they were not so foolish as to take a first-class rowing machine designed for ramming into battle under sail.

Yours faithfully,
JOHN MORRISON

Morrison's letter led to perhaps the most celebrated stream of correspondence published post-war by *The Times*, as Britain's leading authorities on classical naval warfare disputed the construction and operation of the trireme.

THE GREEK TRIREME CONTINUED

4 October 1975

SIR, THANK YOU FOR giving space to such a fascinating and instructive correspondence. May I try to cast the account? All good men seem to agree to the following:

1. That oared ships did not go into battle under sail;
2. That the Greek trireme used full oar power, to produce up to 11½ knots in short bursts, only in battle or in emergency;
3. That oared ships did not put to sea when the wind was unfavourable, rowed out of harbour and then either hoisted sail or continued rowing according to the state of the wind;
4. That a trireme's speed in still water under oar can be credibly calculated to have been five to six knots with one division rowing, a little more with two;
5. And that this calculation does not conflict with Xenophon's "120 nautical miles under oar in a long day." The word he uses can only mean the hours of daylight. So, with 15 hours of daylight plus one hour of twilight at latitude 42° on midsummer day, the speed works out at seven knots and a half, but there would have been little help from the current for the last 103½ miles. According to the Navigation Department of the National Maritime Museum, Black Sea currents run counter-clockwise, but through the Bosphorus there is a north–south current because of the 17in difference of levels at each end. The later MSS of Xenophon have a variant reading "a *very* long day", which suggests that the scribe shared your correspondents' feeling that Xenophon was exaggerating a bit. Etesian winds blowing with the current through the Bosphorus would have kept a galley in port.

Lord St David's galleys were the *a scaloccio* type of the second half of the sixteenth century with gangs of men pulling and in some cases also pushing, very long sweeps. A contemporary admiral reported them slower, in spite of greater manpower, than the earlier *a zenzile* galleys in which three or four men sat at benches set herringbone fashion, each rowing an oar of 30ft or so. Dr Tarn was rightly impatient of the theory then current that the ships of high numerical denominator in the Hellenistic navies had many banks of oars; and suggested instead that the Greeks must have had an *a zenzile* system for triremes and *a scaloccio* systems for the rest. The first part of this suggestion has been rejected because:

1. The Greek trireme's oars were 12⅔ or 13⅓ ft long (the longer oars amidships and, surprisingly, no difference between the levels);

2. an *a zenzile* galley rowing 170 men would have been far too long to fit into the known length of the Piraeus trireme sheds, the three-level system being (obviously) more economical of space.

There are other more detailed, equally cogent, reasons but these two are conclusive. Tarn was quite right about the ships of numerical denominator higher than three. They must have rowed more than one man to an oar at no more than three levels, usually, to judge from the monuments, at two. And the numerical denominator has nothing to do with levels, as people still tend to think; but indicates the power to which the original rowing unit had been raised by the various developments (i.e. 3, 4, 5, 6, etc. men to the oar-room, the space between the rowlocks, irrespective of level). A three-level trireme does not imply a four-level quadrireme.

Two final points:

1. The men who rowed the Athenian galleys in the fifth century were not slaves, indeed the slaves who rowed exceptionally at Arginusae were given their freedom for it.

2. If the hashish-carrying Punic warship reported in your columns is the one about which Miss Honor Frost has recently published excavation reports, it is too small to be a trireme.

Yours faithfully,
JOHN MORRISON

The correspondence ultimately led to the full-scale reconstruction of a trireme in order to test the various hypotheses advanced — see page 364

A BOY FALLING OUT OF THE SKY

11 October 1975

Sir, Mr G. M. Lee's letter (October 4) opens up entirely new possibilities in the field of ancient communications. While he dismisses the ubiquitous trireme in a neat couplet, we would like to draw his attention to the fact that Minoan aviation suffered a 50 per cent rate of attrition. Nevertheless the advantages of flight are obvious. From Ovid's *Metamorphoses* (VIII 11.220–222) we deduce that Icarus crashed some 220 miles (as the hero flies) north-east of Knossos. Taking into account the prevailing Westerlies, the actual distance flown must approximate to 250 miles. A dawn departure would seem imperative to facilitate take-off and we may assume that Icarus fell at midday, for only at that time can one fly vertically up towards the sun: "altius egit iter", which yields an elapsed flight time of six hours. Hence we can calculate a cruising speed of 41.6 mph (37 knots) at an altitude of 2,000 feet, since Ovid records that they were too low to be identified as birds, but sufficiently high to be mistaken for gods. Even considering that Daedalus and Icarus belonged to the age of heroes, and thus handsomely surpassed the sustained 0.1 horsepower of contemporary athletes, the efficiency of wing propulsion must have considerably exceeded the trireme's 70 per cent. Despite the inherent limitations of wax and feathers, the hypothetical 12 knot trireme would have taken slightly over three times as long to cover the same distance.

Yours faithfully,
MARTIN HOOD
JACK HANBURY TENISON
FRANCIS COLES
R. P. C. Forman's, Eton College, Windsor, Berkshire

PAYING FOR PLEASURE

17 October 1975

SIR, MAY I PROPOSE a simple cure for all our economic ills? The magic remedy is PAT – Pleasure Added Tax. It seems only fair and logical that the more you enjoy yourself the more you ought to pay for it. PAT should be applicable to any type of pleasure; public or private, whether derived from a concert, restaurant meal, art exhibition or the joys of love (marital sex to be zero-rated).

The assessment of PAT liability incurred on these and other occasions may pose some technical problems, but we may trust the ingenuity of HM Customs & Excise to devise the appropriate methods of pleasure testing. May I add that apart from solving our economic problems, the proposed legislative measure would also be of high ethical value, since we all agree that what a socialist country needs is more austerity and less *joie de vivre*.

Yours faithfully,
ARTHUR KOESTLER

A PRIME MINISTER'S QUALITIES

20 March 1976

Sɪʀ, A Pʀɪᴍᴇ Mɪɴɪsᴛᴇʀ should be an intellectual with common sense. This is a rare combination of qualities. James Callaghan has common sense but is short on intellect, Wedgwood Benn is an intellectual who lacks common sense.

This narrows the choice down to Healey, Roy Jenkins and Crosland, all of whom are approximately equal in brains and judgment. My own choice, on balance, would be Crosland, because he has the added quality of style.

Yours truly,
JOHN THIRKELL

Harold Wilson had resigned as prime minister on 4 March. He was succeeded by James Callaghan. Tony Crosland, then Foreign Secretary, died at the age of 58 in 1977.

FOOTING THE WEDDING BILL

31 March 1976

SIR, IN THE DAYS when a girl didn't go out to work, and stayed at home until an acceptable suitor could be found, her marriage was a financial as well as a social achievement for her parents — and it was the measure of a father's relief that he stumped up for the wedding.

But nowadays, when equal pay and opportunity give a girl financial independence, and changing social patterns mean that parents have little or no influence on her choice of husband, it is surely something of an anachronism that the bride's parents should still foot the bill.

As the father of three daughters of marriageable age, I admit to bias — and I do not doubt that my counterpart, with sons, would defend the practice to the pop of the last champagne cork!

Yours faithfully,
TERENCE ALLAN

Replied on 3 April 1976

SIR, I AM ACCUSTOMED to looking at the bottom right-hand corner of your correspondence page for an insight into some of the most pressing problems of the world today. As the father of four daughters I am sure that Mr Allan's letter on the cost of paying for weddings falls into this category.

I believe that it is the practice in many countries for such costs to be shared between the two families. In default of this I can only look forward to the prospects of financial ruin, unless it is possible to arrange such expedients as enforced elopements or a multiple wedding.

There is much to be said for a system of bride price which seems to be a custom in societies with a more realistic view than ours.

Yours faithfully,
ALASTAIR C. MORRISON

Replied on 5 April 1976

SIR, I AM THE FATHER of three daughters who are not yet of marriageable age but have no prospect of being able to afford grey topper and champagne occasions when the time comes. Mr Allan could obtain some relief by insisting on a double wedding of any two from three. This would save the cost of one outing for his side of the family.

My solution is to provide a stout ladder suitable for elopement. At the moment the girls think I am joking — over the years they will become conditioned to the fact that I mean it!

Yours faithfully,
W. E. G. MANNING

Replied on 7 April 1976

SIR, MY FATHER, WHO put the cat among the pigeons with his letter about wedding expenses, is quite obviously in cahoots with Mr Morrison who suggests that brides might be sold.

So be it, but if I am to be auctioned, I make the following stipulations:
1. That the price I fetch should be paid to me personally — out of which a small proportion would be set aside for wedding expenses.
2. That the balance should be nonrefundable.
3. That under no circumstances should my father get a cut. "Lot No. 1 — Caroline Allan...." May the bidding be brisk!

Yours faithfully,
CAROLINE ALLAN

Replied on 9 April 1976

Sir, As it is now clear that Miss Caroline Allan is about to be sold by auction, may I inquire where and when this is to take place and whether there is a reserve price? Generally speaking of course, period pieces fetch better prices than those of rather more recent date though one hopes that this will not be the case with Miss Allan. But, most important of all, where can the article be viewed?

I am, Sir, yours speculatively,
PETER J. SIMONS

Replied on 9 April 1976

Sir, Adverting to Miss Allan's letter, wherein she makes the stipulation that after deduction of wedding expenses from the auction price for herself as a bride, "the balance should be nonrefundable."

I am reminded that the Supply of Goods (Implied Terms) Act 1973 states that goods must be substantially suitable for the purpose for which they are supplied.

May I suggest that Miss Allan or her estimable father arranges for a prospectus to be issued so that would-be bidders can make suitable assessment of the "goods" offered. *Caveat emptor.*

Yours faithfully,
P. DONNELLY

Replied on 13 April 1976

Sir, As an Inspector of Taxes I am taking a proper interest in the arrangements being made for Miss Allan's future. I am considering whether her case falls to be considered as a disposal of a chattel having a value in excess of £1000; in that event she will be subject to capital gains tax in her father's hands and the Inland Revenue will want to know her value on Budget Day 1965.

There is another possibility. It cannot be denied that value has been added to her in recent years and there may thus be a liability to VAT, at the luxury rate of 12½ per cent I should say.

If on the other hand Miss Allan were unchivalrously judged not to be a "capital asset", the Inland Revenue would assess her father on any sums paid to him; they would fall to be treated as income or proceeds from a random or spare-time activity.

I hope that no one will suggest any sort of bartering arrangements. There is a precedent, it is true, but the Revenue would certainly regard such an expedient as tax evasion.

Yours truly,
STEPHEN HIGHLOCK

CHAMBER POTS

6 May 1976

Sir, I shall be grateful if you will allow me to draw public attention to the hardship that is increasingly experienced by septuagenarian men when they are away from home, and *a fortiori* by octogenarians and nonagenarians. I refer to the disappearance of the chamber pot as an article of bedroom furniture, or rather of guest room furniture. Of course some bedrooms have a bathroom directly attached to them and in that case I make no complaint. But, like many of my contemporaries, I am often invited to spend the night in a room that has no such convenience. We do not like to disturb our hosts by wandering about dark passages in quest of light switches and uncertain doors and at last by the noise of flushing.

We plead for the restoration of the traditional chamber pot to its rightful place either under the bed or in a bedside cabinet. It is true that most of them now seem to have found their way into antique shops and thence to the United States. But various sizes in plastic are obtainable and, for my part, I am ready to settle for one of those as a substitute for an elegant piece of china.

I would add that I entirely agree with the late Dick Sheppard that the recipients of such relief should always be responsible in the morning for emptying and cleansing any receptacle which they have used, and not leave that operation as a chore for their hostess or any minion of hers.

Yours faithfully,
ALEC VIDLER

TIMES PAST

17 June 1976

SIR, FOR A NEWSPAPER titled *The Times* you seem singularly rash about your timepieces. I read in today's Diary that the Henry Moore sundial intended for the courtyard of your last new building was sold to *The Observer* and is now in Brussels.

I can testify that when your original building was pulled down the clock, centrepiece of your masthead was sold for £50 because I bought it and your readers may like to know that I turned the cast-iron face into a sundial in a courtyard that I built specially at my home in Sussex where the clock enjoys a peaceful retirement surrounded at its base by, what else (?), several varieties of thyme.

I remain, Sir, yours faithfully,
PATRICK IDE

NAVY BLUES

25 June 1976

Sir, Admiral Clutterbuck (23 June) suggests that British industrial management needs, to cure its current malaise, the administrative efficiency of the fighting services, which the Admiral assures us has never since World War I "been accused of deficiency in good management". Surely Admiral Clutterbuck must be joking.

During the whole of the five years that I spent in the wartime RNVR (1939–45) I witnessed an inefficiency of management that would have run any industrial concern out of business in a matter of weeks.

Was the passage of the *Scharnhorst* and *Gneisenau* through the Straits of Dover an example of good management? *The Times* described it by saying: "Nothing more mortifying to the pride of our sea power has happened since the seventeenth century." Was it good management for the Royal Navy to need (I quote Churchill) "forty-seven ships to sink the *Bismarck*." Were Dunkirk, Arnhem and the quite unnecessary destruction of Dresden examples of good management? And what about the cod war?

The present malaise of Britain stems not from managerial inefficiency but from our self-satisfied refusal to admit that the malaise exists.

Yours sincerely,
MERLIN MINSHALL

FOILING THE MUGGER

21 October 1976

SIR, MAY I ADD a rider to my friend Lesley Lewis's admirable letter? I suggest that unescorted women should not carry handbags at all. A judge's wife of my acquaintance puts her valuables in the pocket of a Boy Scout's message belt strapped round her waist.

I personally put my keys in one pocket, the minimum of necessary cash in the other, grip an umbrella in my right hand, and wear a disagreeable expression on my face. The latter comes naturally to me.

Yours faithfully,
BETTINA BEAL

Mrs Lesley Lewis's letter referred to her experience of being mugged one early evening on a street in Chelsea. She argued that increased police presence would deter muggers.

FRAGILE EGGSHELLS

7 April 1977

SIR, How REASSURING to be told by the Poultry Research Centre that the shells of modern eggs are as good as they were 40 years ago! (report by your Agricultural Correspondent on Saturday, April 2). The reason they break so easily is that they are too fresh when we buy them.

Yet I am old enough to remember when the farmer's wife brought baskets of eggs to market travelling in a jolting cart over unmade roads. The baskets were at least 10 to twelve inches deep and the pressure of weight on the bottom layer must have been considerable. Some of the eggs were probably a week old but some would have been collected that morning.

With all respect to the scientists, the results of their 10 years' research only confirms me in my admiration for the old-fashioned hen.

I am, Sir, yours truly,
STELLA F. PALMER

Replied on 12 April 1977

SIR, I CANNOT ENTIRELY agree with the finding of the scientists that the shells of eggs laid by factory bred hens are not inferior to those of their free range sisters. I sometimes find that the former crumble between the fingers even before boiling. I contend that they are inferior because the layers receive no grit in their diet, whereas the grit picked up by free range hens is generally supplemented by ground oyster shell.

Incidentally, it is only in old age that I have at last discovered that the tops of boiled eggs should be sliced off at the thin end, to avoid spilling the yolk. A difference of opinion on this subject was, if I remember correctly, the cause of the war in Thackeray's *The Rose and the Ring*, the delight of which is, I fear, unknown to modern generations of science fiction-fed children.

Yours faithfully,
A. E. STURDY

Replied on 13 April 1977

SIR, I AM GLAD THAT the Poultry Research Centre has, after 10 years' investigation, been able to solve the worrying problem of modern hens' eggs splitting during boiling. People who have been worried lest food quality should be changed by technology will be reassured to know the fault lies with the housewife, not the hen. May I offer some simple advice, known to all husbands who have learnt to boil an egg, that a small pin prick made in the egg's rounded end will let expanding air escape from the air sac and save the shell from splitting?

Yours faithfully,
G. F. BROOKES

Replied on 14 April 1977

SIR, THE MAJOR IS quite right, the modern hen lacks grit.

For several hilarious months during the War I was responsible for a large number of hens kept to provide fresh eggs for the officers' mess. My ignorance of poultry rearing was total so I was dismayed when the eggshells turned soft. I was told that oyster shells were needed in the diet — quite unobtainable in wartime — but luckily the sea was near so I spent many tedious hours collecting and crushing shells found on the beach and feeding them to the hens. And, hey-presto! It worked.

By the time I was posted, the catering officer had been persuaded to provide official RAF transport and once a month Operation Seashell set off, with many volunteers, for a day by the sea. And the officers were again enjoying their new-laid, hard-shelled breakfast eggs.

Thus was the War won.

Yours faithfully,
CURTIS DEAN

The Top People's Paper

Replied on 16 April 1977

SIR, MAJOR STURDY does not, I fear, "remember correctly" that a dispute as to the end at which an egg should properly be broken was the cause of a war in *The Rose and the Ring*: it is in *Gulliver's Travels* that such an incident occurs — the disputants being the Lilliputians and the Blefuscans, and eleven thousand people being prepared to lay down their lives for their beliefs on this subject.

I entirely agree with Major Sturdy as to the comparative fragility of the shells of battery-produced eggs. The best means of preventing an egg from cracking when boiled is to prick the shell at the *larger* end — if the smaller end is pierced, the egg-white tends to escape during cooking. I have not found other suggested preventive measures — such as the addition of salt or vinegar to the water — comparable in efficacy to this.

Yours faithfully,
JENNIFER FELLOWS

Replied on 23 April 1977

SIR, AT RISK OF SOUNDING pedantic I would like to correct terms used in the recent letters about fragile eggshells. All hens have to have grit — not as part of their diet but to be stored in the gizzard to churn up their food.

The oyster shells Mrs Curtis Dean fed to the hens were adding the extra calcium to harden the shells.

Yours faithfully,
E. M. SELBY-BOOTHROYD

Replied on 25 April 1977

SIR, MRS STELLA PALMER is right to admire the old-fashioned hen, which was a remarkably efficient converter of animal feed into human food. But she should admire even more the modern hen, which is yet more efficient, and modern egg producers and distributors, most of whom try hard to ensure that eggs are of good quality when they reach the housewife.

Forty years ago when my mother made a cake or omelette she broke every egg into a cup, for fear of spoiling the mixture by adding an egg that was rotten. Rotting was commonly a consequence of shell cracking, which allowed spoilage organisms to get in. My wife has not been sold a rotten egg since 1954.

Yours faithfully,
T. C. CARTER

Replied on 25 April 1977

SIR, WOULD THE poultry experts now investigate the reduction in thickness of Easter Eggs?

Yours sincerely,
D. LIVERMORE

LEAVING THE EEC

21 June 1977

SIR, MR ERIC HEFFER's contention that the UK can at all times withdraw from the European Community is factually correct. To quote a well known historical precedent, some American states withdrew from the Union in 1860, notwithstanding the ties that had bound them together for 80 years, and which were infinitely stronger than those binding Britain to the EEC.

But having conceded this point, one must regret that British politicians did not take part (although invited) in the great debate that accompanied the negotiation of the Rome Treaty. If they had, it would now be more widely known as Westminster and elsewhere that the Rome Treaty is conspicuous among international conventions for having neither a withdrawal clause, nor a prefixed duration. States which have subscribed, or adhered to it, have no legal way of withdrawing, the Treaty is valid without end.

In the last of their summit meetings at the end of 1956 the then Heads of Government of the six countries recognized that what they were building was, not only a customs union or the beginning of an economic union, but a community of destinies. You don't work for a common destiny until a certain date and then stop. You don't put a limit to the common endeavour and, to make your resolve credible, you don't admit that you may withdraw.

The European leaders of the day may have been what Mr Heffer calls Euro-fanatics. But surely they knew what they wanted and what they were aiming for, and that was certainly somewhat greater than the retail price of butter. The difference is therefore a philosophical one; and philosophical divergences are the stuff of which real revolutionary changes in human history are made.

Yours sincerely,
ROBERTO DUCCI
Ambassador of Italy

Article 50 of the Treaty of Lisbon, which came into effect in 2009, corrected this state of affairs.

THE MORALITY OF TORY IDEALS

18 July 1977

SIR, IN MY IAIN MACLEOD Memorial Lecture, I advised my audience of Young Conservatives to read Adam Smith for themselves at first hand or run the risk of being misled by second-hand versions, not least from his denigrators. From what he writes, The Vicar of Harwell and Chilton (July 11) seems to have ignored a large part of Adam Smith's work. Smith was a moral philosopher of some standing before he turned his attention to the study of economics which placed the whole world in his debt. He had devoted his main inquiries to the place of man in society. In his economic studies he certainly did not exclude the moral and social dimensions, on the contrary.

I shall not attempt to rehearse all Smith's arguments in the space of a letter. Suffice to say that setting out from a philosophy which recognized human motivation as mixed, Smith argued that were we to depend solely on the benevolence of our fellow-men we should receive short shrift. However by harnessing men's natural impulse to improve their own condition and that of their families as well as to deserve the approbation of their fellow-men, the market economy visibly brought great benefits to the greater number.

Smith never suggested that self-interest alone was sufficient to bring the Good Life, or that man can live by bread alone. By contrast, Marx's dialectical materialism gave pride of place to economics.

Marx expressly argued that economic change has underlain all other change throughout human history, that religion, politics, ethics, the arts and letters are nothing but "superstructure" conditioned by the basic economic realities. Perhaps the Vicar will again read Marx for himself after he has laid down Smith. He appears to believe that Marx stood for equality, as well as for benevolence and other Christian virtues. Surely, then, he must have asked himself how, if this be so, can it be that wherever Marxist rule is imposed, as it is on a third of suffering mankind, it leads visibly to cruelty, misery, callousness, selfishness, new crying inequalities. Shall Marxism not be known by its fruits?

I have never claimed that my views or those of my Party are the sole interpretation of Christian truth into social terms. I stated that Conservatives came into politics as a Church Party and that concern for the application of Christianity to politics underlay much of the political debate throughout a large part of our party's three centuries old existence. This is a matter of historical fact.

There are those who draw other conclusions from the Gospels; so be it, dialogue takes us closer to truth.

But when Christians find themselves justifying causes or ideas which not only extend man's inhumanity to man into new fields, but which preach atheism and pitilessly persecute Christian Churches, surely they should stop and ask if their zeal has not somehow led them astray.

Ms Sandra Pontac (July 11) rightly questions why some people should have to work out their own salvation in a slum. Yet beware of being patronizing. For millions on millions have worked out their salvation in every sense of the term from such beginnings, just as others have wasted their opportunities. I look forward to a day when there will be no slums. But I believe that we shall achieve more by helping people to help themselves than by trying to relieve them of their own responsibilities and thereby of their own dignity and self-respect.

In my lecture, which will be published with other speeches in the autumn, I dealt with some of the misapprehensions regarding Victorian times. The miseries which Ms Pontac mentioned antedated the Victorian era. Precisely because the Victorian conscience found them intolerable and sought means of remedying them with philanthropy and self-help, the abuses have come to be associated with that period. This is a poor return to a great reforming age, whose zeal we should do well to emulate in terms of our own age and its need.

The letter by Richard Bull, Vice Chairman of the Greater London Young Conservatives (July 14), encourages me to believe that our work in reaffirming the essential interdependence of individual and collective responsibilities as the core of Conservative philosophy is bearing fruit. What better memorial could there be to Iain Macleod?

Yours faithfully,
MARGARET THATCHER

Iain Macleod had died in 1970, soon after being appointed Chancellor of the Exchequer. Some think that had he lived he might have won the leadership of the Conservative Party, rather than Margaret Thatcher, who became prime minister in 1979.

TRADE UNION IMMUNITY UNDER THE LAW

21 July 1977

SIR, WHEN WILL THE British public at last learn to understand that there is no salvation for Britain until the special privileges granted to the trade unions by the Trades Disputes Act of 1906 are revoked? Mr Robert Moss is probably right when in his recent book he writes that "the Liberals who blithely passed a Bill drawn up by the first generation of Labour MPs in keeping of an electoral promise quite literally had no idea what they were doing".

But they were soon unmistakably told. A. V. Dicey presently spoke of the Act of 1906 as having conferred "upon a trade union a freedom from civil liability for the commission of even the most heinous wrong by the union or its servant, and in short conferred upon every trade union a privilege and protection not possessed by any other person or body of persons, whether corporate or incorporate. The law makes a trade union a privileged body exempted from the ordinary law of the land."

And in 1925 another great jurist, Sir Paul Vinogradoff, again emphasized that "the Trades Disputes Act of 1906 conferred upon the unions an immunity from prosecution on the ground of tortious acts of their agents; the immunity stands in flagrant disagreement with the law of agency and the law as to companies represented by their officers in accordance with the Statutory Order of 1883."

In 1942 a foreign economist intimately familiar with British affairs, the late Professor Joseph Schumpeter, looking back on developments, wrote that "it is difficult, at the present time, to realize how this measure must have struck people who still believed in a state and in a legal system that centred in the institution of private property. For in relaxing the law of conspiracy in respect to peaceful picketing — which practically amounted to legalization of trade union action implying the threat of force — and in exempting trade union funds from liability in action for damages *for torts* — which practically amounted to enacting that trade unions could do no wrong — this measure in fact resigned to the trade unions part of the authority of the state and granted to them a position of privilege which the formal extension of the exemption to employers' unions was powerless to affect."

And only twenty years ago Lord MacDermott reiterated that, in short, the act "put trade unionism in the same privileged position which the Crown enjoyed until ten years ago in respect to wrongful acts committed on its behalf".

Yet still, when the fatal effects of this are before everybody's eyes, nobody dares to consider removing the source of all that misfortune.

There can indeed be little doubt to a detached observer that the privileges then granted to the trade unions have become the chief source of Britain's economic decline. It is an illusion to believe that a Labour government is in a better position to deal with the unions. It is no use suggesting to them moderation when they do all that harm by exercising their chartered rights.

A Labour government cannot touch the sacred charter which is the authorization of all this licence. The public hardly yet understands that the power of the trade unions to destroy the economy has been conferred on them as a special privilege by an irresponsible government buying a few more years of power. That fatal mistake must be undone if Britain is to recover. No government can pull the country out of the mire unless it obtains at the elections an explicit mandate to revoke the unique privileges which the trade unions have enjoyed too long. Only such a power can enable a Conservative government to reverse the trend towards abject poverty.

I am, etc.,
F. A. HAYEK

The Austrian-born Friedrich Hayek, who won the Nobel Prize for Economics in 1974, had a long connection with Britain, having taught at the London School of Economics in the 1930s. His ideas carried much influence with the Thatcher government, which passed laws calculated to reduce the power of the unions — though Hayek himself denied that he was a Conservative rather than a Liberal.

ARMY NICKNAMES

1 August 1977

Sir, Thinking about the film *A Bridge Too Far* can any of your readers explain why World War Two generals had such incredibly childish nicknames?

"Jumbo", "Squeaker", "Pip", "Boy" and "Bubbles" come to mind.

Yours faithfully,
REGINALD BOSANQUET

The television news reader Reggie Bosanquet was the son of the inventor of the googlie — see page 19

Replied on 3 August 1977

Sir, The reasons underlying the nicknames "Jumbo", "Squeaker" and "Boy" referred to by Mr Reginald Bosanquet in his letter are that the first general possessed a large and impressive stature, the second a voice which would rise to a high pitch when under excitement, and the third because of his youthful appearance.

I have never understood the reasons underlying the conferment of "Pip" and "Bubbles" on the other two.

Yours faithfully,
ALEC BISHOP

Replied on 3 August 1977

Sir, The answer to Mr Bosanquet's query is that generals of the Second World War acquired their childish nicknames, not through anything they did in that war, but through the clubby nature of regimental life at the time of their joining, which in most cases was before the Great War of 1914.

Some were purely descriptive, as in the cases of "Jumbo" Wilson, who looked like an elephant, and "Squeaker" Curtis, who had a high-pitched voice. Some

The Top People's Paper

stem from an episode, such as the emission of bubbles by Evelyn Barker on his first attempt at pipe-smoking. (Another "Bubbles" was the infant model for the famous advertisement.)

But the most childish and most numerous nicknames are those automatically linked to a name, and these can be misleading. "Strafer" Gott affords a good example. It occurred to me while I was writing a book on the North African campaign (recently published with title *The Plain Cook and the Great Showman*) that "Strafer" ill described this humane and well loved general. Then I recalled the words attributed to the Kaiser, "Gott strafe England". There could be no escape there-after for any soldier with the surname of Gott from the nickname of "Strafer".

Yours faithfully,
GREGORY BLAXLAND

Replied on 3 August 1977

SIR, MR REGINALD BOSANQUET might be interested to know that my late father, Major-General H. Essame, to whom Ronald Lewin generously referred in his review of *Corps Commander* last week, had slightly turned in feet and took shorter than normal strides. He was known to his troops as "Twinkletoes".

Yours faithfully,
PRIMROSE FEUCHTWANGER

Replied on 3 August 1977

SIR, MR BOSANQUET refers in his letter to some unusual military nicknames. I once heard the son of one of the generals he mentions introduce himself to my husband by saying "I'm Squeaker's boy, the Oat's godson and the Burglar's nephew".

Yours faithfully,
THE OAT'S DAUGHTER

Replied on 4 August 1977

Sir, Reggie Bosanquet queries why it was that British generals in World War Two had such incredibly childish nicknames as "Jumbo", "Squeaker" and "Boy". Surely this reflects nothing more than the preparatory school background of these generals. Equally childish nicknames can be found amongst the literary and artistic talent of that generation. Types of nickname have a lot to do with national characteristics.

For instance, the Germans in the Second World War preferred to give generals nicknames which were a play on words. Thus Field-Marshal Keitel was known as "Lakeitel", a play on the German word *lakai*, meaning lackey, and Field-Marshal Hans Kluge was known as "Kluge" Hans, a play on the German word *klug*, meaning clever. More sinister was the nickname "Strength through Fear", derived from the Nazi leisure organization "Strength through Joy", given to Field-Marshal Schörner, an officer not noted for his sense of humour.

Yours truly,
K. R. SIMPSON ("Whacko" Simpson)

Replied on 4 August 1977

Sir, The incredibly childish nicknames given to World War Two generals surely derived from the fact that most of their contemporaries, both senior and junior officers, went to public schools where witty nicknames were the order of the day.

I served on the staffs of "Monkey" Morgan, "Dolly" de Fonblanque, "Windy" Gale, "Pug" Ismay, "Jorrocks" Horrocks and, lower down the ranks, with "Poppy" Flanders and "Fairy" Fairhurst.

Yours faithfully,
HILARY AGGETT (Captain, retired)

Replied on 4 August 1977

Sir, The answer to Reginald Bosanquet's question is simple. The last war generals acquired their "childish" nicknames at the outset of their Service careers, often while still in their "teens.

In the early nineteen hundreds Christian names were resorted to only after a suitable period of acquaintance had elapsed. As an alternative a ready form of identification was needed amongst the junior officers who invented nicknames for each other based usually on a personal idiosyncrasy or physical feature.

By the late nineteen-thirties when I joined the Army, the invention of new nicknames had become less necessary since Christian names were used at once.

Which is why, Sir, I can but sign myself

Yours faithfully,
SQUEAKER'S BOY

Replied on 5 August 1977

SIR, FOLLOWERS OF THE Bosanquet nicknames correspondence (admirable for August) might also like to know that the present day Indian Army has inherited the nickname habit (and much else) from their British forebears.

Examples include Major "Pickles" Sodhi of the 61st Cavalry, Majors "Binny" and "Mao" Sherghill of the 7th Light Cavalry and the Deccan Horse respectively, and, of course, Colonel "Bubbles" Jaipur.

Yours faithfully,
OLIVER EVERETT

Replied on 5 August 1977

SIR, WERE NOT ARMY nicknames immortalized after the first World War in Sapper's stories? I call to mind Spud Trevor of the Red Hussars, Dog-face (Major Chilham), Pumpkin (twice), Hatchet-face, Tiny Tim (twice), Bimbo Charteris and, of course, Captain Bulldog Drummond.

In Gilbert Frankau's Royal Regiment the two principal characters were "the Hawk" (Colonel Sir Guy Wethered) and "Rusty" (Major Thomas Rockingham).

Yours faithfully,
G. T. ST J. SANDERS

Replied on 5 August 1977

SIR, GENERAL URQUHART's nickname was "Tiger" and General Sir Ivor Thomas, who commanded respect not unmixed with apprehension from his staff, was usually known as "Von Thoma". Nothing boyish about either of those two, I do assure you.

Yours faithfully,
DONALD WILSON

There was a real German General Wilhelm von Thoma, who was captured in 1942. Conversations that he had with other prisoners were secretly recorded and helped identify the sites of the V-1 and V-2 rockets.

Replied on 5 August 1977

SIR, THE GENERALS ARE given these strange nicknames mainly for security reasons so that the enemy (and most other people) cannot possibly tell who they really are.

Yours, etc.,
E. BENTLEY BEAUMAN

Replied on 6 August 1977

SIR, ARMY NICKNAMES were not always affectionate. In 1915, my divisional commander, who had been christened Richard, was Dirty Dick to his friends, and Filthy Richard to all the rest of us.

Yours faithfully,
ALAN LASCELLES

Replied on 8 August 1977

Sɪʀ, I ʜᴀᴠᴇ ᴅᴇʟᴀʏᴇᴅ my answer to Mr Bosanquet's letter just to see what reaction it got. It has certainly produced much information on the subject but mostly inaccurate. None of the nicknames so far mentioned had anything to do with a private or public school background. They all (I'm not sure about Pip Roberts) came into being during the owner's early days in the Army and originated from some inherent characteristic.

The 60th Rifles when I joined before World War I had a number of officers with nicknames given them after they joined such as Loony, Tripe, Oxo, Squeaker, The Oat and many others, and I know the reasons for all of them. Often on marriage their wives inherited their nicknames, and Loony's wife took exception to it. Luckily Tripe never married. As regards my own, I regret to say I have no connexion with Sir John Millais' delightful painting of his grandson (later Admiral Sir William James) who naturally was called Bubbles. He died in 1974. For many years it was used as an advertisement for Pear's Soap. Nor in any case has it anything to do with pipe smoking as Mr Blaxland declares (3 August). The reason for it is Top Secret and only divulged to my closest friends. However, I will give Mr Blaxland the clue that it has some connexion with a camel and not with a pipe. Actually I only smoked a pipe during World War II.

Yours faithfully,
EVELYN H. BARKER, "BUBBLES"

Replied on 9 August 1977

Sɪʀ, Tᴏ ᴍᴇ, ᴀ ʀᴀɴᴋᴇʀ who served throughout the war at the sharper end of the Army, the chumminess of nicknames seems quite out of keeping with the recognized aloofness of generals. Apart from Wilson's "Jumbo" and Montgomery's "Monty", I never got to know what their nicknames were. Moreover, had I been able to get that close and dared to have asked them, my chances of escaping charges for insolence would have been very slender indeed.

Yours truly,
L. G. SCALES

ELVIS HAS LEFT THE BUILDING

20 August 1977

SIR, YOUR LEADING ARTICLE of August 18 is correct when it states that Presley[1] was a singer of great social significance and I am glad that President Carter has also paid official tribute to this extraordinary entertainer.

However, I take strong exception to your statements in the same leader that Presley was an indifferent singer, performing for the most part mediocre songs, and was a totally uninteresting person. This is simply not true and I would be interested to know which popular singers you consider to be superior to Presley in these categories. Or are you unwilling to admit that any popular singers have any merit whatsoever?

Yours faithfully,
TIM RICE

[1] The entertainer had died on August 16

20 August 1977

SIR, "A SINGER OF social significance." Your second leader today so describes a man who, according to the obituary, became the scandal of America from 1956 to 1958. He set the pace for successors who also had "an immoral influence on the mobs of girls who shrieked at concerts—etc, etc". Your leader summarises the results of the singer's influence but, acknowledging that those results are still with us, does not praise or condemn.

I find it difficult to understand how the President of the USA can pay tribute to a man who caused many parents distress and was himself followed by many imitators. Socially significant true, but for good or evil?

Yours faithfully,
OWEN W. JAQUES

20 August 1977

Sir, Your leading article of August 18 implies that Elvis Presley's huge popularity was somehow in spite of, rather than because of, his music. This sneer is untrue and unfair. People did not buy Elvis Presley's records in order to annoy their parents; they bought them because they derived enormous pleasure from listening to Elvis Presley's magnificent and unique artistic performances.

Yours faithfully,
R. G. SHORT

20 August 1977

Sir, In 1956, the year when Elvis Presley's extraordinary talent burst upon the world, I started to teach in a large mixed comprehensive school in north-west London. I shall never forget the elderly senior mistress coming into the staff room one morning and saying sternly, "I must speak to a boy called Elvis Presley because he has carved his name on every desk in the school."

Yours, etc.,
BETTY HURSTFIELD

HOW MANY MEN DOES IT TAKE
TO MAKE TOAST?

4 October 1977

SIR, ON THE FECUND subject of overmanning and productivity I thought that you would wish to have recorded for posterity the following conversation which occurred yesterday evening on a train from Paddington.

Guard to barperson: Tony's serving toast, on the other train.

Barperson: Toast? On his own? I'll have the union on him.

Guard (apparently taken aback by the vehemence of the barperson's reply): Well his customers seem to like it.

Barperson: Pleasing customers is all very well, but you can go too far. Making toast's a two-man job.

Only the reprobate toastmaker's name has been changed, in the probably forlorn hope that it may still be possible to protect him.

Yours faithfully,
WINSTON FLETCHER

CHURCHILL'S PORTRAIT

17 January 1978

Sir, Soon after the presentation[1] I was invited to view the portrait by Sutherland at Churchill's home in Hyde Park Gate. There in the garden drawing-room, fortified by a glass of sherry, I examined the picture alone for some time. Now looking up the number of the magazine I find I described it as "an unconventional work of an unconventional sitter". Its chief defect was that it looked unfinished in as much as his feet were concealed in a carpet that seemed to have sprouted a dun-coloured grass — the artist had obviously been unhappy about them and they had been painted over since it would have been impossible to "cut off" his legs below the knees without radically altering the proportions and placing of the picture on the canvas.

One has to remember that the portrait was a gift to Churchill by colleagues past and present in Parliament as a token of their affection for him as a man of long service in that institution. It was not a state or official portrait but a personal symbol of good will and respect of which there was little evidence in the painting; I wrote the "mood and the manner of the study do not awaken sympathy or warmth" as anyone looking at the colour reproduction accompanying my critical comments may confirm. Also, Churchill had a keen sense of history and his own place in it; lacking a present-day Holbein, he and his wife were not going to risk being preserved for posterity in a painting that they felt did neither him nor the artist full justice.

As footnote to the above, soon after I had viewed the portrait I visited Arthur Jeffress, the art dealer, who told me that a portrait of him by Sutherland had actually been begun and "laid in" on the canvas the artist then used for Churchill — not that it mattered, for that initial sketch was undetectable.

Jeffress asked me not to mention this in print and I didn't until some six years later after he had died. As I said then it would have been another reason for the Old Man to have disliked the portrait though by that time apparently it did not exist.

Yours, etc.,

G. S. WHITTET

[1] In 1954, to mark his 80th birthday, Parliament had presented Sir Winston Churchill with his portrait by Graham Sutherland. Both Churchill and his wife disliked it and Lady Churchill later had it destroyed. George Whittet was a former editor of the art magazine *Studio International*.

LIVING IN
INTERESTING TIMES

1980–89

MANNERS AND MEN

22 May 1982

SIR, AS A WYKEHAMIST, I am happy to own a number of the soft impeachments contained in your leading article[1]; but I cannot refrain from protesting at your shameless reconstruction of the well-known story of the chair.

It was, of course, the imperious and patrician Etonian who commanded that a chair be brought for the fainting lady; it was the unobtrusive, efficient and — dare I say it? — well-mannered Wykehamist who provided it.

Yours faithfully,
CHARLES GORDON

[1] The Queen had visited Winchester College — motto: Manners makyth man — on the 600th anniversary of the school's foundation. The next day, a leading article in *The Times* had related the story of a woman who (perhaps imprudently) finds herself in the company of a Wykehamist, an Etonian and a Harrovian: the first calls for someone to fetch a chair for her; the second gets it; and the third sits on it himself.

22 May 1982

SIR, THE WYKEHAMIST did not "call out for somebody to fetch a chair"; he asked the lady, very politely, whether she would like one. That, surely, makes all the difference.

Yours politely,
F. R. SALMON

25 May 1982

SIR, AS A PAST inhabitant of both Harrow and New College (and therefore strictly neutral) I cannot allow the inaccurate story in the third leader today to go unchallenged). (Is your leader writer perhaps an Old Etonian?)

In the correct version an attractive girl enters a room containing an Etonian, a Wykehamist (of the junior foundation) and an Harrovian. The Etonian says,

"This lady needs a chair", the Wykehamist fetches one and the Harrovian sits down with the girl on his knee.

Yours faithfully,
TOM MORTON

26 May 1982

SIR, YOUR EDITORIAL today has got it wrong! It is Etonians who notice that ladies have no chairs, Wykehamists who fetch them. That is why the latter make good civil servants: they assess and follow up creative thinking.

Yours very truly,
T. J. ALLISON

Replied on 26 May 1982

SIR, AM I, AT 48, yesterday's woman? I am not surprised when any man, Wykehamist or not, opens a door for me (but then, my school motto was *In Fide Vade*). Certainly I thank him.

Yours in courtesy,
CLARE SPRING

Replied on 27 May 1982

SIR, SOME FIFTEEN years ago I was interviewing candidates for a vacant post. One was a Wykehamist, who made a poor impression on me and my colleagues. He seemed to us obtuse and conceited. Anyway, he did not get the job.

A few days later I received a letter from the frustrated applicant, abusing me roundly for turning him down, pointing out that it was bad manners to reject Wykehamists and that I must mend my ways.

Yours faithfully,
JAMES PALMES

Replied on 27 May 1982

SIR, THE GENTLEMEN's actions indicate that the attractive young lady can only have been a Marlburienne – anyone else would have been left standing.

Yours faithfully,
JAMES JOHNSTONE

Replied on 28 May 1982

SIR, I SUGGEST THAT the comparison between Wykehamists and Etonians should be extended beyond the question of manners to that of pragmatism.

During the first Atoms for Peace conference at Geneva in 1955 the Mr Big of the international energy scene was confined, raging, to his room by a cold. He instructed me and a fellow delegate to go to a pharmacy and get him some blackcurrant syrup. My colleague (an Etonian) demanded "courants noirs". I (a Wykehamist) waited for the pharmacist to ask us (in English) what we required.

Yours, etc.,
PETER DANCKWERTS

The modest Professor Danckwerts had won the George Cross in 1940 for defusing unexploded enemy parachute mines dropped during the Blitz.

Replied on 29 May 1982

SIR, THE TALE OF THE Wykehamist and the chair calls to mind the anecdote illustrating the distinguishing characteristics of the five Oxford "women's" colleges.

Five girls, one from each college, meet. Their conversation concerns a young man of their mutual acquaintance:

The girl from Lady Margaret Hall asks, "Who are his parents?"

The girl from Somerville asks, "What is he reading?"

The girl from St Hugh's asks, "What sport does he play?"

The girl from St Hilda's asks, "Who is he going out with?"

And the girl from St Anne's says "Me".

At least, that is the version which I was told, when I was at St Anne's.

Yours faithfully,
IMOGEN CLOUT

Replied on 31 May 1982

SIR, IN MY UNTYPICAL experience, the Cheltenham girl says, "Gosh you look pale", the Wycombe Abbey girl says, "I'll get you a glass of champagne", and the Heathfield girl drinks it.

Yours faithlessly,
MAX TAYLOR

Replied on 2 June 1982

SIR, THE STORY AS I understood it was that a pretty girl came into a room containing three ex-public schoolboys who provided her with a chair to sit upon and then proceeded to argue amongst themselves as to which of them should receive the credit for this deed.

The girl stifled a yawn, made her excuses and left the room.

Yours faithfully,
PAUL STEWART

Replied on 2 June 1982

SIR, I SEEM TO remember that at Charterhouse we had enough chairs for everyone to be able to sit down.

Yours faithfully,
NICHOLAS FREELAND

Replied on 2 June 1982

SIR, THE YOUNG gentlemen of Harrow, Eton and Winchester may indulge themselves in idle banter about who does what with a chair, but their fathers have arranged matters so that old Lliswerrians can no longer hew the wood to make the chair.

Yours faithfully,
JOHN HERBERT

Replied on 4 June 1982

SIR, I TOO REMEMBER the story of the five Oxford women undergraduates discussing the young man.

I am sorry to have to tell Miss Clout, however, that in my day at Lady Margaret Hall the young lady from St Anne's was reputed simply to have said "*Where is he?*"

Yours faithfully,
GILLIAN WILSON

Replied on 8 June 1982

SIR, AT ST HUGH'S in 1947, I was told:
    The young man stood outside the college.
    Somerville said: "What does he read?"
    L.M.H. said: "Who are his people?"
    St Hilda's said: "What does he play?"
    St Hugh's said: "Bring him up."

Yours nostalgically,
DOUCE FORTY

Replied on 8 June 1982

SIR, IN THE VERSION which reached us at St Hugh's, the St Anne's girl concludes the conversation with: "He's my husband, actually."

Yours faithfully,
JENNIFER ORCHARD

HORSING AROUND

26 April 1980

SIR, SOME YEARS AGO, I had a horse called Ministry so that if the Bishop called when I was out riding, he could truthfully be told: "The Rector is out exercising his ministry." I now have a new horse to be named. Could your readers make any suggestions along similar lines?

Yours faithfully,
REV. I. H. G. GRAHAM-ORLEBAR

Replied on 1 May 1980

SIR, "I'M AFRAID the Rector is unable to see you — he's just fallen from Grace."

Yours faithfully,
LINNEA CLIFF HODGES

Replied on 1 May 1980

SIR, CONSIDERING THE supposedly low level of stipends may not the Rector have gone to collect "Social Security"?

Yours faithfully,
FRANCIS HOPKINS

Replied on 5 May 1980

SIR, MAY I SUGGEST that the Reverend Ian Graham-Orlebar calls his horse Praxis? Thus when the Bishop telephones he may be told that the Rector "is developing Praxis in an on-going interface situation". Such a use of current liberal ecclesiastical jargon will surely, by its very incomprehensibility, convince the diocesan hierarchy that here indeed is one parochial clergyman attempting to meet with contemporary society in relevant and meaningful confrontation.

Yours,
GEORGE AUSTIN

Replied on 9 May 1980

SIR, WHEN THE RECTOR of Barton-le-Cley is out on Parish Business (or away on Retreat), are Tact and Great Discretion exercised by his staff?

Yours faithfully,
PATSY STEPHENS

Replied on 9 May 1980

SIR, IF THE GENTLEMAN gave his correct name and address and his Bishop reads *The Times*, whatever he calls his horse the game is up.

Yours faithfully,
R. J. PAINE

Replied on 13 May 1980

SIR, THE HORSE IS TO be named Sabbatical at the suggestion of Canon Eric James of St Alban's Abbey, who thinks I need one, having been in the same parish ten years on the trot.

Yours faithfully,
I. H. G. GRAHAM-ORLEBAR

NOTES OF DISCORD

8 July 1980

SIR, I WAS MUCH saddened the philistine attitude adopted by your correspondent Harry Henry in last Friday's letters column (July 4). Personally, as a regular pedestrian, I have long deplored the sad reduction in the number of street musicians since my pram-borne days. Where is now that robust, if slightly faded, soprano who used on summer evenings to delight the residents of Ladbroke Grove with "Just a Song at Twilight"? Where that maestro whose spirited rendering of "The Light Cavalry Overture" on the musical glasses held every pram spellbound? Where that master of the musical saw whose rendering of "Träumerei" brought tears to every housemaid's eye?

The barrel organists would appear to have followed their monkeys into oblivion and even the Salvation Army seems thinner on ground and more shortwinded than of yore. I am therefore delighted to welcome the re-emergence of the street vocalists; their voices may not always be sufficiently powerful and their political views are, to me, frequently unsympathetic. Nevertheless, better far an occasional discord than the unpunctuated monotony of Concorde.

Your obedient servant,
OSBERT LANCASTER

JEKYLL OUT OF HIDING

28 November 1980

SIR, MR ROGER LANCELYN Green (25 November) asks whether it is known how Robert Louis Stevenson intended the name of Dr Jekyll should be pronounced. Fortunately a reporter from the *San Francisco Examiner*, who interviewed Stevenson in his hotel bedroom in San Francisco on 7 June 1888, asked him that very question:

"There has been considerable discussion, Mr Stevenson, as to the pronunciation of Dr Jekyll's name. Which do you consider to be correct?"

Stevenson (described as propped up in bed "wearing a white woollen nightdress and a tired look") replied: "By all means let the name be pronounced as though it spelt 'Jee-kill', not 'Jek-ill'. Jekyll is a very good family name in England, and over there it is pronounced in the manner stated.

Yours faithfully,
ERNEST MEHEW

BEATING INFLATION KEY
TO RECOVERY

4 April 1981

Sir, It should surprise no one that the lost generation of British economists who had succumbed to the teaching of Lord Keynes should form a panicky mob when a reversal of the policies they had inspired reveals the damage they have done. They significantly can only refer to, but cannot specify, the "other methods" by which their professed aim can be achieved.[1]

Following their advice has induced a structure of employment that can be maintained only by accelerating inflation but will collapse only when it becomes a gallop and destroys any possibility of a rational use of resources. Nobody has ever claimed that so long as it is necessary to reduce inflation to get out of this vicious circle the effect can be anything but to destroy the particular employments created by past inflation.

Only after inflation has been brought to a full stop can the market be expected to guide workers to jobs which can be maintained without accelerating inflation. All those who plead for "mild" inflation and oppose "too much" inflation are merely preparing the ground for a later depression.

If the present Government, I don't believe its head, can be blamed for anything it is for going too slowly about the job. As I have stressed more than once in these pages, even a very high unemployment will be borne for a short period if it leads in a few months to a condition of monetary stability in which a new recovery can start, in the course of which workers are drawn into employment that will continue without new inflation. All employment which can be maintained only by (even moderate) inflation is a waste of resources for which we shall have to pay later by renewed growth of unemployment.

Lest the readers be unduly impressed by the sheer numbers of the signers of the statement I may perhaps add that, so far as I can see, less than a quarter of the economists who are Fellows of the British Academy have signed that statement.

F. A HAYEK
Professor F. A. Hayek

[1] Hayek, whose theories were seen as a key influence on Margaret Thatcher's economic policies, was responding to a letter signed by 364 economists which criticised those.

WEST INDIANS IN SCHOOL

27 June 1981

SIR, WEST INDIAN KIDS fail to do well in school. First, lack of discipline all over the place; at an early age they are all taught in school that parents are too strict; they had Victorian upbringing (although Victoria died 22/1/01); parents do not understand them.

The biggest culprits are the welfare officers who leave little white babies to be battered to death but can't wait to take black kids from their home to put them with nice white aunties and uncles, where they are allowed to run wild in most cases. They can't relate to new environment, but worst of all there comes 18th birthday, no more artificial love and affection, so they are thrown in at the deep end. The few misfits glamorize their position.

So parents fail to do their duties for fear of their children being taken away from them. So the young darlings play up and blackmail parents into giving in (if not they'll tell Miss or Sir and they'll call the Welfare) or run away and lie on parents and the court will be told Topsy or Sambo needs love and affection as the blacks are too illiterate to provide same.

Leave blacks alone and children will come OK. Let them realize there is nowhere to run. They must have discipline.

As for Asians, most were not born here. Wait for the next generation before you pass judgement. Our kids have the same 4lbs of grey and white matter in the hollow of the skull so let them use it. The whites are afraid, they also look towards USA too much. A lot of the teachers do not seem to know much themselves.

Respectfully yours,
S. BEST
(West Indian parent)

WORLD SERVICE

1 July 1981

SIR, AT A MOMENT when, thanks to the failure of diplomacy, we are spending £33.7m a *day* (and rising) on defence, and wondering whether we are getting value, the Foreign Office is aiming to save £3m a *year* by cutting BBC foreign language broadcasts to three of the most important unaligned countries of the world: Burma, Somalia and Brazil. At a saving of £10,000, which is a fraction of the cost of keeping a very average ambassador in the style to which he is not accustomed, they are also disconnecting Malta.

By what conceivable right? Are we to believe it is not worth one tenth of our daily defence expenditure to be revered as the distributors of sober, accurate and impartial news to unaligned countries who are otherwise without it?

Does the Foreign Office itself believe that the pulp distributed by its information services and spokesmen commands a particle of the same respect, let alone the same audience? Have we forgotten that two years ago the Foreign Office ordered cuts in the Turkish broadcasts, only to come running back a year later, asking for them to be expanded?

The BBC's foreign language broadcasts achieve something which goes far beyond the capacity of any foreign office. They enter the homes of thousands of ordinary people. They are taken to their hearts. They inform and educate. They set standards of objectivity. They inspire gratitude and even, now and then, actual love, as any traveller to those regions can establish for himself.

Really, it is obscene to imagine that the Foreign Office, whose emissaries have scant contact, at best, with the ordinary people of the countries to which they are accredited, should presume to sit in judgement over our most effective, popular and trusted spokesman.

If Mrs Thatcher is looking to bring reason to bureaucracy, let her do it here, and sharply. Better to shed an embassy or two, and slim a few more, than sack our real ambassadors.

Yours faithfully,
JOHN LE CARRÉ

THE ROYAL WEDDING

29 July 1981

SIR, I WOULD LIKE to put on record, in *The Times* of July 29, 1981, one citizen's sense of revulsion and foreboding at the ostentation, the extravagance and the sycophancy surrounding today's wedding of the heir to the British throne.

Yours faithfully,
JAN MORRIS

◆

BABES AND SUCKLINGS

11 August 1981

SIR, READING TODAY'S article (4 August) on breast feeding in Oxford reminds me, not of my Oxford days, when such problems did not arise, but of finding myself on Singapore docks queueing for one of the last boats out before the Japanese arrived.

The scorching tropical sun was beating down, and occasional bombs, and with my baby desperately needing a feed, I poked my head into a tent full of British "other ranks" and explained my need.

"Come in, love," they all chorused, "we're all married men in here." (They all looked about 18 to me then!)

I was offered an upturned packing case to sit on and thereafter completely ignored. How has everyone become so much more "sensitive" in the last 40 years?

Yours faithfully,
SYLVIA SHEPHARD

IN THE STEPS OF HANNIBAL

27 August 1981

Sir, Two weeks ago, on August 8, your third leading article concerned itself with the crossing of the Alps in 218 BC by Hannibal and his army with its 37 elephants; this was occasioned by the photograph two days before on your back page of Mina, an elephant, waiting at Dover before crossing the Channel to make her own crossing of the Alps; after taking 33 hours to get through the pass known as the Col du Clapier, she and her entourage reached Sousa in Italy on Tuesday 11th.

"Proof for Hannibal" is the sub-title of the news paragraph (August 12), but does anyone require proof that Hannibal brought his elephants across the Alps? Has anyone doubted it since 218 BC? Yet we are told that Mina's reconnaissance journey is "the culmination of eight years of research by two groups", and that "a definitive expedition will be mounted next year with six mountain elephants from Nepal".

The historical questions about Hannibal's journey are: by what route did he go from the river Rhône to the Alps, and through which Alpine pass did he march. Sir Gavin de Beer in his book *Alps and Elephants*, published in 1955, thought he had proved scientifically and irrefutably that Hannibal used the Col de la Traversette, and the French authorities thereupon called it the "Route d'Hannibal". Since 1955, however, opinion among historians has swung back to one of the Mont Cenis group of passes further north, which indeed Napoleon had thought the most likely. Mina's Col du Clapier is perhaps the most favoured of these.

If for Hannibalic reasons elephants are to be led across the Alps, then they might at least be the correct sort of elephant. Every schoolboy knows that African elephants (*Loxodonta africana*), the ones with the huge ears, are bigger than Indian elephants (*Elephas maximus*), but Greek and Roman writers all say the opposite. This is because the African elephant of antiquity was not our big-eared animal, the elephant of the African bush which may indeed never have been seen in the Mediterranean area; the African war elephant of antiquity was a different animal, the forest elephant (*Loxodonta africana cyclotis*), a sub-species which derives its scientific name, *cyclotis*, from its comparatively small round ears and its name "forest" from the fact that nowadays it is found chiefly in the forests of the River Congo.

In classical times these elephants were widespread over north Africa from Eritrea, through the Ethiopian mountains, across the Sahara and into the north African coastal regions and the Atlas mountains. The Ptolemies of Egypt got most, if not all, of their war elephants from Eritrea; the Carthaginians got theirs from the Atlas area and the lands along the north African coast. In 1947 it was estimated that there were about 100 of these animals still living in the mountains of Mauretania. A good stuffed specimen of *cyclotis* is in the Kensington Natural History Museum, but the Regent's Park Zoo has no specimen and, it seems, never has had. In 1970 the National Zoo in Washington DC had a specimen, a most attractive beast with its distinctively rounded ears. It was considerably hairier than either its larger Indian and much larger African cousins with whom it was housed. The African forest elephant seldom exceeds 7ft at the shoulder, the Indian elephant stands up to 10ft and more, while the African bush elephant, old Big Ears, grows up to 12ft and more, the huge specimen in the Smithsonian Institute in Washington measuring just under 14ft at the shoulder.

I am not sure that next year's expedition with the six Nepalese elephants deserves to be called "the Kon Tiki approach to an historical question". I hope they and their human companions will enjoy their trip, but the contemporary question to put to them is: "Is your journey really necessary?"

Yours faithfully,
DOUGLAS GRAHAM

Replied on 4 September 1981

SIR, THIS SUMMER" s experiment of taking an elephant on Hannibal's supposed route across the Alps, discussed in your third leading article on August 8 and in the Reverend D. L. Graham's letter to you (August 27), is not the first recent one.

About twenty years ago a party of young graduates took an elephant for the same purpose via the Col du Clapier pass. One of them, John Hoyte, wrote a book about it, *Trunk Road for Hannibal*, published in 1960 by Geoffrey Bles Ltd.

Yours faithfully,
C. Z. PURCELL

SIR, COULD I MAKE a small negative contribution to the "Hannibal-and-his-elephants" discussion (leading article, August 8)? It is, I suggest, interesting since it reflects on Sir Gavin de Beer's theories.

As your correspondent on Wednesday (August 27) wrote, Sir Gavin's first choice was the Col de la Traversette. But in his second book on the subject he added another possibility, the Col de Mary. I walked over this pass in the autumn of 1975 (with donkeys, not elephants) and became convinced that Sir Gavin had never done the same. If he had he would certainly have eliminated it, for it largely fails to comply with the rules for success as he himself describes them.

These, as all who have played the game will know, are to discover in the chosen pass a number of specific features which match Polybius's (and if possible Livy's) account of the crossing. Certainly there was a rock formation at the entrance to the Col de Mary where Hannibal could have rallied his advance-guard during the Second Battle of the Alps, but no place for him to assemble them beyond the summit and encourage them with an extensive view of the plain of Piedmont below, no rocks on the descent which would have needed splitting with fire and vinegar, and above all virtually none of last year's impacted snow, on which the Carthaginians and their baggage animals, falling through the new snow, could have lost their footing and slithered into gorges below.

On the climate of 217 BC Sir Gavin was original and persuasive, but in other ways I suggest unreliable.

Yours,
THOMAS HINDE

SIR, IN 1911 MY LATE father, Professor of Military History at All Souls College, Oxford, published a detailed essay on his decision that Hannibal crossed the Alps over the Col du Clapier (*Hannibal's March:* Oxford, Clarendon Press). He came to that view after testing the many other possibilities put forward over the years and studying the accounts of Polybius and Livy on the sites.

All this was to the great advantage of his children, who spent happy school holidays in the French Alps, walking and climbing, unwittingly assimilating both history and geography at first hand.

Yours faithfully,
VICTORIA SPENSER WILKINSON

Sɪʀ, Fᴜʀᴛʜᴇʀ ᴛᴏ ʏᴏᴜʀ article by Frances Gibb on our expedition (August 28) and your correspondents to *The Times* on September 4 and 5, I should like to supply you with further information to clarify the record[1].

Mr Thomas Hinde, whose most interesting book, *The Great Donkey Walk*, includes his crossing of the Alps with donkeys, mentions that Sir Gavin de Beer's first choice was Col de la Traversette. Of the two passes favoured by Sir Gavin I would agree with Mr Hinde that Col de Mary is most unlikely.

There are other cols in the area, for example, Col de Malaure, which our expedition have investigated over the years and which fit with Polybius's description fairly well, but these have changed in many ways since Hannibal's time.

At least three, including la Traversette, have been considerably damaged by being blown up for political reasons on more than one occasion during the last 250 years. This makes a serious investigation of the Italian descent and also the views from the top rather difficult, particularly as part of the top has disappeared. Our researches, started eight years ago, led to our taking an elephant across five passes last month: Col de Clapier, Col de Petit Mont Cenis, Col de Grand Mont Cenis, Col de Mont Genevre and the French side only of Col de la Traversette. We consider that one of these passes must have been used by Hannibal, but we have very large quantities of information on other sections of the route which influence which pass is possible as a crossing point. These have still to be analysed fully before we make our final decision as to which route Hannibal really took. The exercise this summer was mainly a feasibility study and to field test our radio-telemetry equipment.

Your second correspondent, of September 5, refers to John Hoyte's book, *Trunk Road for Hannibal*. We are well aware of this book, in which John Hoyte categorically states that he failed to cross Col de Clapier with an elephant and went over the Mont Cenis down to Italy to Suza, where he had an enormous party and was made most welcome. Nevertheless, stonemasons carved an elephant on the Italian side of Col de Clapier even though Hoyte's elephant never reached that point. It is therefore considerably to the credit of our team, despite previous attempts by others, that we did succeed in crossing Col de Clapier from the French side and down the Italian side in 9¾ hours, absolutely according to plan and without incident.

I hope this clarifies the facts that your correspondents queried.

Yours faithfully,
W. F. ZEUNER

[1] Mr Zeuner was the leader of the "Hannibal Expedition"

SWAN AND EDGAR

30 October 1981

Sɪʀ, Tʜᴇ ꜰᴏʀᴛʜᴄᴏᴍɪɴɢ demise of that famous Piccadilly store brings to mind an incident at New Delhi in the War.

Two new swans had arrived to grace one of the Viceregal ornamental ponds. Lord Wavell was asked to name them. Members of his personal staff stood silent as the well-stocked mind of the scholar-statesman was applied to the problem.

Which pair of names would be produced from classical history or legend or indeed from other men's flowers? The Viceroy broke the silence. "Call them Swan and Edgar", he said.

Yours faithfully,
MICHAEL CHARLESWORTH

———◆———

END OF THE PEER SHOW

29 January 1982

Sɪʀ, Iᴛ sᴛᴀʀᴛᴇᴅ ᴏꜰꜰ well. Only a few months after I succeeded to my father's title, I handed over my shiny new passport — in which the prefix "The Right Honourable", was written out in full — to the receptionist at the Slon Hotel, Ljubljana, and was duly inscribed, in his register as the one thing I had always wanted to be: Mr Right.

Since then, however, I have gone steadily downhill. There was a bad moment some years ago when another receptionist, ashen-faced, handed me a sinister-looking envelope on which I was addressed as The Vice Count; but even then the depths were not yet, plumbed. The ultimate – I hope — humiliation came only quite recently, when I received a missive addressed to me in the style according to which now sign myself — as.

Your obedient servant, The Discount Norwich,
JOHN JULIUS NORWICH
Viscount Norwich

ALL MY EYE

13 February 1982

SIR, THE DEATH OF John Hay Whitney, whose obituary you publish today (February 9), enables me to relieve my conscience of a burden it has been carrying for almost two decades, and I would be grateful if you would allow me, in your columns, to make open confession — so good, they say, for the soul.

Not long after, in 1961, Whitney bought the *New York Herald Tribune*, I was visiting that city and having lunch with a friend who worked on the paper. I called at his office to pick him up, and as we had some time in hand, he offered to show me round the building. Eventually we got to the executive floor (if you think you have a posh executive floor at *The Times*, and indeed posh executives, you should have seen the ones at the *Trib*) and my friend, with the insouciance of a man who knows the back way in to Fort Knox, ushered me into Whitney's office (the boss was out to lunch, you see).

I sank up to my collar in the carpet, and eventually, hacking my way through the undergrowth, came to a desk about the size of Victoria Station. On it there was nothing but a blotter-pad, some tastefully-arranged pencils, and a green eyeshade.

Now you and I know, of course, that newspapermen do not wear green eyeshades except in bad films; presumably, however, nobody had told Mr Whitney this (well, *you* wouldn't tell Mr Murdoch if his shirt was hanging out, would you?), and there the thing was. It was an exceptionally up-market green eyeshade, I may say, made out of some very firm Perspex-type plastic, and with a beautiful padded strip round the top to avoid chafing the boss's forehead or temples.

The ink blushes red in my pen as I write the words, but write them I must. Sir, madness swept over me, the high principles by which I had always endeavoured to guide my life vanished in an instant, and Belial had me in his grip. *I determined to steal John Hay Whitney's green eyeshade.* With the last vestiges of decency that remained to me, I bade my friend turn his back, so that he could truthfully say, when the uproar started, that he had seen nothing untoward take place. I then tucked the green eyeshade under my jackets, and we went to lunch.

Ever since, the guilt of that crime has dogged me, day and night. But I must expiate it at last, if only because Whitney may even now be explaining to his Maker that he ought to be let off a good deal of Purgatory because his life had been soured by the theft of his green eyeshade, and that his Maker ought to be going after the villain who had nicked it instead of him.

I feel better already. I have to add, though, that when I left the paper on which we then both worked, I bequeathed the green eyeshade of John Hay Whitney to Katharine Whitehorn. As far as I know, she has never lost a moment's sleep over her role as an accessory after the fact. But that is her problem now.

My best wishes to you all down there. I bet Mr Murdoch doesn't wear a green eyeshade. Ta-ta for now.

BERNARD LEVIN

———◆———

PLASTIC SURGEON'S HUNGRY ALLIES

23 March 1982

SIR, YOUR RECENT news item on leeches (17 March) interests me because I have been using these little creatures in my practice of plastic surgery for 30 years.

The bugbear of skin flaps is that blood stagnates in them and destroys them. The leech, with his two-fold skills, combats this, first of all by sucking out the sluggish blood, and secondarily by injecting an anti-clotting agent called hyalurodinase into the wound. This means that the wound made by his bite will still drip blood perhaps two days later. All of this helps the plastic surgeon very considerably.

Reasonably, therefore, one must be kind to leeches. They don't come from Hungary, as your informant suggests; they come from Africa. Don't you remember Humphrey Bogart climbing back into the *African Queen* with his back covered with leeches? Therefore they must be kept warm. We keep our leeches in a warm cupboard and periodically they are taken into the sunshine.

Long ago I knew a pharmacist who felt very keenly about his leeches. He would roll up his sleeve and feed them off his arm as a special treat. I remember, still, watching the sensual peristaltic movements of these gleaming dark-green bodies as they engorged themselves, it would seem in a sort of haemorrhagic orgasm.

You have to be very careful with leeches, because each end is very alike. When you want a leech to bite you must present the right end. They like to sit on their bottoms and bite with their mouths. If, through anatomical ignorance, you try to reverse the process you will end up with a resentful, sullen and dispirited leech.

My ward sister starts them off with milk or jam. She tells me that a little jam on the skin will start them off with enthusiasm, and many a skin flap in peril has been saved by these small, little-known simple creatures.

Yours faithfully,
D. DENCER

THE FLYING SCOTSMAN

22 April 1982

SIR, MAY I THROUGH your columns draw to the attention of your readers the impending end that is planned for a 120-year-old British institution?

Apart from a short period in 1917, at 10 o'clock on each weekday morning since June, 1862, the Flying Scotsman has pulled out of King's Cross for Scotland. It is not overstating matters to claim that this is one of the most hallowed of all remaining historical traditions in the field of British transport.

From next June it is proposed to run the 10.00 train from King's Cross to Aberdeen with the title The Aberdonian; the Flying Scotsman leaving at the historically obscure time of 10.35 and running to Edinburgh.

On the face of it, it may appear wholly logical to confer the name Aberdonian on an Aberdeen train. However the Flying Scotsman is, by tradition, a service that terminated in the granite city and is the train that has always left King's Cross at 10 o'clock. To run it at any other time is unthinkable — indeed a suitable analogy would be a proposal to rename Big Ben as the national time-centre.

We are by nature a conservative people. We have the good fortune to be steeped in the most colourful history imaginable. The rescheduling of the Flying Scotsman is a subtle but significant erosion of our heritage.

The Flying Scotsman has always left King's Cross at 10.00. Let it be so for the future.

Yours faithfully,
W. S. BECKET

NOT TENNIS

26 June 1982

SIR, A STORY IS TOLD of an incident in a match when Don Budge was playing Gottfried von Cramm. Budge questioned a line decision which he felt had been wrongly given in his favour.

After the match Gottfried took him to task. "That was very unsporting of you," he told Don.

"But Gottfried," replied Don, "I was questioning a decision given in my favour!"

"I know," replied Gottfried. "But think how you embarrassed the linesman."

Yours faithfully,
BUNNY AUSTIN

In the mid-1930s, Gottfried von Cramm twice won the French Championship and three times reached the final of the Gentlemens' Singles at Wimbledon.
He refused to be a tool of Nazi propaganda and in 1938 was arrested and imprisoned for having had a homosexual relationship. The American champion Don Budge was among those who wrote to Hitler in protest.

LESSONS OF THE FALKLANDS WAR

29 June 1982

SIR, YOUR LEADING ARTICLE on defence policy today (June 21) brilliantly expresses the neo-imperial mood evoked in many British people by the courage, professionalism and ultimate success of our Falklands task force, but it would have done better to have deflated this mood instead. For the Falklands operation has altered nothing in terms of Britain's present and likely future place in the world or her real defence dilemmas.

It does not alter the fact that our GNP is only four times that of Switzerland or about half that of Western Germany. It does not alter the fact that the likely rate of increase in GNP over the next decade will be significantly less than the increase in the real cost of weaponry; and that therefore we face the prospect of repeated defence reviews, each cutting the Armed Forces in one way or another, and each demanding that choices have to be made as to priorities between the three Services.

The lesson of the Falklands crisis is not that we need a bluewater surface fleet in case similar residual bits of pink on the map come under attack, but that we should bring our foreign policy into congruence with our defence policy and shed such unprofitable bits of pink in good time.

The real guilty men of the crisis are the MPs of both parties who, in the past, blocked possible deals with the Argentine with emotional cries of "sell-out" without apparently reckoning the possible cost of defending the Falklands against the value of the islands to the United Kingdom.

Can it now be really argued that a capability to do another Falklands somewhere in the wide oceans is more important to our security of this country than the preservation of Western Europe, our own outer rampart and our greatest market? Are we really to return to the beguiling fallacies of Basil Liddell Hart and Neville Chamberlain in the 1930s to the effect that the defence of Western Europe was a matter primarily for Europeans, with only a "limited liability" land-war contribution from us? Have you, Sir, pondered the impact on less resolute members of NATO of a withdrawal of a major portion of BAOR back to the United Kingdom and the follow-on consequences for the cohesion and effectiveness of the whole Alliance?

In conclusion, I would argue more broadly that our besetting national failing since 1945 has been world-role nostalgia and reluctance to confront the realities of our decline. It seemed in recent years that the penny was at last beginning to drop. I now fear that, thanks to the Falklands victory, it may finish

Britannia-side uppermost, with disastrous consequences for our national sense of realism.

Yours faithfully,
CORRELLI BARNETT

SINISTER ORIENTALS

22 July 1982

SIR, LEFT-HANDERS ARE always a nuisance at a Chinese banquet. The most serious problem arises when precious superior sharks-fin is served since this must be most delicately brought up to the mouth with one's chopsticks and when they are left-handers their left-hand neighbours are invariably impeded in their intake.

This was the sole reason why my great-grandmother and grandmother never sat anyone important to the left of my brother, who is left-handed. Indeed, Chinese of their generation thought left-handers were improperly brought up and should be frowned upon.

My brother was perpetually instructed to change over to his right hand. He now unhelpably does everything with his left hand but writes with his right hand — in, I think, a most dreadful handwriting. He admits it, too, but consoles himself with the fact that when writing Chinese he doesn't get ink on his hand, since we write from right to left.

Yours faithfully,
DAVID TANG

The Hong Kong entrepreneur David Tang was knighted in 2008, and died in 2017

QUESTIONS ON FALKLANDS THANKSGIVING

26 July 1982

Sir, Most of your readers will understand how eager David Watt must have been to assert that "the Falkland spirit is on the wane" (23 July). For in common with the majority of intellectuals and established figures of his generation — with the honourable, and significant exception of yourself, Sir — he has been implacably opposed to the whole "adventure" since its inception. First openly "… these paltry Islands" then, as the operation proceeded successfully, by slight and innuendo.

Let us assume that this attitude originates in conviction rather than malice; in the fact that during the last 40 years no British government has ever felt able to take major foreign policy initiatives, still less military action, without consultation and deferral to other nations, and this has become the accepted norm. And that any assertion of the national will has certain non-specific, but undesirable moral overtones.

I suggest that this argument is completely inverted. Far from being on the wane, the Falkland spirit — by which I understand a quiet pride, disseminated at all levels in society (outside the Athenaeum) in our country's proven ability to assert its independence, to rescue its own nationals, and to shed blood through the skills and valour of its servicemen in defence of the principles to which the West is committed — not only flourishes but is wholly beneficial.

It is this background which allows an amused toleration of the various silly-season diversions which Mr Watt identifies, and restrains too hysterical a reaction to the outrages.

But had our nerve failed over the Falklands, the Task Force been recalled and the Islanders delivered, under various pretences, to Argentine rule, then everything that has happened since would be portrayed as still further indicators of decadence. A corrupt and incompetent police force; the Queen herself at risk; the intelligence services still further disconcerted; flagrant and devastating acts of terrorism in the centre of London.

It is not difficult to draft the alternative text of an article by Mr Watt. Instead of gloating over the "waning" of the Falkland spirit, he would be cautioning us against "extremist solutions" to deal with these various maladies.

As it is, the dignity and self-confidence which that great victory generated should and do restrain us from excesses in dealing with our own domestic irritants.

I am, Sir, your obedient servant,
ALAN CLARK

FONS ET ORIGO

3 August 1982

SIR, I AM APPALLED BY the news that St Barnabas, Pimlico, is to become redundant.

Architecturally it is a jewel of a church, not least the Comper Lady Chapel. And historically it is central to the history of the Church of England in the nineteenth century: riots, Bennet, the Vicar in a *Punch* cartoon, Lord Shaftesbury attacking it in pious evangelical horror and, during the Second World War, Winston Churchill attending the church for the baptism of his Sandys grandchild. It was from its vicarage that the *English Hymnal* was produced and it was always a place of devout prayer.

The church needs to continue as a living focus of love — God's love and ours for him. And it is in the centre of literally hundreds of working-class flats whose inhabitants are the congregation.

Yours faithfully,
JOHN BETJEMAN

GRACE KELLY LEGACY

17 September 1982

Sir, The British people would seem to have paid their own warm tribute to the late Princess Grace of Monaco over the last 20 years or so in a way that may not be immediately obvious.

While she was still Grace Kelly she appeared as Tracy Samantha Lord in the film *High Society*, released in 1956. Until that film appeared Tracy was almost unknown as a first name in Britain, but it immediately began to be used in great numbers. Samantha was not such an immediate success, but it came into general use at the beginning of the 1960s and has also been intensively used since.

Meanwhile, Kelly appeared as a first name in 1958 and quickly multiplied. The latest available figures, based on first name usage by the Smiths in England and Wales, show that Kelly is currently the fourth most popular name for girls. Tracy and Samantha, though they have clearly passed their peak, are still in the top 30.

There have been such films as *Gone with the Wind* which have had a major influence on first name habits, and individuals such as Shirley Temple and Gary Cooper who have caused their own names to become highly fashionable. But Grace Kelly's impact in her last film seems to have been truly remarkable.

Yours faithfully,
LESLIE DUNKLING
General Secretary of the Names Society

"FOR THE USE OF"

15 October 1982

Sɪʀ, PHS's ᴍᴇɴᴛɪᴏɴ (October 5) of today's married quarters being equipped with garden fork but no rake, ironing board but no iron, and so on reminds me of 1940, when as a newly-commissioned officer, I was intrigued to find that in our makeshift accommodation my colleagues and I would be credited "Field Allowance" of 2s. daily by the Paymaster *if* the Quartermaster was unable to supply us with the officially prescribed essentials of furnishing, viz,

> One coalscuttle (officer's), One poker (soldier's),
> One chair (Windsor or Fold-flat), One inventory board.

As we were accommodated outdoors in bell tents, the likely usefulness of the first two items was as baffling as the apparent class distinction between them. Fortunately for us, however, they were in short supply and so we got our 2s. daily to compensate. However, the Quartermaster was able to provide the chair — thus saving himself the ignominy of issuing an inventory board with nothing listed upon it except itself.

Yours faithfully,
R. G. ROBINSON

Replied on 21 October 1982

Sɪʀ, Iɴ 1943, ᴡʜᴇɴ I took over the inventory of the RAF Hospital in Reykjavik, I had to sign for one item entitled: "Bedpans, rubber, lunatics for the use of".

Yours faithfully,
ANTHONY RICKARDS

SIR, MR ROBINSON's reflections on the vagaries of the Quartermaster's syntax and vocabulary for his stores nomenclature made me think further about the purpose underlying the rigid rank stratification which differentiates "poker officers steel" from the more mundane "poker soldier".

An even more striking example of the class structure, midway between officer and soldier, and with the implicit suggestion that in some way the description fitted the user, is provided by the time-honoured, but now obsolete, piece of military furniture known as "stool, wooden-headed, sergeant".

Yours faithfully,
J. P. CROWDY

SIR, I WONDER WHETHER Major-General Crowdy knows the full extent of the privileges which rigid stratification confers upon his rank?

In 1957 Middle East Headquarters were good enough to house some of the political staff attached to them. We were "marched in" to quarters in Episkopi. All went well until my wife enquired about the lack of certain fittings.

"Lids?", came the startled reply. "Only major-generals have lids to their loos."

Yours faithfully,
H. K. MATTHEWS

SIR, VOS (FROM WHICH "pokers, soldiers" — letter, November 3 — comes) is the tongue enshrined in the Vocabulary of Ordnance Stores and certain other military and naval epics. It is unique in containing no singular forms. All its nouns are plural in form, though not necessarily in meaning.

It is a spoken as well as a written language. I once observed two highly articulate VOS speakers (both elderly quarter-masters), one of whom was taking over the contents of a cook-house from the other. As each item was read out by the incoming sergeant cook the outgoing one produced it.

Living in Interesting Times

"Skims cooks one", said the first sergeant, and the other held up an implement.

"Come off it, Sergeant Cook", said the incoming quartermaster, "I wasn't born yesterday. You know bloody well that isn't a skims cooks; it's a slices fish."

Yours etc,
JOHN CARSWELL

Replied on 12 November 1982

SIR, PERHAPS ONE OF the simplest yet at the same time most incongruous items in military inventories used always to be found (and I dare say still is) amongst glasses — Port, glasses — wine, etc, was glasses — looking, Officers, for the use of.

I have the honour to be, Sir, Your obedient servant,
A. G. B. WALKER

Replied on 18 November 1982

SIR, UNDER THE RAJ, VOS (Vocabulary of Ordnance Stores), like Shakespeare, had its devotees amongst the Gurkhas and Indians as well as amongst the British. One of its characteristics which they most readily grasped was its almost invariable reversal of the normal order of words.

Thus, when I was a company commander, I could never dissuade my havildar-clerk, when presenting for signature a stores indent including a demand for razor blades of the kind then normally supplied for troops under the brand name Seven O" Clock, from listing the item as "blades, razor, Clock, O' Seven". The demand was always honoured without query.

Yours faithfully,
A. R. ISSERLIS

LITERARY LAPSES

2 November 1982

SIR, YOUR LITERARY EDITOR, in his recent animadversions on the Booker Prize, rightly pointed out that what is celebrated today is all too likely to be forgotten tomorrow. What then remains? I am, Sir, in a position to tell you.

Yesterday I took my children to Madame Tussaud's, where English Literature is represented by just seven figures, three of them members of the same family — the Brontë sisters. The others are Shakespeare, Dickens, Sir Walter Scott and, proving indeed how ludicrously misleading all these twentieth-century prizes are, Barbara Cartland.

Yours truly,
JULIAN GLOAG

BEST-SELLER

8 March 1983

Sir, Mr Philip Howard (Special Report, February 28) is not very well informed about publishing history. He writes of "the vast sales that Graham Greene attracted 40 years ago". In 1943 I could have just qualified for inclusion in a similar list as today's "young novelists" but where were my "vast sales"? I had been in debt to my publishers for nearly 10 years when at last I broke even in 1938 with *Brighton Rock* (the "vast sales" amounted to 8,000 copies at the published price of 7s 6d). As a result my publishers risked an improved first printing of 3,500 copies of *The Power and the Glory* in 1940.

Just as most young writers today, I had to find other sources of income. It was not until 1949, at the age of 45, 20 years after my first published novel, that I was able to rely on my novels alone.

Has very much changed since those days, except perhaps that publishers now have not the courage or perhaps the means to help support a promising young author through the lean years.

Yours truly,
GRAHAM GREENE
Antibes, France

Graham Greene had worked as a sub-editor at *The Times* while writing his earliest novels.

POLO CHICANERY

30 May 1984

SIR, MAJOR LOYD'S MENTION in today's *Times* (May 22) of the ancient Persian word for a polo stick — *chaugan* or *chupaan* — opens an interesting linguistic sequence. When the game spread from the Persian to the Byzantine empire, "to play polo" was hellenized into *tsikanizein* or *tsoukanizein*, and the pologround, which was set up in the Hippodrome at Constantinople became the *Tsoukanisterion*. Anna Comnena records that her father, the Emperor Alexis, a keen player, was laid up for some time after a nasty fall.

Possibly through his Crusader contemporaries, the Greek word stepped into French and English, dropping its sporting context and surviving in either language as *chicane* and chicanery, no doubt from the devious zigzag manoeuvres to which the ponies were put.

For further ramifications we must refer to *Hobson Jobson*, the wonderful late nineteenth-century dictionary of English words of Far Eastern origin.

Your obedient servant,
PATRICK LEIGH FERMOR

THE PRESIDENT'S JOKE

23 August 1984

SIR, MAY A PHILOLOGIST remark that technically Mr Reagan's joke[1] was rather a good one? He extrapolated to a preposterous but logical conclusion from two assumptions both of which are actually false but both of which some people might possibly believe to be true, viz., the standard propaganda parody of himself, which he was parodying, and the competence of one country's legislature to abolish another.

He assumed his hearers would be bright enough to spot these for falsehoods, and so share the joke.

The only people who come with discredit out of the episode are those humourless souls, whether in the Kremlin or in your columns, who treat parody as on a par with serious discourse, and those who confuse nastiness with sacredness, which is about what it amounts to to say nuclear war should not be joked about.

Yours faithfully,
P. R. KITSON

[1] President Reagan had been accidentally recorded joking that "we have signed legislation that would outlaw Russia forever — we begin bombing in five minutes."

MINING RHYMING

27 September 1984

SIR, NOT ODD, SAID God, I'd have you know
It may seem quite easy down below
To keep the Bishops all in tow
Just propping up the Thatcher show;
Up here, you see, there's hell to pay —
She wants to tell ME what to say.

Yours faithfully,
MICHAEL FOOT
Mr Michael Foot, MP

Foot's letter was in response to remarks made by the Bishop of Durham at his enthronement in July 1984.

HP SAUCE

20 October 1984

SIR, AM I ALONE AMONG your readers in deploring the loss of that much loved and most piquant of French primers — the label on the HP sauce bottle?

If unfortunate circumstances decreed that there was nothing else to read at the breakfast table one could always turn to the HP sauce bottle for a little French revision. It will be sadly missed.

Yours faithfully,
J. H. HUNTER

Replied on 25 October 1984

SIR, DR JOHN HUNTER is not alone. There must be many who miss the opportunity to polish up their Franglais by constant study of the description of the virtues of HP sauce.

Perhaps it was omitted from the label after a prolonged but unsuccessful attempt to capture the French market for bottled sauces. This would not be surprising; HP sauce, like most others produced in this country, is admirably suited for Anglo-Saxon cooking, as it disguises rather than enhances the taste of our food.

It is said that a Frenchman, on recovering from his first application of the sauce, studied the bottle intently and opined that it could be more briefly and just as accurately labelled in his language as *une sauce incendiaire*.

Yours faithfully,
H. J. G. RICHARDS

Replied on 25 October 1984

SIR, *Pace* DR JOHN HUNTER, give me the multi-lingual Angostura label at any meal!

Your obedient servant,
J. H. MCGIVERING

Replied on 27 October 1984

SIR, LIKE DR JOHN HUNTER I too regret the passing of the French label on the HP Sauce bottle.

It used to contain the sentence *'elle est absolument pure'* which I used in my French classes to teach my students that "it" in French was just as likely to be "elle" as "il". They never forgot it.

Yours faithfully,
JOHN LOMAS

Replied on 2 November 1984

SIR, IF HP SAUCE is not already regarded universally as a national institution, surely the fact that it merits discussion in the correspondence columns of your famous newspaper finally confers on it this status. Naturally I am delighted because my grandfather was the founder of the company which invented it and my father played a leading role in its introduction, which transformed a fairly prosperous family vinegar brewery into a company of national and international fame.

I am not sure which of the two dreamed up the brilliant idea of a discourse in French on the label, but this was much in character with the inspiration and imagination which accompanied the rest of its launch — the name itself, Houses of Parliament Sauce, shortened to HP (my grandfather's favourite dictum was "condense"); the fact that it was the first thick sauce to be distributed nationally; and sales promotion by, among other things, giving away free miniature bottles of sauce from miniature carts drawn by miniature Shetland ponies or donkeys which toured the streets of all the towns in the UK. The original idea was to use zebras, but this proved impossible!

As possibly the last family contribution to the popularity and prosperity of this national institution, may I be permitted to join your other correspondents in deploring the present label and suggesting that the present proprietors would do themselves a lot of good by reverting to the original label in its entirety.

Yours faithfully,
E. H. MOORE

SIR, I, TOO, REGRET the passing of the French label on the HP sauce bottle. What does this portend? Already the officer and his Indian servant on the Camp coffee bottle have become much smaller, and the last time I bought a bottle of Dr Collis Browne's medicine the testimonials from Whymper and the doctor struggling against cholera in India had disappeared.

Will the lion disappear from the Tate and Lyle syrup tin?

Yours faithfully,
PHYLLIS BIRT

SIR, LET ME ASSURE Miss Phyllis Birt that there is no item on the board agenda to consider the removal of the lion on our syrup tin.

Judges, ch XIV ("Out of the strong came forth sweetness") is of greater antiquity and carries more authority than some of the recent bottle coverings — designed, dare one suggest, to conceal the contents!

Yours faithfully,
COLIN McFIE
Secretary, Tate & Lyle

SIR, I WAS VERY INTERESTED to read the letter from Mr E. H. Moore regarding the origin of the name of HP Sauce, since, when I was researching this name for my book, *Dictionary of Trade Name Origins* (Routledge, 1982), I was informed in a letter from the Group Product Manager (Sauces) of Smedley-HP Foods Ltd that, alas, there was no firm evidence that the initials did actually stand originally for "Houses of Parliament".

Company records show that a Mr Sampson and a Mr Moore (no doubt Mr E. H. Moore's grandfather, whom he mentions) first started to make HP Sauce in Birmingham in the 1870s, having purchased the name from a Mr Garton in Nottingham. The latter was marketing the product then as "Garton's 'HP' Sauce", although there is nothing to indicate why he chose this particular name.

The name itself was first registered in the *Trade Marks Journal* of May 22, 1912, by "Edwin Samson Moore, trading as The Midland Vinegar Company, The Trade Malt Vinegar Company, and as F. G. Garton & Co." The company was then based at Aston Cross, near Birmingham, where it traded as "vinegar brewer and sauce and pickle manufacturer".

Yours faithfully,
ADRIAN ROOM

Replied on 10 November 1984

Sir, Miss Birt should not be too despondent. Proctor's Pinelyptus Pastilles are still being recommended by Mme Sarah Bernhardt, Miss Ellen Terry and Sir Henry Irving.

Yours faithfully,
J. B. POOLE

JUST SO

14 December 1984

SIR, COULD WE HAVE a moratorium on the use of the phrase "they behaved like animals" to describe any especially nasty form of human brutality? Carnivores certainly kill when they need their dinners but do so as quickly as they can. Herbivores just eat vegetation and do not interfere with others.

Do we hear of dolphins torturing other dolphins, gorillas cutting, or biting, bits off other gorillas, elephants inflicting prolonged periods of terror on other elephants, or indeed on any other animal?

Rather should dolphins left to die in nets, gorillas killed in order that their dried heads should be sold to tourists, elephants dying in agony from poisons for the sake of their tusks, exclaim, in condemnation of acts of savagery (should these ever occur) committed by members of their own species: "They behaved like humans".

Yours faithfully,
ELSPETH HUXLEY

Elspeth Huxley's many books about life in Kenya included *The Flame Trees of Thika*, which was adapted for television in 1981.

MRS THATCHER'S HONORARY DEGREE

1 February 1985

SIR, CAN THERE EVER have been such reason to feel ashamed of one of our great institutions?

The world knows that Margaret Thatcher is one of the very finest people who has ever passed through any university. Oxford could and should be justly and immensely proud to honour her as their own. And all credit to those of its leaders who wished to do so in the traditional way.

But what shame on those who have thwarted that wish. Such bigotry is beyond belief. The discourtesy defies description. That so many should so behave for political purposes — men and women who no doubt pride themselves on practising and protecting the freedom to differ — is surely deplorable.

None of this will do our Prime Minister any harm. And she is too big a person to allow the very real personal hurt which she must feel to interrupt her endeavours or colour her approach. But what a terrible reflection it is on the university. What harm it may do to Oxford.

So many of its leaders have shown themselves to be such small people swimming in a pond which seems too big for them. It is as sad as it is anger-making to find that so many of those to whom the achievements and glories of Oxford over the centuries have been entrusted are not up to that trust — and that so many of our young people should be at risk of indoctrination by them.

A sad day indeed for the Oxford of which all of us, of whatever university, or of none, have always been so proud.

Yours etc.,
IAN PERCIVAL

The governing assembly of Oxford University had voted, by a margin of rather more than two to one, to snub Margaret Thatcher by not awarding her the honorary degree customarily conferred on prime ministers. The miners' strike was then in its tenth month and the Government (in which Sir Ian Percival had latterly been Solicitor General) had made cuts to the funding of academic research. Ramsay MacDonald had been similarly rebuffed by Cambridge in 1926 (see page 72).

Living in Interesting Times

SIR, IT IS NEVER EASY to know why people vote. Your remarkable editorial, "Sale of honours" (January 30) suggests that the campaign against giving Mrs Thatcher an honorary degree was got up by "militantly left-wing dons" and "Marxist dons" who gained "more respectable support" from those who object to the Government's policies in higher education.

Your assumption is questionable. The vote was very large and very decisive, 738 to 319. Few Oxford dons are either militant or Marxist (are you joking?); overwhelmingly they are of a conservative disposition, very unlikely to reject either a "customary civility" or a Conservative prime minister; and certainly very few Oxford dons, except leading scientists, have much knowledge of or care for the higher education system outside Oxford. Oxford has been cut the least.

Many of the votes cast must have been from Conservatives wishing to show that they think that she has *uniquely* divided and polarised the country. No one else has so broken from Baldwin's conciliatory tradition except Edward Heath in his brief "Selsdon" phase.

This vote shows once again that some of the most important political divisions are *within* the two main parties, not just between them. You are very sensitive to divisions in the Labour Party, perhaps a bit less so among Conservatives.

Yours sincerely,
BERNARD CRICK

1 February 1985

SIR, WHEN THE BEATLES were given the MBE some members of the order sent their medals back.

Now that Oxford University has devalued its honorary degree by refusing it to one of our greatest prime ministers, will those who have it feel it worth keeping?

Yours faithfully,
JUNE BADENI

LIVE AID

15 July 1985

SIR, THE OUTSTANDING response of the Irish people to the Live Aid appeal (at over £1 per head) is typical of their approach to all famine situations.

When I was Deputy Director of Christian Aid I found that, although our appeals for the famine in Maharasdra and again in the Sahel were only directed at the UK, the response from Southern Ireland was many times greater, *per capita*, than the UK itself.

My own belief is that this amazing generosity stems from their deep seated folk memory of their own "Great Famine" — they feel that they know what famine means.

Yours truly
W. H. O'NEIL

17 July 1985

SIR, THE QUITE EXTRAORDINARY success of the Live Aid concert organised by Bob Geldof must have a profound lesson for the nation's leaders, both political and religious.

It is obvious that young people both need and want something to believe in that is greater and beyond themselves. Their cynicism is well founded. Where is the genuine religious leadership that can offer a self-sacrificing spiritual ideal or a vision like that displayed by Bob Geldof in his concern for suffering humanity?

Why have religious and political leaders so miserably failed to offer the youth of this country something worth while to live for? Religious leaders have been preoccupied with Church membership and theological discussions questioning the existence of God, while political leaders vie with each other to offer greater bribes in the quest for power.

There is probably more latent idealism among young people than ever before. But who is there to raise their sights and to show them a vision of goodness and holiness?

For "without vision, the people grow wild" (AV. "the people perish"), *Proverbs* 29:18.

Your faithfully,
E. GASTWIRTH

UP TO THE MARK

5 March 1986

SIR, HAVE YOU LEFT your own files behind in New Printing House Square? You say today (February 28) that the pound has never been lower in terms of the mark. Look up 1923, when it cost a thousand million marks to send a letter from Düsseldorf to London.

Yours faithfully,
M. R. D. FOOT

———◆———

GENTLE BLOOD

31 March 1988

SIR, I HAVE ALWAYS assumed that anyone who claims to be a gentleman (1) does not make trouble, (2) does not publish private conversations. Lord St John of Fawsley (Diary, March 25) evidently does not make this claim.

I am forced by his remarks to say that his statements are quite wrong. My friends know that I have never made any criticism of the governing body of Peterhouse, with which I have the most friendly relations, although some individuals, who have not hesitated to publish their dislike of me in the press, can hardly complain if I have sometimes commented on them in private conversation.

Yours faithfully,
DACRE of GLANTON

The writer was perhaps better known as Hugh Trevor-Roper, the historian, who had recently had an unhappy spell as Master of Peterhouse, where his attempts at reform had been opposed by a clique of several Fellows. The witty, gossipy former politician Norman St .John-Stevas was subsequently Master of Emmanuel College, Cambridge.

TRIREME TRIALS

22 June 1988

Sɪʀ, Mʀ Wᴀʀʀʏ (Jᴜɴᴇ 20) raised two questions about the reconstructed Greek trireme *Olympias*, the first about the stature of the oar crew to fit the ship and the second about the publication of the trial results.

Mr Warry rightly suggest that modern competitive rowers from northern Europe tend to be large individuals. Their muscular power can be well exploited with the help of sliding seats in racing shells designed for riverine conditions.

In the trireme the attested distance from one oar to the next is only two ancient Athenian cubits (0.888m). Nevertheless, an oar-handle stroke of 0.86m can be achieved if the stature of the rowers is fairly uniform and at about the average for a modern northern European or American population. For this year's trials at Poros the Trireme Trust has recruited such a crew.

Detailed results of the British trials in 1987 will be published shortly. From 1988 onwards experimental research into the performance of the *Olympias* will be co-ordinated by a committee in Greece on which the trust has been kindly invited to be represented.

The results of these trials, conducted by Greek and other crews, including British, will be published by the committee.

The trireme having teased academics and seafaring men for centuries (as your columns once showed), seems now to be seeing the light of practical reality. This light will show that, although she may have been the swiftest oared ship of any size, the speed of 20 knots so flatteringly attributed to her in America should be at least halved.

Yours truly,
JOHN MORRISON
(Chairman, The Trireme Trust)

JOHN COATES
(Naval architect to the trust)

Olympias proved capable of a speed of 9 knots and extensive trials in her suggested that ancient historians had not exaggerated the trireme's capabilities. She is now on display in Athens.

THE BERLIN WALL

16 December 1989

SIR, I FIND IT A PITY *The Times* should publicise the sale of pieces of the Berlin Wall ("A bit of Berlin for Christmas", November 30). The wall is a very symbol of the suffering it has created for the last 28 years. It is a monument to the resilience of both East and West Berliners, not an experiment in capitalist enterprise.

I was in Berlin 28 years ago to report on the erection of the wall and returned this month to report on its "breakdown". I can assure you that a sledgehammer will merely bounce back off the actual wall sections. The wall itself was reinforced with metal and built to withstand cannon fire and tank attacks.

The hundreds of people chipping away at the wall by the Reichstag building, opposite to the Brandenburg Gate, succeed in getting only the smallest of pieces, regardless of the size and weight of their implements. I myself was lent a hefty mountaineer's chisel and after many hard blows managed to take away only a very small chip.

Yours sincerely,
CARLOS A. BOHORQUEZ
European Correspondent, *El Mundo*, Colombia

MODERN TIMES

1990–99

THE ENGLISH PEAR

28 June 1993

SIR, IF FRENCH FLAIR requires the enthusiastic embrace of cigarettes, extra-marital affairs, and the "art" of binge fasting ("French flair v British grunge", June 23), then I would strongly recommend the pear shape of the English woman. Why promote such an ignorant and irresponsible attitude to health? Lung cancer and eating disorders do not constitute "style".

Yours sincerely,
JILL COWEY

SILENT MICE

1 January 1994

SIR, BATS IN THE belfry are an accepted part of church life, but mice in the organ must be unusual.

In the rural church of which I am churchwarden, I was recently dismayed to find that seven of the black notes of the organ had been almost entirely demolished by mice, leaving a mound of shredded ebony over the keyboard. The ivories were untouched.

Assuming that the nutritional value of rather aged ebony is almost nil, I would be fascinated to know the motivation for this strangely selective diet. Is the current trend to mindless violence spreading to the rodent population?

Yours faithfully,
BEVIS BROCK

Replied on 8 January 1994

SIR. MR BEVIS BROCK's fears of an epidemic of mindless violence in the rodent population after damage to a church organ (letter, January 1) are groundless.

I understand that the teeth of rodents continue to grow in the same way as do our fingernails and that the rodents' gnawing of substances of suitable hardness is analogous to humans cutting their nails, serving the same purpose of preventing them from becoming too long.

There is a precedent for mice in the organ, for on the night of December 23, 1818, it was discovered that mice had gnawed through the bellows of the organ in the church of Oberndorf near Salzburg. So that there would be music on Christmas Day the priest, Joseph Mohr, composed a carol which the organist, Franz Gruber, set to music for two voices and a simple children's chorus. This was "Silent Night."

Perhaps Mr Brock could be persuaded to bend his talents to composing a carol using a scale deprived of his seven gnawed black notes.

Yours faithfully,
JOHN CLAYTON

Replied on 8 January 1994

SIR. AS AN ORGAN builder practising in a rural area, I know that mouse damage to church organs is quite common. Mice grown plump on the largess of harvest festival offerings soon become desperate once it has all been cleared away.

One local organ had all the maple stoppers carefully nibbled off the tops of a whole rank of pipes, quite a feat of acrobatics. Unaware of the high lead content, the mice cheerfully gnaw holes in metal pipes. Ebony sharps, as mentioned by Mr Brock, are another treat. One of their favourite tricks is to gnaw holes in the sheepskin of the bellows, invariably where it is impossible to glue a patch.

No doubt science will have some boring explanation for their behaviour. I suspect they have a malicious sense of humour.

Yours,
ROBERT SHAFTOE

Replied on 8 January 1994

SIR, THE MOTIVATION for the "strangely selective diet" of ebony organ keys is more sinister than may be apparent at the keyboard. The mice are practising: they are sharpening their teeth before attacking all the luscious leather parts of the organ hidden from view.

The renowned poverty of church mice is not lack of money but lack of nourishment. Watch out for anything tasty. The candles will be next.

Yours sincerely,
GRAHAM MATTHEWS

Replied on 8 January 1994

SIR, MR BEVIS BROCK's letter reminds me of two instances when I found mice not only eating and sharpening their teeth on working organ pipes, but actually nesting amongst them.

On both occasions, once in West Africa and once in Wiltshire, the nesting material consisted entirely of pages torn from *Hymns Ancient and Modern* (standard version). Bibles (authorised version) were equally available beside both the organs in question, but were left untouched. Not such mindless vandalism?

Yours sincerely,
RICHARD GODFREY

Replied on 8 January 1994

SIR, FOR YEARS MY wife pounded away on the harmonium in a variety of Royal Navy chapels. She remembers with particular poignancy one instrument dating from the early years of the century, which boasted on engraved metal plates that it was equipped with "mouse-proof pedals".

It certainly showed no signs of rodent attack, though it was sadly deficient as a musical instrument.

Yours faithfully,
MURRAY HAYES

Replied on 8 January 1994

SIR, CHURCHWARDEN BROCK's letter is proof positive of the proverbial "back-to-basics" standard of poverty. If reduced to this, church mice are indeed poor.

Mine here, also rural, have more sporting and agricultural tastes — the cork handle of a salmon rod and the plastic rotor guard of a grass trimmer.

Yours faithfully,
GEORGE C. AITKEN

Replied on 8 January 1994

SIR, COULD NOT the mice in question have been looking for a suitable Flat?

Yours faithfully,
R. C. USHER

"DEVILISH" TEMPTATIONS OF THE INTERNET

16 August 1995

SIR, MY RECENT REMARKS about the Internet (report and leading article August 12) were intended to provoke discussion, and have done so. There is a danger, however, that the wave of indignation over what I am thought to have said may distract attention from my real point.

I was not saying that the Internet itself is devilish. It is a powerful piece of technology which, like any other, can be used or abused. Nor was I primarily concerned about the kind of material which might be conveyed through the Internet, though that is a serious problem and indicates the need for some controls.

My concern is with the Internet as a means of communication, which is potentially life-enhancing, but could also dangerously reinforce tendencies towards a self-absorbed individualism.

The main characteristic of the Internet, as I understand it, is that individuals can scour the world for whatever they want. It is the ultimate expression of choice, and it carries no commitment, no permanence of relationship, no necessity for give and take.

This is not to say that genuine relationships and worthwhile discussions cannot emerge from it. But the revealing phrase "surfing the Internet" carries a different message. As an activity it can be entirely free-floating; surfers can create their own little self-chosen individualistic world. Add this to "virtual reality", and the nightmare scenario I painted is not all that far away.

I contrast this with the ancient wisdom which enabled people to grow in moral and spiritual stature through the constraints imposed on them. Of course the constraints, like the prospects of unlimited choice, can be overdone. But there is surely room for serious debate here about the potentially dehumanising effects of an undisciplined information overload.

Why did I call it devilish? I had in mind the third and most alluring of the temptations of Jesus, to view the whole world and make it his own, while denying its true meaning, and essential givenness as God's creation.

Yours faithfully,
JOHN EBOR
Archbishop of York

"DEMON EYES"

30 January 1997

Sir. I read with interest Andrew Pierce's report in your issue of January 24 about the Tory "demon eyes" campaign being described as "one of the most successful in the party's electioneering history". By what criteria was its spellbinding triumph assessed?

It could hardly have been the polls. Nor could it be the reputation and ratings of Mr Blair and Mr Major, given that Mr Blair is ahead on every count, in every region, in every age group and among both sexes.

Nor could it be the state of the parties, given that the Tories are in a state of decay and panic and Labour continues to set a political agenda for change.

Perhaps the Conservatives and those who comment on their posters should remember that their aim is to win the election, not win awards.

Yours faithfully,
ALASTAIR CAMPBELL
Press Secretary to Tony Blair

VICTORY ANTHEM?

22 April 1997

SIR, I SEE THAT Westminster Abbey is singing *Blair in B minor* for Evensong on Saturday, 3 May. Do they know something we don't?

Yours faithfully,
MICHAEL BECKETT

Replied on 30 April 1997

SIR, I AM GLAD THAT the music for *Evensong* on election day is coming along so nicely (letters, April 22, 23, 24 and 28) but I fear I cannot find much in the daily psalms to encourage either Mr Major or Mr Blair. On the contrary, the psalmist on the seventh evening of the month is quite specific: "but the righteous is merciful and liberal" (Psalm xxxvii. 21).

Yours faithfully,
ROY MASSEY
Organist of Hereford Cathedral

Replied on 30 April 1997

SIR, MANY YEARS AGO, when I was at school, the general election day hymn chosen for morning assembly was *Hymns Ancient & Modern* number 738 — *Come, labour on!* The headmaster was thought to have had radical leanings.

The Conservatives won the election on that occasion. So much for dedicated behest. Perhaps someone thought His name was being taken in vain?

Yours sincerely,
HUGH STEPHENSON

SIR, A CLERGYMAN, when asked which party he was going to vote for, replied that a man in his position could not declare his politics.

However, he added, if the Tories win the opening hymn on Sunday will be *Now thank we all our God*: if Labour wins, *O God our help in ages past* and, should the Liberal Democrats win, then it will be *God moves in a mysterious way*.

Yours sincerely,
A. OSBALDISTON
In the event, the theme to Tony Blair's election victory was "Things Can Only Get Better", by D-Ream.

LAURIE LEE REMEMBERED

22 May 1997

SIR, YOUR OBITUARY OF Laurie Lee told the bitter-sweet tale of Laurie going unrecognised in his own village of Slad — "Excuse us, could you tell us where Laurie Lee is buried?"

There was however one occasion on which he was recognised.

As Laurie told us himself at the Chelsea Arts Club one evening: "As I was walking down to the village pub I was approached by a little girl of about 9 or 10 who asked me if I were Laurie Lee. I said that I was, whereupon she said: "Were it you what wrote that poem teacher made us learn by 'eart?" I said with modest pride: "Yes, I expect so." The girl, taking careful and deliberate aim, then kicked me ferociously on both shins before running off as fast as her little legs could carry her."

Yours sincerely,
CHRISTOPHER J. McMANUS

PLEASE MR POSTMAN

15 July 1997

SIR, A LETTER OF MINE you published in January 1986 brought me hundreds of letters. For a few days the postman delivered in sacks.

I had joined in a light-hearted banter you ran about junk mail. I supported the stuff because it brought the postman to me each day as one who was "old, isolated, and alone".

At the time I was old, a lone widower, in the remote Devon countryside. The combination of those three words had a dramatic effect. Kind letters came from all sorts of people from all over the world, although chiefly from southeast England. A high proportion were written by doctors, teachers and children (at the behest no doubt of adults).

Every child in one class of 12-year-olds in the Midlands, encouraged obviously by an imaginative teacher, wrote individually the most charming letters. Many hard-pressed GPs scribbled a few kind words on prescription forms. One lady in Scotland said she made it a rule to write to someone every day before she had breakfast. A child said my letter reminded her that she did not write to her grandparents enough. There were tips from businessmen on useful lucrative occupations. Large numbers of elderly people suggested pen-pal relationships.

To my intense embarrassment someone writing anonymously from France arranged with Fortnum & Mason to send me a parcel of brandy and cigars. The firm refused to disclose the name of my benefactor.

I received no proposals of marriage nor, interestingly, any letters from the clergy. One lady of slight acquaintance wrote to express disappointment that I had not let her know I was lonely. Letters came, mostly anonymously, in decreasing numbers for a couple of years.

Now I am very old, married again, and live in a town. The junk mail comes in greater volumes but I do not have time to look at it.

Yours faithfully,
ALAN LIDDICOAT

Sɪʀ, Pʟᴇᴀꜱᴇ ᴘᴜʙʟɪꜱʜ this letter. I am old, sad and unbearably lonely, and would derive maximum benefit (on all fronts) from an anonymous Fortnum & Mason hamper.

Yours, in anticipation of imminent relief,
ROGER COOKSON

THE DEATH OF DIANA

1 September 1997

Sɪʀ, Aᴛ Sᴀɴ Fʀᴀɴᴄɪꜱᴄᴏ a fortnight ago the immigration officer who checked my passport asked if I was connected with the press. I mumbled that I was, sort of. "In that case," said he, "I want to make a request. Please lay off Diana. The British Royal Family hasn't generally been very popular over here, but we love her, and we hate to see her hassled."

Well I retorted, God knew she often asked for it. He looked at me with sad reproach then, and today I'm sorry I said it.

Yours faithfully,
JAN MORRIS

NEVER SAY DYE

18 September 1997

Sir, You report my former colleague Alan Clark as saying (interview, "History man who refuses to bow to the passage of time" September 13) "Nigel Lawson dyed his hair very early."

I do not know whether anyone nowadays takes the entertaining Mr Clark, of Matrix Churchill fame, seriously; but in case they do let me make it clear that, while I have nothing against hair dye, or even for that matter Mr Clark, I have never in fact dyed my hair in my life.

Yours etc,
LAWSON

———◆———

IN 75 WORDS

30 August 1999

Sir, "Nowhere ... can anyone write 75 words", Simon Jenkins asseverates today. Wrong. Seventy-five words is the ideal length for a book blurb, long enough to say what's inside, short enough to hold passing attention. I well remember the late Poet Laureate and publisher, Cecil Day Lewis, telling me his two favourite literary forms, challenging in their brevity, were the sonnet and the blurb.

Yours,
H. R. F. KEATING

FROM BLAIR TO BREXIT

2000–16

THE MEANING OF DEATH

16 September 2000

SIR, BEING OF A GENERATION for whom grass was for cutting, coke was kept in the coal shed, and someone who was gay was the life and soul of the party, I was relieved to find that, in a certificate of insurance recently received from Lloyds TSB, some things don't change.

Under the heading "Words with special meanings" was the following: "Death means loss of life".

Yours faithfully,
MICHAEL MARTIN

TRAVELLING LIGHT

30 January 2001

SIR, FOUR SUITCASES FOR Posh Spice?

In the 1950s I knew an elderly farmer who embarked on the only holiday of his long lifetime — a trip to the Isle of Man. He stood, in best suit and polished boots, waiting for my father to drive him to the railway station.

"Where is your suitcase?" asked my father. The old man produced a spare shirt collar from his pocket. "Nay, lad," he said, "I'm only going for the week."

Yours faithfully,
J. A. MELLIN

PERFECT PORRIDGE

20 January 2001

Sir, Like Bruce Miller (Weekend, January 13) my family has a porridge recipe: boil 1 jug (1.14l) water, add 1 mug (227g) oatmeal and 1 teaspoon (5ml) sea salt, return to boil, stir, cover, leave for 1 hour. Transfer to casserole; heat in oven for 4 hours.

Yours faithfully,
ANTHONY PARSONS

Replied on 31 January 2001

Sir, Two recipes have appeared in your columns recently for the making of porridge. What the end product of these can be like I do not know, but it is certainly not Scottish porridge.

This is how you make the real thing, as used over the years — in my own case nearly a century.

First, throw away your measures, cups and litres and what not. Porridge-making is an art, not a science. All you need is boiling water, a bowl of oatmeal, a little salt and your own common sense, plus a little experience.

Take a handful of meal and trickle it slowly into the pot, stirring with the spurkle all the time, to prevent knotting. After a few minutes, the meal all in and the porridge beginning to thicken, stir in a little salt and set aside to simmer for five to ten minutes, giving a stir now and again. Pour into the plates.

There is a sensuous pleasure in the making of porridge — the delightful aroma from the pot as the boiling water begins to take hold of the meal, the pouring into the plates, which fills the room with scent of warm meal.

The proper way to sup porridge is to have alongside the plate a bowl of top of the milk or cream — a spoonful of porridge, then a dip in the bowl.

I am, Sir, yours,
W. G. McPHERSON

Replied on 2 February 2001

Sir, When I was a youngster in Port Ellen, Islay, my piping teacher, Alastair Logan, would stir his porridge atop his peat-fired oven, all the time listening intently to whatever piobaireachd I was practising. After the porridge was made he put it in the oven and added some more peat to keep it warm till morning.

Also put into the oven were his large woollen socks, which, so far as I could make out, were never washed. He worked at the Lagavulin distillery and the socks gave off a pleasant odour which I attributed to a combination of heather and Islay malt.

Sincerely,
CALUM CARMICHAEL

Replied on 2 February 2001

Sir, Always eager to improve my own porridge technique (oatmeal, water, salt, leave overnight then boil while stirring), I note that Dr Anthony Parsons recommends one hour standing time followed by four hours in the oven.

Does this mean that a) Dr Parsons eats his porridge at lunchtime, b) he has staff to rise in the middle of the night to prepare it for him, or c) he uses the traditional technique of making the porridge in bulk and pouring it into a drawer, from which portions can be cut and reheated as and when needed?

Yours faithfully,
COLIN MacNEILL

Replied on 2 February 2001

Sir, Prepare porridge how one may, it can still be enhanced, as a family dish, by a treacle well. For this, each breakfaster, while remaining seated, should raise a fully charged spoonful of golden syrup as high as possible above his or her plate, and try to ensure that the descending globule of syrup penetrates the exact centre of the porridge. This can be surprisingly difficult, and a poor aim may be penalised.

From Blair to Brexit

Over-enthusiastic parents have been known to show off by standing on their chairs, but this should be discouraged.

Yours faithfully,
DAVID SERPELL

Replied on 6 February 2001

Sir, My wife, who is English, makes excellent porridge from a recipe culled from *The Scotsman* some 40 years ago.

The whole principle of porridge-making is to continue to add pinches of fresh meal as the porridge boils, so that when the dish is ready you will have a complete gamut of textures from fully boiled to almost raw meal. The moment when the salt is added is also important, for the first and bulkiest portion of the meal should have swelled and burst before this happens.

Tradition prescribes a birchwood bowl with a horn spoon, and that they (porridge to me is always a plural noun) should be eaten standing up.

I submit this letter with some diffidence, first because I make porridge in the microwave with porridge oats, and second because my wife says I might as well save my breath to cool my porridge.

Yours faithfully,
ROBERT SANDERS

Replied on 6 February 2001

Sir, The recent correspondence on the making of perfect porridge has been a revelation for this Sassenach. For me, however, perfection lies in equal measures of porridge oats, milk and water, sweetened to taste and microwaved in a Pyrex basin until boiling causes the mixture to rise. At this stage the lily can be gilded by the addition of slices of peach.

Eat from the basin (and drink from the measure, a standard cup is ideal) for economy of washing up. At least this part should appeal to the Scot.

Yours sincerely,
JOHN FARMAN

Replied on 8 February 2001

SIR, FOR THOSE WITHOUT benefit of peat fires, piobaireachd or, God help us, a porridge drawer, may I commend my recipe: two dessert spoons full of porridge oats; mix with approx four fluid ounces of milk; microwave for 5¼ minutes on high; add a spoonful of honey to sweeten.

The result is a sort of porridge soup, one of the few things I am able to eat and enjoy on the actual morning of preparation.

Yours faithfully,
MAUREEN HAWKINS

Replied on 8 February 2001

SIR, CONTRARY TO Mr Colin MacNeill's suggestions, the secret of giving my breakfast porridge four hours in the oven is not rising in the middle of the night but "setting the timer to turn the oven on four hours before breakfast", a useful phrase that was cut from my original letter (Weekend letters, January 20).

Yours faithfully,
A. M. PARSONS

Replied on 9 February 2001

SIR, AS EVERY WOMAN married to a Scotsman knows, the only person who made perfect porridge was that Scotsman's mother.

Yours sincerely,
JIM CHRISTIE

Replied on 9 February 2001

SIR, IT DOES NOT MUCH matter how you prepare your porridge the night before. The important thing is that in the morning you should, before anybody eats it, throw it out.

Yours faithfully,
HUW JAMES
Llanishen, Cardiff

From Blair to Brexit

TERMS OF ENDEARMENT

15 January 2002

SIR, I AM A WIDOWER aged 57 and I have just met a nice young lady whom I introduce to my friends as "my companion". After much deliberation, I settled upon this introduction because I think it has a degree of grace, dignity and perhaps even an air of mystery about it.

The problem I have is that my children fall about laughing; they think it is weird, oozes senility and destroys any small vestige of the street cred that I might once have had.

At my age, descriptions such as "partner" or "girlfriend" seem inappropriate, and one rakish suggestion that I could introduce her as "my mistress" just gave me a panic attack. Am I doomed to a life of hot flushes?

Yours sincerely,
D. J. THOMAS

Replied on 16 January 2002

SIR, PROFESSOR THOMAS could try introducing his young lady as "my dear friend". Not only does this meet his requirement of race and dignity, but it continues to keep people guessing. "Companion" sounds as if she pushes his bath chair and writes his letters to *The Times* for him.

Yours faithfully,
LESLEY RUSSELL

REFUGEE STATUS

26 April 2002

SIR, OBITUARIES TODAY: Sir Michael Kerr, German refugee, Appeal judge and fighter pilot; Professor Victor Weisskopf, Austrian refugee and renowned physicist; Lewis Goodman, OBE, Polish refugee and noted textile technologist. Just shows you what can happen if you're not careful about the sort of people you let flood in to dilute the native population.

Yours faithfully,
BARRY HYMAN

———◆———

NEVER BEFORE REVEALED

14 March 2003

SIR, I SEE THAT WHAT was thought to be a new discovery about Hitler's health was already noted about 50 years ago. This is an example of perpetual rediscovery, along with such topics as the presence of arsenic in samples of Napoleon's hair, Salieri's role in the death of Mozart and the knotty problem of the direction of circulation of water going down the plughole.

Researchers note that the period of recurrence of questions being asked about these topics is upwards of 20 years but are divided as to whether this frequency corresponds to the generation gap of 25 years or to 22 years, which is two sunspot cycles.

Further work is evidently required, supported by a large grant from a major research institution.

Yours sincerely,
JAMES HARRISON

THE CASE AGAINST HATE SONGS

1 October 2004

SIR, MICK HUME (Comment, September 25) criticises the OutRage! campaign against Buju Banton and seven other reggae singers whose lyrics are widely believed to incite the murder of lesbians and gay men. He says freedom of expression must be defended.

We agree that people should have the right to criticise homosexuality. That is why I opposed the prosecution of the Bournemouth lay preacher, Harry Hammond (report, April 25, 2002) His homophobic views were deplorable, but the price of a free society is that we sometimes have to put up with views we find offensive.

Free speech does not, however, include the right to commit the criminal offence of incitement to murder. These singers have gone too far with their calls for "queers" to be shot, hanged, drowned and burnt alive. Gay people, like everyone else, have a right to live their lives without being subjected to threats to kill them.

Yours sincerely,
PETER TATCHELL

DA VINCI CODE FICTIONS NEED
NO DISPROVING

13 August 2005

Sɪʀ, Yᴏᴜ ʀᴇᴘᴏʀᴛ that among the more controversial claims of *The Da Vinci Code* is that Jesus married Mary Magdalene and that they had a child.

Dan Brown's novel does not make claims: it's fiction. The "controversy" that Mary Magdalene and Jesus were married does not even originate with Dan Brown but dates from the earliest years of the Christian Church.

The denunciation by the Roman Catholic Church in England and Wales of the novel's flawed logic and history is sheer silliness. Fiction is either good or bad fiction. It cannot be good or bad fact.

HENRY JONES

13 August 2005

Sɪʀ, Tʜᴇ ᴄʏɴɪᴄᴀʟ ᴀᴛᴛᴇᴍᴘᴛ to position the whole *Da Vinci Code* phenomenon as a speculative but nonetheless legitimate contribution to historical study richly deserves to be disowned by those now profiting most from it.

As the shelfloads of trashy pseudoscholarship in our high street bookshops attest, it is now extremely difficult to find an orthodox account of the Knights Templar, the Holy Grail or the origins of the New Testament outside a major university library.

More disturbingly, increasing numbers of students have been manoeuvred into the "must be some truth in it" position by the skilful publicity behind *The Da Vinci Code* — a tendency all educated opinion should view with alarm.

ROBERT A. DAVIS
Department of Religious Education, University of Glasgow

PEAK PERFORMANCE

9 September 2006

SIR, THE FIRST ASCENT of the Matterhorn was made not by the Italian Jean-Antoine Carrel (report, Sept 7) but by the Englishman Edward Whymper on July 14, 1865. In his book *Scrambles in the Alps* Whymper talks of throwing stones from the summit towards the Italians below to ensure they knew the summit had been conquered.

The British team did suffer a setback when a rope broke and four members of the team died, but that was on the way down, not on the way up. Perhaps your correspondent should remember Whymper's closing words in the final chapter of his book: "Do nothing in haste; look well to each step; and from the beginning think what may be the end."

THERESA MAY
Shadow Leader of the House of Commons

———◆———

GOLDEN OLDIE

20 September 2007

SIR, WHAT A RIDICULOUS debate has sprung up over the ability of Sir Menzies Campbell to lead a political party at the age of 66 (report, Sept 18). I have today, at the age of 86, been reappointed to the council of one of our most progressive universities, Essex, for a further three years.

Palmerston was 71 when he became Prime Minister and held the job for more than eight years. Churchill celebrated his 80th birthday while PM and our much-beloved Queen is in her 81st year. I would suggest that Northern Rock would not have undergone such turmoil if its fortunes had been guided by older and wiser heads.

SIR SIGMUND STERNBERG

Sir Sigmund, who came to Britain from Hungary in 1939, lived to be 95.

COVENTRY RAID

15 April 2008

SIR, ONCE, YEARS AFTER the event, I was able to discuss the Coventry raid with Professor R. V. Jones. who had at the time been in charge of most secret scientific intelligence (letters, April 7 & 8).

He told me that he knew from secret sources that a major Luftwaffe operation impended, against either Wolverhampton, or Coventry, or London. Only at 3pm on the day of the raid, when the Germans tested their navigational beams, did he discover that it was to be Coventry.

By then there was only time to take one counter-measure, jamming the Germans' beams. He had to guess which of three wavelengths to jam and guessed correctly. By a clerk's transmission error, the wrong wavelength was sent to the jamming stations; the beams were unaffected. Hence the raid's success.

M. R. D. FOOT

For years, the story had circulated that Churchill knew in advance that Coventry was to be the target of what proved a devastating raid, but let it take place so as to conceal the fact that Germany's Enigma code had been cracked.

◆

OVAL OFFICE DESK

8 November 2008

SIR, NEVER MIND THE rug, will President-elect Obama's agenda include a new desk in the Oval Office (letter, Nov 7)?

The current desk was made from the timbers of HMS *Resolute*, a British Arctic exploration ship abandoned in 1854 when it became trapped in the ice. When she was discovered by American whalers some 18 months later, having come free and drifted more than 1,000 miles, the United States Government returned her to the British as a gesture of goodwill. Queen Victoria was so impressed by this that when the ship was broken up in 1879 she ordered a desk to be made and presented it to President Rutherford B. Hayes.

JULIAN THOMAS

HAMELIN'S PIED PIPER

19 December 2008

SIR, HAMELIN TRADITION, first attested in the 14th century, is very firm that on Saints John and Paul's day, June 26, 1284, a Pied Piper led 130 children out of the town (report, Dec 17); the rats were added in a 16th-century Bavarian chronicle, and the date of July 22, 1376, as in Browning, substituted by another chronicler in 1588. The original "children" may have been colonists for Brandenburg and Pomerania, where Hamelin surnames recur.

LEOFRANC HOLFORD-STREVENS

BERLUSCONI BLUES

12 December 2009

SIR, MANY YEARS AGO Willy Rushton and I wrote a song for *That Was the Week that Was* called *Fornicazione is Italian for Love*.

Do you think I should send a copy of it to Signor Berlusconi?

DAVID LEE

FUR IS MURDER

2 August 2010

Sir, I welcome Ann Widdecombe's views on the depravity of bear-baiting in order to serve the vanities of the British Army Guards (Opinion, July 30). In the humanised world, of course, hats are not worth killing for. Yes, animal rights move different people differently, and there are even those who think that animals simply have no right to be, but there is no sanity in making life difficult on purpose for the Canadian brown bear, especially for Guards hats that look absurd in the first place, and which can easily be replaced by faux versions (thanks to the visionary Stella McCartney) with no death involved.

It is difficult not to look to the Queen herself — after all, they are her Guards, and she must surely be aware of the horrific process utilised to supply real bearskins for her Guards. The mere sight of each bearskin hat must surely jab at the Queen's heart.

Protection of animals makes for a responsible life. The world is speeding up, and in order to assist humankind to advance we all strive in many ways to be a better "we".

The brain speculates, but the heart knows, and there is no clever distinction in trapping and skinning bears for petty considerations based on vanity. Concern for all beings — human or animal — is a kindness and a goodness that springs from somewhere much deeper than Royal duty, and like it or not, the Guards wearing real fur reflects the human spirit at its lowest.

MORRISSEY

Morrissey, the lead singer during the 1980s of The Smiths, has for many years campaigned for better treatment of animals.

SOMETHING BLUE

22 April 2011

SIR, AT THE TIME of the last royal wedding you kindly printed a letter from me complaining, as I remember it, about the preposterous flummery, extravagance and vulgarity of the event.

This time words fail me.

JAN MORRIS

See page 332 for Jan Morris's letter on the previous royal wedding.

WRANGLINGS AND ROYAL SUCCESSION

25 October 2011

SIR, THE SEPARATION OF the crown of Hanover from that of the United Kingdom on the accession of Queen Victoria in 1837 (report, Oct 15, and letter, Oct 20) would not provide a happy precedent for any division of the monarch's realms today.

A bitter controversy over ownership of some of the finest jewels in the royal collection soured Anglo-Hanoverian relations for 20 years. After two lengthy commissions of inquiry Queen Victoria was forced to hand over some of her favourite pieces, leaving her "desperately annoyed". She was prohibited from buying the distinctive Hanoverian cream and black horses which had drawn the royal coaches on state occasions since 1714. Her uncle, the King of Hanover, who was extremely unpopular in England, infuriated her by demanding precedence over the Prince Consort. That led to unseemly scenes at a royal wedding when the Hanoverian king nearly fell over after "a slight push" from Prince Albert. He was caught and led away by force by the Lord Chamberlain "fuming with ire". Could members of the Royal Family today avoid similar wrangling if the Queen's realms were split?

LEXDEN

The writer is the historian of the Conservative Party

ANNOYED

4 March 2014

Sir, I am getting increasingly annoyed at the barrage of articles about teenagers, and the adults who keep trying to explain our behaviour ("Moods and Meltdowns: what's inside the teenage brain?", Mar 1).

I am 16 and a straight-A student, like most of my friends. We are not as irrational and immature as adults seem to think. We've grown up with financial crises and accept that most of us will be unemployed. We no longer flinch at bloody images of war because we've grown up seeing the chaos in the Middle East and elsewhere. Most of us are cynical and pessimistic because of the environment we've grown up in—which should be explanation enough for our apparent insolence and disrespect, without "experts" having to write articles about it.

Has no one ever seen that we are angry at the world we live in? Angry that we will have to clean up your mess, while you hold us in contempt, analysing our responses as though we were another species?

I would like adults to treat us not as strange creatures from another world but as human beings with intelligent thought — a little different from yours, perhaps, but intelligent thought nonetheless.

Stop teaching adults how to behave round us, and instead teach them to respect us.

JENNI HERD

RHODES MUST NOT FALL

26 December 2015

SIR, IT IS REGRETTABLE that the "Rhodes Must Fall" folly has spread from South Africa to Oriel College. My people — the Afrikaners — have greater reason to dislike Rhodes than anyone else. He was the architect of the Anglo-Boer War that had a disastrous impact on our people. Yet the National Party government never thought of removing his name from our history.

If political correctness of today were applied consistently very few of Oxford's great figures would pass scrutiny. George Washington — another Oriel alumnus — would certainly not. By the same measure, how many statues would remain in Britain at all?

We do not commemorate historic figures for their ability to measure up to current conceptions of political correctness — but because of their actual impact on history.

Rhodes, for better or for worse, certainly had an impact on history. He has, in particular, had a positive impact on more than 7500 Rhodes scholars from all over the world and on Oriel College to which he bequeathed the then enormous sum of £100 000.

Students have always been full of sound and fury, signifying very little. However, one would have expected an institution as venerable as Oriel to be a little more gracious in its treatment of its most generous benefactor. If Oriel now finds Rhodes so reprehensible would the honourable solution not be to return his bequest, plus interest, to the victims of British imperialism in southern Africa?

Yours sincerely,
FW DE KLERK
Former President of South Africa

The former President of South Africa had written to oppose the student movement calling for the removal of a statue of Cecil Rhodes at Oriel College, Oxford. Its campaign echoed a successful one at the University of Cape Town which had claimed that a statue of the imperialist politician and tycoon symbolised past and present racial oppression and injustice.

THE WORST OF BRITISH

21 August 2016

THE LAND ROVER Defender, reviewed by you last month ("As modern as scurvy but still the coolest", July 31), is pure Brexit: plodding old Britain, with dullness as a badge of honour and lack of any material comfort as a reassurance to people who don't like sex or garlic and usually prefer their dogs to other human beings.

MICHAEL LIMB

END TIMES

"YOURS TILL THE COWS COME HOME"

5 August 1982

SIR, THE ENGLISH LANGUAGE is a subtle and flexible instrument, but it does have various lacunae; I am writing to invite your readers to repair one such gap. I am concerned that there seems to be no way of ending a letter with a phrase which conveys the idea of "in friendship" or "with warm and friendly feelings".

There is "love from", but that is perhaps a little naive; there is "with kind regards" but that seems rather formal; "best wishes" is too like a Christmas card, and "yours ever" implies all sorts of long-term commitments; *amicalement* comes closest to the phrase I mean — but I want something in English.

Yours sincerely,
JAN PAHL

Replied on 9 August 1982

SIR, A WELL-TRIED French acquaintance of ours invariably ends her English letters to us with "Yours friendly", which we love. But perhaps Mrs Pahl might prefer to employ the simple American coda of "Cordially"?

Yours faithfully,
VIVIAN VALE

Replied on 9 August 1982

SIR, I ONCE TAUGHT an attentive student who ended her little notes to me with the valediction "Yours eventually". I assumed that this was intended to convey warm and friendly feelings.

Yours sincerely,
J. R. BUTLER

SIR, JAN PAHL WANTS a letter-ending to convey friendship, not love or formality. How about "yours cordially", with which I have been ending letters for years (including one to her)?

The "yours" form is capable of all sorts of individual variations: "yours apologetically", "yours disgustedly", "yours in sackcloth and ashes", "yours delightedly" and I have used them all. But perhaps "yours" itself is absurd; so what about just "Cordially"?

Until this is an accepted form, however, I remain,
Yours cheerfully,
KATHARINE WHITEHORN

Replied on 12 August 1982

SIR, MRS PAHL FINDS a gap in English in ways of signing off her letters. There is no gap in the language; it is a question of looking a little further to find an expression unhappily fallen into desuetude. When I wish to convey "warm and friendly feelings" to my correspondent, I sign myself

Yours affectionately,
PAMELA JERRAM

Replied on 12 August 1982

SIR, Is "YOURS AFFECTIONATELY" *too* affectionate for Mrs Pahl? It offers warmth of feeling without pushiness.

Incidentally, why never *"Dear* Sir" nowadays — even when one is feeling particularly friendly towards *The Times*?

Yours sincerely,
BRIGID GRAFTON GREEN

Replied on 13 August 1982

Sir, I have always thought of Evelyn Waugh's immortal phrase "with love or what you will" as the ultimate end to my correspondence.

It has disarmed my sternest critic and redeemed my dullest prose.

Yours faithfully,
PHILIP A. DAVIES

Replied on 13 August 1982

Sir, Amiably yours,
GEORGE GALE

Replied on 16 August 1982

Sir, Mrs Jan Pahl, who seeks an English equivalent for *amicalement* with which to end her letters, may be interested to know that when I was a District Officer in Barotseland in the nineteen-fifties all official letters in English to the local African chief commenced with the salutation "My Friend" and ended "I am Your Friend".

I never discovered the origin of this strange mode of address, which was in frequent use at the time but may be a little too regal for Mrs Pahl's purposes.

Yours sincerely,
JOHN HOUSDEN

Replied on 17 August 1982

Sir, My son, who is 22, began writing to me a year or so ago with the ending: "Your friend, William". This seems to be a simple and unaffected ending that conveys the desired feeling.

Your friend,
IAN MILLS

S<small>IR</small> (<small>AND</small> M<small>RS</small> J<small>AN</small> P<small>AHL</small>):
Yours till the cows come home.

> Yours sincerely,
> BERNARD KAUKAS

S<small>IR</small>, I <small>HOPE IT MAY</small> help Mrs Pahl to hear of the endings of two letters I found especially engaging. A servant ended a letter to George IV, "Invariably Yours". (Incidentally it began, "My dearest Sir ...") And I will end this letter as did my 10-year-old granddaughter,

> Ever wishing good,
> DAVID PEACE

S<small>IR</small>, S<small>OME YEARS AGO</small> a young distant relative wrote to thank me for a Christmas present. With an obvious wish to express some sentiment of friendliness, without appearing too effusive, she brought her letter to a close with the words "most of my love".

> Yours faithfully,
> GERVASE CRAVEN

S<small>IR</small>, M<small>RS</small> P<small>AHL</small> <small>IS</small> perfectly correct. There *is* a gap in the language. The problem is one of long standing.

Did not Miss Austen, in the person of Miss Mary Crawford, say to Fanny Price: "You must give my compliments to him. Yes, I think it must be compliments.

Is there not a something wanted, Miss Price, in our language — a something between compliments and love, to suit the sort of friendly acquaintance we have had together? ... But compliments may be sufficient here."

I present my compliments to your correspondents and to yourself, and sign myself *simpliciter*.
PHYLLIS GASCOIN

Replied on 24 August 1982

SIR, I REMEMBER A lady anxious for a reply from my office to her letter seeking to be excused from jury service as she was eight months pregnant, ending appropriately,

"Yours expectantly"
ALASTAIR BLACK
Under-Sheriff of Greater London

Replied on 25 August 1982

SIR, DURING THE PERIOD he was spring cleaning the Royal Navy, Admiral Jackie Fisher didn't do too badly. To Viscount Esher: "Yours till a cinder".
To J. A. Spender: "Yours till the Angels smile on us".
To F. E. G. Ponsonby: "Yours till death".
To George Lambert: "Yours till Hell freezes".
From 1908 onwards the last appeared most frequently.

Yours faithfully,
LOUIS LE BAILLY

Replied on 31 August 1982

Sir, When the contents are appropriate, we can end our letters, as our Victorian forefathers often did, by giving a final encore to the dominant theme or delicately reiterating the emotional gist: by, for example, "Yours in great distress of mind" or "Yours in heartfelt gratitude and relief". In this way we can, so to speak, round off our letters pointedly.

Yours in earnest hope of publication,
R. W. K. PATERSON

Replied on 14 August 1982

Sir, Mrs Pahl is treading on delicate ground. The moment you depart from the accepted forms of salutation you inevitably endow any new formulas with some specific value, whereas the present time-honoured conventional forms, inane as they are, no longer have any significance in themselves.

We could, of course, revert to the extravagant protestations that our great-grandfathers liked to use when rounding off a letter, but life is too short for that; and quite honestly I do not see members of our contemporary society tamely subscribing themselves as most obedient, humble servants.

Believe me to be, Sir,
Not your anything but simply,
STELIO HOURMOUZIOS

THE REST IS SILENCE

6 February 1946

SIR, I HAVE JUST written you a long letter.

On reading it over, I have thrown it into the waste paper basket. Hoping this will meet with your approval.

I am, Sir, Your obedient servant,
A. D. WINTLE

INDEX OF LETTER
WRITERS